GW00818439

Neville Chamberlain's Legacy

Neville Chamberlain's Legacy

Hitler, Munich and the Path to War

Nicholas Milton

PEN & SWORD
HISTORY

AN IMPRINT OF PEN & SWORD BOOKS LTD.
YORKSHIRE – PHILADELPHIA

First published in Great Britain in 2019 by
Pen and Sword History
An imprint of
Pen & Sword Books Ltd
Yorkshire - Philadelphia

ISBN 9781526732255

Typeset in INDIA By IMPEC e Solutions

Printed and bound in the UK By TJ International

Pen & Sword Books Ltd incorporates the Imprints of Pen & Sword Books
Archaeology, Atlas, Aviation, Battleground, Discovery, Family History, History,
Maritime, Military, Naval, Politics, Railways, Select, Transport, True Crime,
Fiction, Frontline Books, Leo Cooper, Praetorian Press, Seaforth Publishing,
Wharncliffe and White Owl.

For a complete list of Pen & Sword titles please contact

PEN & SWORD BOOKS LIMITED
47 Church Street, Barnsley, South Yorkshire, S70 2AS, England
E-mail: enquiries@pen-and-sword.co.uk
Website: www.pen-and-sword.co.uk

or

PEN AND SWORD BOOKS
1950 Lawrence Rd, Havertown, PA 19083, USA
E-mail: Uspen-and-sword@casematepublishers.com
Website: www.penandswordbooks.com

Contents

Foreword by Chris Packham CBE

I am haunted by grainy black and white images of war. The war that my parents endured and survived, and shared with me in my formative years. The war that culminated in the unsurpassable horror of two mushroom clouds over Japan and precipitated my sleepless childhood nights waiting to 'duck and cover', the futility of which was never hidden from my terrified racing mind. I know why we like sunrises, worship their glowing joy; it's because we have survived another night, that night when the missiles didn't launch and I could run down the garden, vault the fence and land in the footsteps of Neville Chamberlain.

And how damned bizarre is that? The very man who I'd heard broadcasting from the cabinet office in 1939 ... 'No such undertaking has been received, and that consequently, this country is at war ...' That very posh bloke, in a bow tie and tux, with his big moustache and black eyes, his harrowed brow, whose voice defines agony for me, whose beaten syllables were the touch paper for a global catastrophe that will always be beyond my imagination. How could we achieve any direct connection?

Life. A love of life. A love of living things.

History is almost as good as natural history; and when it draws a par it's because its stories connect, make circles, join us together as people across the ages. When we smile, laugh, wince or cry at the same things, when big people who have changed all our destinies share moments with little people like us, then we become part of the world and see with greater clarity our time and place in it. Chamberlain had impacted upon me. I knew that from the *World at War* in 1973, but until now I had no idea that we had another, deeper connection; moths and birds: finding, studying, counting, cataloguing, and, critically, being principally excited by. Those jewels, those simple masterpieces of nature, which Churchill and Hitler probably swatted or stepped over, were the source of a lifelong fascination, of a largely secret appreciation, a refuge for unparalleled joy and happiness, his breathing space in the choking tensions of thirties' Britain.

Wow! Chamberlain – Nev, as I would call him if we were sharing binoculars in a hide – put up bird boxes and tables to the bemusement of his staff, spotted Redwings in St James's Park, 'Hey Hoed' Ramones-style when he discovered a Blackbird mimicking a Song Thrush in Downing Street – where he also discovered a Leopard Moth – and enthusiastically reported it in *The Countryman* which, he wrote to his sister, 'also included remarks about my tits'. Oo-er!, So 'Carry on Springwatch'!

But let's be clear. What these beautiful insights provide is part of the essential context of this book. The man was overshadowed by others, but these 'nature notes', these windows to his lifelong passion seem to offer some humble proof of his purity of purpose, his honest dedication to provide proper public service in times of extraordinary difficulty. They make a statesman of enormous historical importance a real man. And I can't help but wonder how many species have been on the Downing Street bird list of Thatcher, Blair and May. Maybe if there were such lists our world would be a different place.

Sometimes we need bridges to join minds and motion, little links to spark a simple connection across political, social, religious and ideological divides. That can fuel and invite change, and this book made me change my mind about a man I thought was a posh, bow-tied bloke who told my parents that their world was about to get blown to bits. Nev is now on my 'imaginary dinner party' guest list. Well, sort of. I don't do dinner parties, but he would be welcome to help me empty my moth trap.

Chris Packham
New Forest, 2018

Foreword by Rt Hon Hilary Benn MP

This fascinating book by Nick Milton sheds new light on the complex character of Neville Chamberlain.

Many people know about his work on social housing, but not that he championed the introduction of widows' pensions and worked to improve midwifery. And the insight into Chamberlain's profound love of nature will come as a revelation; a reminder that there is more to political figures, even Tory Prime Ministers, than many a quick judgement allows.

History, however, will rightly remember him for his disastrous appeasement of Hitler. Milton reminds us that at the time of Munich, Chamberlain was greeted as a hero because he seemed to have secured peace but it was an illusion, and the nation and the world learned – at great cost – that the only way to deal with Hitler's fascism was to defeat it.

Preface

What was really going on in the mind of Prime Minister Neville Chamberlain in the run up to the declaration of the Second World War? How did he cope with the catastrophic consequences of appeasing Adolf Hitler? And how relevant is his controversial legacy today? This book seeks to provide answers to those questions.

As a military historian I thought I knew all about appeasement, the 1938 Munich agreement and the subsequent path to war. Then I read Chamberlain's weekly private letters to his two younger sisters, Hilda and Ida, and discovered there was much I didn't know about the backdrop to these momentous political events. These included Chamberlain's other war legacy: helping to create the Air Raid Precautions organisation, the Women's Land Army and the Special Operations Executive. However, as a natural historian, the most revelatory to me was Chamberlain's love of nature and the vital role that birdwatching played in his Premiership.

In his youth, Chamberlain was an expert in lepidopterology, the study of butterflies and moths. His interests later extended to botany, ornithology, angling, shooting and forestry. He didn't do well at school, but thanks to his family name and his wife, Annie, he finally found his niche in business and then politics. As Lord Mayor of Birmingham during the First World War, he created a municipal savings bank and championed national service while his wife looked after the troops. Despite pushing fifty years of age by the time he finally entered Parliament, his rise to the top remains to this day one of the quickest in political history.

As Minister for Health, he helped create affordable homes and championed widows' pensions and a midwifery service. As Chancellor, he led the economic recovery in the mid-1930s following the Great Depression. In doing this, Chamberlain taxed the 'divi', or dividend, at Co-op stores, forging their alliance with the Labour Party, a relationship that continues to this day in the form of the Co-operative Party. Chamberlain also made cuts to Britain's defences, a move that was to cost it dear in the years to come. When, in 1937, he became Prime Minister, his time soon became dominated by foreign affairs, particularly his controversial policy of appeasement towards Nazi Germany.

Chamberlain's private letters are as close as we will ever get to finding out what he was really thinking when he tried, unsuccessfully, to appease Hitler before looking into the abyss of war. They reveal a lot about Chamberlain the politician, too often self-righteous, especially when it came to his belief in the fabled 'Chamberlain touch'. Yet they also show a man who wanted, at almost any cost, to prevent another world war because of the horrors he had witnessed during the first, particularly the death of his cousin Norman. Far from the impersonal bureaucrat his critics accused him of being, his letters to his two sisters show he was a sensitive, loving father and, in unprecedented times, found it tough at the top.

When it came to his political colleagues, the letters reveal Chamberlain's complex relationship with Winston Churchill and the enmity he felt towards Lloyd George, Prime Minister during the First World War, and the Labour Party. Like many Tories of his generation, Chamberlain came from a privileged background and while he championed the plight of working-class people, he also commented that they were 'unrefined' and 'ugly'. He enjoyed mixing with royalty and visiting his beloved Chequers, the grace-and-favour country estate bequeathed to sitting British Prime Ministers. He also set up the Conservative Research Department, the first think tank on the right of politics. However, what the letters truly lay bare is the amazing lengths to which he went to win over Mussolini or 'Musso' as he nicknamed him. His dogged attempt to drive a wedge between the Italian dictator and Hitler was matched only by his persistent denial of a Nazi attack in the west despite so much evidence to the contrary.

The other fascinating aspect to Chamberlain's Premiership, I found while researching his archive at the University of Birmingham, were the gifts he received following the signing of the Munich peace agreement on 30 September 1938. In the first few days alone over 20,000 letters and telegrams poured into Downing Street from an immensely grateful public who believed he had secured 'peace for our time'. These ranged from a mother, whose three sons had died in the First World War, knitting him some socks to a grand piano from the German firm Blüthner, which caused a major diplomatic incident. While many of the gifts simply resulted in a headache for Chamberlain's already overworked staff, others created a political storm or, like the piano, raised serious questions about Chamberlain's judgement.

When it comes to nature many Prime Ministers have fleetingly embraced conservation when it has suited them, but Chamberlain remains the only true naturalist to have ever occupied Number 10. Visiting the Chamberlain archives at the University of Birmingham and Birmingham Museums revealed a wealth of information about the extent to which nature, and in particular moths and birds, played a pivotal part in his life. Researching this led me to Sarah Kelly whose great uncle, Gilbert Collett, was an ornithologist and who, from September 1937 to July 1940, corresponded with Chamberlain about the wild birds they found in St James's Park. Sarah had kept all the original letters Chamberlain had sent to her great uncle and emailed them to me. What I found particularly fascinating while reading them was their timing; the bird sightings forming a backdrop to some of the most momentous events of the twentieth century: the rise of Adolf Hitler, the signing of the Munich agreement, and the declaration of war.

While the laconic letters form only a small part of his vast archive they reveal a lot about life at Number 10 and how Chamberlain was coping with the almost unbearable pressure he was under as Prime Minister. They are published here for the first time in their entirety, together with the letters Chamberlain wrote to national newspapers on birds and his article for *The Countryman* magazine. Chamberlain remains the only serving Prime Minister to have had a species named after him – the Chamberlain's Yellow butterfly *Pyrisitia chamberlaini* – and an article published in a respected journal about the wildlife associated with Downing Street.

In the years leading up to war, when he resided at first Number 11 and then Number 10 Downing Street, Chamberlain took a walk nearly every day in St James's Park. Then, like now, the Royal Park, with its ornamental lake and tame wildfowl, was of great ecological value. He and Collett found some very special wild birds there including rarities such as the common sandpiper *Actitis hypoleucos*, scaup *Aythya marila* and the smew *Mergellus albellus*, notable sightings for a small park in the middle of one of the most densely populated cities on earth. To help his staff increase their knowledge of birds he would, on occasion, bring them with him or ask them to recce the park on his behalf. These forays attracted criticism inside Downing Street, but were always stoutly defended by his Principal Private Secretary, Osmund Somers Cleverly, knowing the immense stress his boss was under. Remarkably, the letters show that on the morning of 8 May 1940, during the two-day debate in Parliament on the disastrous Norway campaign which led to his downfall, Chamberlain was busy looking for a kestrel *Falco tinnunculus* nest in St James's Park. Birdwatching had become more than just a hobby; it had become Chamberlain's way of dealing with the nightmare that was Adolf Hitler and the Second World War.

As in his political life, there were many contradictions at the heart of Chamberlain's love of nature. An early associate member of the Society for the Promotion of Nature Reserves, he helped to found a network that today encompasses over 2,300 nature reserves run by The Wildlife Trusts. Yet he was also an avid angler and shooter who regularly, on his annual holidays to Scotland, took part in driven grouse shooting. Today there is a campaign to ban driven grouse shooting due to the negative impact it has on upland wildlife and ecology, particularly the persecution of birds of prey such as the hen harrier *Circus cyaneus*. If the evidence of the damage caused by this practice had been available in his day, I hope Chamberlain the naturalist would have backed the campaign.

Chamberlain was also a strong supporter of the protection of the countryside and a founder member of the Council for the Preservation of Rural England (today known as the Campaign to Protect Rural England). Conversely, he also wanted to build more affordable houses to replace the inner-city slums, like the ones in his native Birmingham, that were then still home to many poor people. Here he had more success in balancing these often competing demands by coming up with the first truly consultative arrangement whereby local authorities had to take into account environmental considerations when allocating land for development. This would later become the model for the Town and Country Planning Act 1947, the foundation of our modern planning system.

In writing Chamberlain's biography I have tried to convey his career using primary sources and have used historical hindsight as sparingly as possible. My sources have included period books, pamphlets, articles and records, including Hansard, but the principal references have been the four volumes of Neville Chamberlain's letters to his sisters, Hilda and Ida, in the Chamberlain archives in Birmingham. These have been edited and published by the highly respected Chamberlain biographer Robert Self. As well as the invaluable insight they provide to the tragic politics of the time, they also contain a wealth of information about Chamberlain's true personality.

A note is needed about Chamberlain's letters and his use of language. Most weekends throughout his adult life Chamberlain wrote alternately to his two sisters, Hilda and Ida, putting down on paper his innermost thoughts. The weekly letters are a record of what was happening at the time but they are not always set out in a coherent or logical way. Therefore, making sense of Chamberlain's protracted and sometimes random thoughts has been challenging. In addition the letters contain outdated language that today we would consider racist and anti-semitic. There is no evidence that Chamberlain was racist, as demonstrated by his time during the 1920s working with people on the Bahamas trying to grow sisal. However, by his own admission he 'didn't care for the Jews' and in his handling of the resignation of Leslie Hore-Belisha, his War Minister and the only Jew in the Cabinet, there remain nagging questions about anti-semitism, a subject that has again reared its ugly head in modern politics.

Today, nearly eighty years after his death, Chamberlain's name is still synonymous with the dirty word 'appeasement'. His legacy of appeasing Hitler, being duped at Munich and proving an indecisive war leader will probably never change, but I hope that this biography establishes his deserved reputation as one of the early pioneers of the conservation movement. Consequently, this biography is a natural history book in the literal sense of both words.

On his daily walks around St James's Park, Chamberlain particularly looked forward to seeing the return each winter of one particular bird; the great black-backed gull *Larus marinus*. The largest gull in the world, its size, powerful bill and distinctive black back mark it out from any other species. The bird in St James's Park had, according to Chamberlain, a 'habit of standing on the rock facing into the west wind'. In September 2018 I took part in the 'People's Walk for Wildlife', organised by the naturalist Chris Packham, which culminated in the handing in of the People's Manifesto for Wildlife to 10 Downing Street. Since Chamberlain's time, Britain's wildlife has undergone a catastrophic decline and, as a fellow naturalist, I like to think he would have backed many of the ideas in it. Afterwards I followed in the footsteps of Chamberlain and wandered across from Downing Street to St James's Park. There, on the rock in the middle of the ornamental lake, was a great black-backed gull, facing into the wind.

Acknowledgements

Writing a book on Neville Chamberlain's legacy has been a long and at times challenging journey, but along the way I've met many really wonderful people. In helping me to tread in his footsteps I'd like to thank all the Special Collections archivists and librarians at the Cadbury Research Library housed in the University of Birmingham, especially Susan Worrall, Catherine Martin, Martin Killeen and Helen Fisher who could never do enough to help, particularly when it came to ordering box after box from the Chamberlain archive. Thanks also go to Lukas Large, the Curator of Natural Science at Birmingham Museums, who opened up the vaults so that I could search through Chamberlain's moth books, and the librarians at Stratford upon Avon library, especially Rachel Bannister and Lewys Morgan, who managed to renew for me the four volumes of The Neville Chamberlain Diary Letters edited by Robert Self for month after month. I'm also extremely grateful to Sally Clark, Hilary Benn's Parliamentary Assistant, to the historian Gary Willis, to Phil Richards and Oliver Hilliam at the Campaign to Protect Rural England, who provided invaluable material on Chamberlain and the CPRE, to the conservationist Tim Sands, who set me straight on the history of the Society for the Promotion of Nature Reserves (The Wildlife Trusts as they're known today), to my friend Carl Wright who proofread the draft and to the journalist Martin Kenny, who helped with some of the initial research on Chamberlain. Special thanks go to Sarah Kelly for sending me her great uncle Gilbert Collett's correspondence with Chamberlain about the birds they saw in St James's Park, and to Hilary Benn MP and the naturalist Chris Packham who provided the foreword; both have been very supportive over the years. When it came to writing the book the staff at Pen and Sword were incredibly helpful in guiding me through the production process, especially Claire Hopkins, Alan Murphy and Janet Brookes. I particularly want to thank my late mother Valerie who was born during the war and survived a V1 attack on her street. Throughout my childhood she cheerfully endured my obsession with Battle Picture Weekly comic. Finally I'd like to thank my wife Andrea and my daughter Georgia for putting up with me writing the book at all hours of the day and night, including on holiday. This book is for you.

Chapter 1

I believe it is peace for our time

'Blessed are the peacemakers, for they shall be called sons of God.'
Matthew 5:9

Not even the persistent drizzle could dampen the spirits of the crowd that had gathered on the tarmac at Heston aerodrome in the early evening of Friday 30 September 1938 to witness the Prime Minister's historic homecoming. As Neville Chamberlain's plane taxied on the runway at 5.40pm, following a three-and-a-half-hour flight from Munich, a throng of people rushed forward to greet the elderly Prime Minister. Leaving behind his trademark umbrella despite the rain, Chamberlain emerged from the sleek, silver aircraft in a black overcoat and immaculately pressed suit carrying his homburg hat. With his grey forelock and temples, salt and pepper moustache, stiff wing-collared shirt and fob watch he looked every inch the Victorian gentleman. In his pocket was a hastily typed-up accord, an Anglo-German agreement, consisting of three short paragraphs signed earlier that day by himself and the German Führer, Adolf Hitler. This now infamous 'piece of paper' proclaiming 'peace for our time' would determine Chamberlain's legacy for generations to come.

The four-power agreement that Chamberlain had also signed in Munich in the early hours of that autumn day with Hitler, the Italian dictator Benito Mussolini and the French premier Édouard Daladier had achieved a transient peace, but at a great political cost. Large swathes of Czechoslovakia's border territory, the disputed Sudetenland, had been ceded to Germany. The occupation was to begin on the 1 October and was to be completed in ten days, by which time anywhere with a population of 50 per cent or more ethnic Germans was to be returned to the Reich.

In Prague, the Czechoslovakian government felt utterly betrayed and humiliated, printing silk handkerchiefs so that their people could weep into them. On the handkerchiefs was printed the wording: 'The Czechoslovak nation to save the world's peace in 1938 sacrificed historic frontiers which a thousand years and a hundred wars could not change.'[1] The new Czech Prime Minister, General Syrový (1888-1970) spoke for the nation when he said, 'As a soldier and

Premier I must think first of the lives of millions of hard-working citizens, men, women and children. I have experienced the most tragic moment in my life. I am fulfilling the most painful duty which can ever have fallen upon me, a duty which is worse than dying.' His words were broadcast on loudspeakers throughout the streets of Prague. First there was a stunned silence, then many men and women started crying before the atmosphere turned to anger. Thousands descended on the President's palace, waving flags and chanting, 'Give us arms to defend ourselves', and 'We demand the people's Government'.[2]

That Sunday, Roman Catholic Cardinal Karel Boromejský Kašpar (1870-1941), the Primate of Bohemia, ordered a prayer to be read in all churches. It said 'The land of St Wencelas has just been invaded by foreign armies and the thousand-year-old frontier has been violated. This sacrifice has been imposed on the nation of St Wenceslas by our ally, France, and our friend, Britain. The Primate of the ancient Kingdom of Bohemia is praying to God Almighty that the peace efforts prompting this terrible sacrifice will be crowned by permanent success and, should they not be, he is praying to the Almighty to forgive all those who impose this injustice on the people of Czechoslovakia.'[3] Yet to a generation of British people who still vividly remembered the horrors of the First World War, the detail of the agreement and the fate of the Sudetenland mattered little. What meant everything was that, against all the odds, Chamberlain had flown back home from his meeting with the German dictator having secured 'peace for our time'.

The Munich and Anglo-German agreements were the result of three return flights to Germany that the Prime Minister had taken in just two weeks from Heston airport in West London. Such shuttle diplomacy, now commonplace, was at the time still a great novelty. Ironically, the first politician widely credited with using aircraft in this way was Hitler. He flew extensively between German cities during the Presidential election campaign of 1932, securing the support that would help to bring him to power a year later. By contrast, Chamberlain was a newcomer to flying and had previously made only one short flight – which he had completed in his top hat – at a Birmingham trade fair fifteen years earlier.[4] Now he had clocked up nearly twenty hours' flying time in two British Airways aircraft, a twin propeller Lockheed 10 and 14. It was an impressive feat for a 69-year-old man who had a well-known aversion to flying, a fear he had to conquer in the name of peace.

As well as the Lockheeds, the runway at Heston aerodrome, with its large expanses of open grassland, was home to a bird that epitomised freedom, the skylark *Alauda arvensis*. Its beautiful song, delivered in flight, would have been a very familiar sound to Chamberlain who was an avid ornithologist and regularly went bird watching in St James's Park when he was at Downing Street. The song inspired George Meredith's famous 122 line poem *'The Lark Ascending'*, which begins:

> He rises and begins to round,
> He drops the silver chain of sound,
> Of many links without a break,
> In chirrup, whistle, slur and shake.

and includes the lines:

> The voice of one for millions,
> In whom the millions rejoice
> For giving their one spirit voice.[5]

Now, just like the skylark in Meredith's poem, Chamberlain had ascended into the clouds and upon his descent had proclaimed peace for our time, which had resulted in millions rejoicing.

Chamberlain's mercy flights in the name of peace had started on 15 September 1938 when he flew from Heston to Munich on a Lockheed Model 10 Electra, registration G-AEPR, piloted by Captain Nigel Pelly, who would go on to serve with 216 Squadron in Egypt during the war.[6] It was the model made famous by the aviator Amelia Earhart who, in July 1937, had disappeared in a modified one during an attempted round-the-world flight. A week later, Chamberlain flew to Cologne airport for a meeting at Bad Godesberg on the new and more advanced Lockheed Model 14 Super Electra, more commonly known just as the Lockheed 14. The plane was developed from the Lockheed 10 but had greater seating capacity, accommodating 14 people instead of 10, and improved performance. Though at the time of Chamberlain's flight the Lockheed 14 was still technically a prototype, it had already proved itself a few months earlier when the billionaire Howard Hughes completed a global circumnavigation in one. Chamberlain's plane was registered G-AFGN and was flown by Douglas King and Eric Robinson who would both later be killed on active service in 1940.[7]

For his final trip to Munich, on 29 September, Chamberlain again used aircraft G-AFGN, but this time it was piloted by Victor Flowerday.[8] At the behest of Sir John Simon, his Chancellor, all the Cabinet bar one had come to see him off, a gesture which touched Chamberlain greatly.[9] Before departing for Munich Chamberlain spoke from the aircraft steps, as he had done on previous flights: 'When I was a little boy I used to repeat "If at first you don't succeed, try, try try again". That is what I'm doing. When I come back I hope I may be able to say, as Hotspur said in Henry IV, "Out of this nettle, danger, we pluck this flower, safety".'[10]

The short speech with its historical analogies was typical of Chamberlain and was designed to give the waiting media a quote that would please their editors and rally the nation. Robert the Bruce was meant to have rallied his troops with the words 'Try, try, try again' before their great victory over the English in the Battle of Bannockburn in 1314 and Shakespeare's Hotspur was modelled on Sir Henry Percy, an English rebel who led the uprising against the usurper Henry IV. Unfortunately, Hotspur was slain at the Battle of Shrewsbury in 1403 after being shot in the face and his forces fled, a fate which Chamberlain was no doubt keen to avoid, both for himself and the nation. The quote, however, proved popular and was extensively repeated in the media. It even inspired the title of a book, *This Nettle Danger*, a fictional take on the crisis by the author Philip Gibbs which sold extremely well.[11] (It was about an idealist American journalist, John Jennings Barton Junior, who gradually comes to accept the need for diplomacy and negotiation with Hitler in the name of peace).

In response Lord Lloyd who, with Churchill, was a well-known member of the 'Diehard' wing of the Conservative party, memorably quipped, 'If you don't concede, fly, fly, fly again'.[12] Churchill himself described Chamberlain's three flights in monetary terms, 'At Berchtesgaden £1 was demanded at pistol point. When it was given (at Godesburg) £2 were demanded at pistol point. Finally (at Munich) the dictator consented to take £1 17s. 6d. and the rest in promises of goodwill for the future.'[13] More pointedly, in a letter to the former Liberal leader and Prime Minister David Lloyd George, he said, 'I think we shall have to choose in the next few weeks between war and shame, and I have very little doubt what the decision will be.'[14]

The media, already briefed on what the Prime Minister had achieved, had played a crucial part in generating the near hysteria which greeted his return. The *Daily Mirror* had run with 'It is Peace – Hitler Accepts New Plan and Withdraws Ultimatum', while the *Daily Mail* headline said '4 Powers Reach Agreement', and the *Daily Sketch* 'No War – Official: Powers Agree'. The *Daily Express* in a '5am special' literally went big with the story when it ran with the headline 'Peace' in 3-inch-high letters with 'Agreement signed at 12.30am today' underneath. Across the pond the *New York Times* reported, 'Four powers reach a peaceable agreement; Germans to enter Sudeten area tomorrow and will complete occupation in ten days'. One of the few newspapers not to heave a sigh of relief was the *Manchester Guardian*. Their diplomatic correspondent presciently reported, 'The Munich agreement gives Hitler everything he wants (to begin with) except in so far as it does not perhaps quite enable him to get it as quickly as he would have done under the untrimmed ultimatum of Godesburg. All the misery and outrage that followed the German occupation of Vienna are now certain to follow the German occupation of the Sudetenland. He will be master of Czechoslovakia's main defences, and there is nothing to stop him from making himself master of all Czechoslovakia in the course of time.'[15]

As on his other trips, Chamberlain's plane had been well stocked with provisions for the flight, the Savoy Hotel providing luncheon hampers containing grouse sandwiches, caviar, paté and smoked salmon with beer, claret and cider to wash it down. On the outbound flight Chamberlain had confided to his Parliamentary Private Secretary Alec Douglas-Home, Lord Dunglass, that this was his last throw of the dice, but he could not see how it would pay Hitler to 'push things to the point of war.'

Chamberlain's ticket, number 18249, was specially issued by British Airways and on it had the official stamp of its office at Terminal House, 52 Grovenor Gardens, London, SW1W. It was an open return and in the box marked 'fare' was written simply the words 'special flight'.[16] Chamberlain was so proud of his special flight that he later decided to use a picture of the Lockheed 14 on his official Number 10 Christmas card. Upon his return, Richard Dimbleby, who was covering the Prime Minister's flight for BBC radio, memorably described the Lockheed 14 as 'the machine', reinforcing the perception that the Prime Minister had taken a great technological leap in the name of peace.[17] Chamberlain's first flight on 'the machine' had been two weeks earlier when he had flown to see Hitler at his mountain retreat, the Berghof, in Berchtesgaden. It had not been a pleasant experience as he had felt ill during the flight. But by 30 September he had overcome his air sickness and had used the time on the return flight to Heston to meticulously plan what he would say to the waiting crowds.

The Downing Street machine had also gone into overdrive organising a large welcoming party composed of Cabinet ministers, press, senior civil servants, members of the public and foreign ambassadors, all corralled on the tarmac to greet him. They included the French and Italian ambassadors and the German Chargé d'Affaires, Theodr Kordt. Coronation flags flew from the houses surrounding the airport and the government had encouraged those living nearby to go to the aerodrome to witness history in the making. By the time of his arrival a line of cars at least a mile long were parked on the roads leading to and from the airport. Security was tight and only pass holders were allowed inside the airport, but still the crowds kept coming. In all the *Daily Herald* estimated that 10,000 people had gathered on the tarmac and outside the airport perimeter gates. They included a contingent of Eton boys who had been especially bussed in for the occasion to add atmosphere for the cameras.[18]

Although none of the waiting crowd knew it, the presence of Theodor Kordt, the German Chargé d'Affaires at the London embassy, marked the end of any effective opposition to Hitler in Germany. Both he and his brother, Erich Kordt, had been part of a secret plan to assassinate Hitler if Germany went to war with Czechoslovakia over the Sudetenland. Known as the 'Oster Conspiracy', it was named after Generalmajor Hans Oster and was composed of senior officers in the German army who opposed the regime because they thought Hitler would take Germany into a war it couldn't win.[19] To have any chance of assassinating Hitler the conspirators needed strong British opposition to his seizure of the Sudetenland. To achieve this, Erich had been using his brother as a secret envoy to urge the British government to stand up to Hitler over the Sudeten crisis, in the hope that the army officers would then stage a coup against him. Chamberlain's piece of paper had effectively destroyed any chance of the plot succeeding, as following the signing of the Munich agreement Hitler was now seen in Germany as the 'greatest statesman of all time'. Kordt was reported as being 'very pleased' to meet the Prime Minister, but his real thoughts on the agreement with Hitler were not recorded. Yet the tragic irony of being asked to greet the triumphant Prime Minister at Heston cannot have been lost on him.

Chamberlain had been aware of Kordt's warning about the threat Hitler posed and this had been a major factor in him going to see the dictator in person. Now, as he exited the door of the plane on that wet Friday evening and climbed gingerly down the steel steps, an ecstatic crowd waited. At its head was Lord Chamberlain, the Earl of Clarendon, who had come with a special message from the King inviting Chamberlain to Buckingham Palace and putting at his disposal the royal car. The handwritten letter brought 'the warmest of welcomes to one who by his patience and determination has ensured the lasting gratitude of his fellow countrymen throughout the Empire.'

On the tarmac, also present among the crowd of well-wishers, were Sir John Simon, the Chancellor, together with Malcolm McDonald, the Colonial Secretary, the Secretary of State for War, Leslie Hore-Belisha, and Edward Wood, Lord Halifax, his Foreign Secretary. Those present loudly cheered the Prime Minister as he walked among the throng, the 'hip, hip, hoorays' echoing around the aerodrome. Greeting them with a hearty handshake, a warm word and a beaming smile, Chamberlain then made his way to a bank of six microphones, still clutching the letter from the King, the rest of the press and newsreel cameras being confined to the terminal building where they had taken up position on the roof to get the best angle. Here was assembled not just the cream of the British media but many reporters from America, Europe and across the British Empire.

Some of the public had also been allowed in to witness his speech, but most were kept behind barriers guarded by the police. Putting the letter from the King in his pocket and handing his homburg hat to one of his staff, he pulled out an envelope from his top pocket with his 'piece of paper'. After being cued in by a sound technician, he spoke to the waiting crowd: 'There are only two things I want to say. First of all I have received an immense number of letters during these anxious times and so has my wife. Letters of support and approval and gratitude. And I can't tell you what an encouragement that has been to me. I want to thank the British people for what they have done.'[20] Rather than taking any credit himself, he had decided to thank the British people for their 'support, approval and gratitude'. As Movietone News reported, 'all the world wants to tell him (thank you) but when he comes back his first thought is to thank others'. It was a great piece of political spin, designed to isolate his critics and bind the British people to the Munich agreement. He continued: 'And next I want to say that the settlement of the Czechoslovakian problem, which has now been achieved, is, in my view, only the prelude to a larger settlement in which all Europe may find peace.'

The audience cheered enthusiastically. Chamberlain used his second statement to reiterate his belief that the Munich agreement would lead to peace for all of Europe, something he knew everyone craved. Again, it was an adroit move. He paused, helping to build up the tension to his big moment: 'This morning I had another talk with the German Chancellor, Herr Hitler, and here is the paper which bears his name upon it as well as mine'. Pausing again for effect, Chamberlain produced the piece of paper, with his and Hitler's signatures on it, from his pocket and waved it with his right hand for the assembled cameras. Now it became clear why he had left his trusty umbrella behind; he needed a free hand to show the world what he had achieved. Loud cheering greeted the Prime Minister's theatrics but in an ominous turn of events a sudden gust of wind nearly blew the paper away. Holding on tightly to it Chamberlain looked around and milked the moment for all it was worth before continuing, 'Some of you, perhaps, have already heard what it contains but I would just like to read it to you: "We the German Führer and Chancellor and the British Prime Minister have had a further meeting today and are agreed in recognising that the question of Anglo-German relations is of the first importance for the two countries and Europe. We regard the agreement signed last night and the Anglo-German Naval Agreement as symbolic of the desire of our two peoples never to go to war with one another again".'

At this point a huge cheer went up in the crowd at the mention of the words 'never to go to war with one another again'. Chamberlain, who had hastily drawn up the piece of paper during the visit, had caveated this all-important phrase with the much more nebulous one 'symbolic of the desire of our two peoples'. Yet, caught up in the sheer emotion of the moment, no one in the crowd or listening on their radio heard the caveat, or even cared. The fact that Chamberlain's piece of paper was symbolic rather than literal was lost on a war-weary population who only wanted to hear that the threat of another war was now consigned to history. He finished: 'We are resolved that the method of consultation shall be the method to be adopted to deal with any other question that may concern our two countries, and we are determined to continue our efforts to remove possible sources of difference and thus to contribute to assure the peace of Europe.'

The cheering crowd now drowned out the Prime Minister. Cries of 'Well done, Mr Chamberlain!' and 'Three cheers for Neville!' competed with 'For he's a jolly good fellow'. As a piece of political theatre, it would have been difficult to surpass. Chamberlain had not only won over the crowd, but more importantly, thanks to the massive wall of microphones and newsreel cameras present, the British public and its supporters throughout the world. His many critics, including Winston Churchill, listened on in stunned disbelief. Against all the odds it looked as if the Prime Minister had pulled off the greatest political gamble of his career, curbing Hitler's insatiable territorial demands and in the process securing peace.

In contrast to the jubilant scenes on the streets of London, the city of Prague was in mourning. While the tense negotiations had been going on between the four powers, the Czech delegation had been confined to their room, guarded by Hitler's elite SS bodyguard. When the Munich agreement was announced the government had issued a terse statement which read, 'The Czechoslovak government, after having considered the decisions of the conference in Munich, taken without and against them, find no other means but to accept and have nothing to add.'

Seven hundred and forty miles away as the crow flies, after making his historic announcement, Chamberlain was ushered into the waiting royal car, policemen holding back the crowd, including the Eton schoolboys who had climbed under the perimeter fence to get a better view of the Premier. Word of Chamberlain's triumph soon began to spread and, even with a police escort, it would take an hour to make the nine-mile drive from Heston to Whitehall, so dense was the throng of people. Recorded by the newsreel cameras, the sea of well-wishers presented a scene more reminiscent of the closely choreographed mass adoration associated with speeches made by Hitler.

All along the route people came out of their homes and offices to see Chamberlain's car as it slowly made its way across London towards Buckingham

Palace. By the time his car travelled up the Mall the crowds were already five rows deep and thousands had gathered outside the palace gates waving flags and shouting hysterically. The crowd, reported by the *Daily Herald* to be in excess of 10,000, was of a similar size to a royal wedding. The *London Illustrated News*, in a special issue entitled 'Record Number – Crisis and the Agreement', reported that the scenes recalled Armistice Night in 1918.[21] 'Even the descriptions of the papers gives no idea of the scenes in the streets as I drove from Heston to the Palace,' Chamberlain wrote to his sister Hilda on 2 October, 'they were lined from one end to the other with people of every class, shouting themselves hoarse, leaping on the running board, banging on the windows and thrusting their hands into the car to be shaken.'[22]

It was not just well-wishers and onlookers who crowded around the gates to Buckingham Palace, but also the traffic, in particular taxis. The London staff of the *Manchester Guardian* reported, 'It was a harassing time for the police who could not stop the flow of evening traffic. Matters were complicated by the unscrupulousness of those who hired taxis and drove slowly round and round the Victoria Memorial, hoping that one of their circuits would provide a view of Mr Chamberlain's car. The crowd amused itself by shouting "What! Again?" each time the culprits appeared.'[23]

As his car finally went through the palace gates at 6.45pm the police, who up to that point had just about managed to restrain the cheering crowd, lost control. So many people wanted to see Chamberlain – to shake his hand or simply touch the car – that the police struggled to close the gates and a few lucky people managed to get in. Such was the unbridled joy that, according to the *Herald*, they were allowed to stay inside the palace courtyard, where they 'had front row seats for the appearance on the balcony'. Entering the palace, Chamberlain was met by beaming officials and was shown to their majesties' private apartments, where Mrs Chamberlain was already waiting. The couple then had twenty minutes alone with the King and Queen. Outside could be heard the chant 'We want Chamberlain! We want Chamberlain!' which grew ever louder. After fully briefing His Majesty, the Chamberlains finally made their way through the labyrinth of palace rooms and out on to balcony.

By this time a huge crowd had gathered at the gates despite the rain, and the police had to link arms to hold people back and prevent anybody being crushed. On seeing Chamberlain, a massive cheer went up and there was a deafening roar as both couples came out and stood between the Corinthian columns, illuminated by a huge searchlight beam which had been hastily erected on a fire engine below, especially for the occasion. Queen Elizabeth wore a beige dress and hat with pearls, finished off with a fox fur around her neck, the harsh light showing off her ensemble to maximum effect. In contrast, Mrs Chamberlain looked funereal in a black coat and hat, again finished off with a real fur collar. Chamberlain's black suit and stiff winged-collar shirt, more reminiscent of the Victorian era of his father than the 1930s, also contrasted with the smart white shirt, black dinner jacket and pinstriped trousers of King George VI. To an unknown observer looking on, the two couples would have resembled a family group with the Chamberlains playing the part of the elderly parents. Standing on the balcony, the King and Queen who were strongly in favour of Chamberlain's policy of appeasement, voluntarily surrendered the central position so the Chamberlains would be the focus of the crowds and the world's media.

Under the glare of the searchlight and intimidated by the huge crowd laid out before her, Mrs Chamberlain initially stood back, but was ushered forward by the King. There they stood for five minutes, the Queen, the Chamberlains and the King, illuminated for all the world to see, with the cheering crowd singing, 'For He's a Jolly Good Fellow'. Then, in an unprecedented break with official protocol, the King, Queen and Mrs Chamberlain stepped back and the Prime Minister stood on his own in front of the ecstatic crowd. The *London Illustrated News* proclaimed that Chamberlain was 'probably the first commoner to appear on the balcony at Buckingham Palace to be acclaimed by a vast crowd.'[24] In doing so the royals had explicitly acknowledged Chamberlain as the great peacemaker of Europe.

Movietone News summed up the moment when it said, 'So let us close on this scene of enthusiasm. The Prime Minister by his King's desire acknowledging his popularity from the balcony of Buckingham Palace. Our words of admiration and thanks are exhausted for the man who averted another armageddon.' After stepping back inside, the Chamberlains were escorted through the palace by their Majesties before being cheered on their way by the whole of the royal household who had gathered together and lined the exit to see them off. As the Chamberlains' car left the palace gates it was mobbed by the crowd and the police had to ride on the sideboards to keep the public at bay.

Due to the sheer weight of well-wishers, the car drove at a snail's pace the short distance to Downing Street, the Chamberlains holding hands in the back and waving to the crowd, for all the world like a royal couple. There they met a crowd that had become 'hysterical'.[25] Edward Murrow, the American broadcaster working for Columbia Broadcasting System, reported: 'Thousands of people are standing in Whitehall and lining Downing Street, waiting to greet the Prime Minister upon his return from Munich. Certain afternoon papers speculate concerning the possibility of the Prime Minister receiving a knighthood while in office, something that has happened only twice before in British history. Others say that he should be the next recipient of the Nobel Peace Prize.' Outside in the street a newspaper boy summed up the public mood shouting, 'Read all about it! Public hero number one!' Getting out of his car by the famous black door to Number 10, the Prime Minister was surrounded by his Cabinet as he waved to the crowds. Upon entering he was met by his staff, who had lined up along the corridor to welcome back the hero of the hour and his wife Annie.

The jubilant crowd outside Number 10 used the day's newspapers with their triumphant headlines to cover their heads from the rain, shouting 'Good old Neville!' or singing 'For He's a Jolly Good Fellow'. But soon the cries turned to 'Speech! Speech!' After talking to staff and having a cup of tea, Chamberlain decided to go to a first-floor window to acknowledge the crowd. Having initially dismissed the idea of making another speech, he decided on the spur of the moment to mark the occasion by making a few impromptu remarks. Ministers, sensing the atmosphere of the crowd outside, rushed out to join in the celebrations with the Colonial Secretary, Malcolm McDonald, and Geoffrey Lloyd, Under Secretary of State at the Home Department, climbing out of the window and on to the gateposts of Number 10 for a better vantage point. The *Daily Herald* reporter on the scene, Hannen Swaffer, summed it when he said, 'I saw, at the end of it all, what is no doubt unique in the annals of Downing Street – a Prime Minister addressing a crowd from the official residence itself.'

When it was suggested to Chamberlain that he quote former Prime Minister Benjamin Disraeli two days earlier, he had apparently snapped back, 'No, I don't do that sort of thing'.[26] However, on entering Downing Street, he been carried along by the moment and, by the time he got to the first floor, he had changed his mind. Going to the window, his wife beside him, he looked down at the crowd and invoked the words of Disraeli's most famous statement upon returning home from the Berlin Congress of 1878: 'My very good friends, this is the second time in our history that there has come back from Germany to Downing Street peace with honour. I believe it is peace for our time.' Then he added, 'We thank you from the bottom of our hearts. And now I recommend you to go home and sleep quietly in your beds.'[27]

While the Disraeli quote had been suggested to Chamberlain, the line about peace for our time had not. It was an uncharacteristic slip up by a man who always chose his words very carefully and one which was to cost him dearly in the Parliamentary debate that was to follow. History would also judge him to have made a fateful error of judgement. But at the time, the remarks were exactly what a generation still scarred by the death toll of the First World War wanted to hear.

Amid scenes of national rejoicing, the Conservative Party Conference, which was due to take place in Newcastle upon Tyne on Thursday, 6 October, was postponed. Pathé News made plans to rush out a new twelve-minute film entitled *'Chamberlain, the Man of the Hour.'* 'In all my experience in the trade', said W.J. Gell, the Managing Director of Pathé Pictures, 'I have never known such an enthusiastic demand for any picture as the one we are making. We shall be working twenty-four hours a day between now and Monday, turning out the prints required for simultaneous exhibition throughout Great Britain. At least 1,000 will be needed.'[28]

Yet the Munich agreement was not welcomed with unbridled joy everywhere. In its editorial of 8 October 1938, *Nature* magazine, which counted Chamberlain among its readership due to his passion for natural history, stated:

> This is, indeed, a step forward in the promotion of peaceful methods of settling disputes between nations; and however much we may deplore the intolerance of intellectual freedom, and the persecution of a defenceless minority, by which Germany is suppressing the advancement of knowledge and the rights of man, the declaration of the new Anglo-German undertaking makes the outlook much brighter. Sixty years ago, another Prime Minister, Disraeli, avoided a war between Russia and Britain by the Treaty of Berlin, as the result of consultation with the councils of Europe, and secured his "peace with honour". We hope and believe that the resolution now made between the German Führer and Chancellor and the British Prime Minister will have more lasting influence than that reached by Disraeli, of whose treaty it was said soon afterwards:

> 'Once "peace with honour" home was brought; And there the glory ceases. For peace a dozen wars has fought, And honour's all to pieces.'[29]

Outside of the euphoria which overtook the capital, the population expressed its feelings in very different ways. In Leicester, members of an amateur dramatic society at The Little Theatre were so alarmed about the 'national emergency' that they postponed the opening of their latest production. A local paper stated, 'Owing to the national emergency many acting members of the Leicester Drama Society are not at present available and it has therefore been found necessary to delay the opening of the 1938-39 season until Saturday, 15th October, when the Society will present "In Theatre Street" by H. R. Lenormand [Henri-René Lenormand, 1882-1951].' Luckily for Little Theatre goers who had already bought tickets, all the seats from the cancelled run were transferred to the week of 15-23 October.[30]

In Cardiff, in a sign of the hostility that was to come, *The Daily Telegraph* reported that a crowd had developed outside the Town Hall after the Lord Mayor, O.C. Purnell, ordered that the flags of the four powers be flown above the building 'as an expression of joy that the peace of the world had been preserved.'[31] As soon as the swastika flag was raised there were telephone calls to the Lord Mayor's office complaining and asking for it to be taken down. The calls were duly ignored so a crowd began to gather outside. When the councillors arrived in the afternoon for their meeting about school attendance they were barracked by an angry mob. Quickly turning against the mayor, the councillors demanded the flag be taken down but the Lord Mayor refused to give in, stating that they had 'taken the wrong view of the situation.' The councillors decided to take matters into their own hands and Alderman Sir William Williams stormed out of the meeting and, accompanied by several colleagues, climbed up the stairs which led to the roof. Finding the door closed, they pushed themselves up through a skylight and eventually reached the flagpole using ladders that had been left in the loft by workmen laying slate on the roof. By this time a big crowd had gathered outside to witness the spectacle of three councillors balancing on ladders a hundred feet above the ground, like something out of a Charlie Chaplin slapstick comedy. When the Nazi flag was finally hauled down a very loud cheer went up in the crowd below.

Swastika flags over Cardiff apart, most of the war-weary population were delighted by what Chamberlain had achieved that late September day. It was his finest hour and, for a few short months afterwards, he would be the most popular politician of his era, basking in the reflected glory of a thankful world. Immediately following the Munich agreement, Chamberlain would be inundated with over 20,000 letters and gifts from a grateful nation and from countries around the world, and this would continue unabated up to his seventieth birthday in March 1939. Yet just six months later, Britain would be plunged into a war with Germany for the second time in just over twenty years. Then, in May 1940, Chamberlain would be forced from office following a vote of no confidence in Parliament. Finally, on 9 November, as bombs rained down on British cities, he would die from cancer. No politician in recent history would achieve such levels of popularity or fall from grace so quickly.

Chapter 2

Moths, birds and the Bahamas

'A farmer went out to sow his seed. As he was scattering the seed, some
fell along the path; it was trampled on, and the birds ate it up.' Luke 8:5

The year of Neville Chamberlain's birth, 1869, was memorable politically for
both the Conservative Party and his famous family. That year, the first council
houses in Europe were built by a Conservative local authority in Liverpool, a block
of tenement flats called St Martin's Cottages.[1] In Birmingham, Chamberlain's
birthplace, his father, Joseph Chamberlain, was elected to the town council for
the first time.

Arthur Neville Chamberlain was born on 18 March 1869 in a house called
'Southbourne', in Augustus Road in the middle of the Calthorpe estate,
a fashionable suburb for wealthy industrialists in the upmarket district of
Edgbaston. Owned by the 5th Baron Frederick William Henry Gough-Calthorpe
(1826-1893), a Liberal politician, the estate lay to the south of Birmingham but
escaped the prevailing southwesterly wind, which blanketed the city in smog, the
result of smoke and fumes from its ever expanding industries.

In line with many of Victorian Britain's cities, Birmingham was undergoing
a population explosion and had doubled in size in just fifty years. Dubbed the
'Workshop of the World', Birmingham was indisputably Britain's second city,
with a thriving civic heart. Despite its cultural advancements, however, living
conditions for the majority of its inhabitants had deteriorated markedly. By the
time of Chamberlain's birth the centre of Birmingham was surrounded by poor,
working-class housing, with Edgbaston the sole wealthy middle-class enclave.
The houses of the poor were built of local brick and roofed with Welsh slate
brought by canal. Most were back-to-back, two-up-two-down, or even one-
up-one-down, with shared outside toilets and washing facilities in a communal
courtyard, and commonly known as slums.[2] In Birmingham there were 40,000
back-to-back houses and 6,000 communal courtyards while one in ten people
lived more than two to a room. The infant mortality rate was a frightening 199
in every thousand, a statistic that was soon to include Chamberlain's own sibling.
One tap supplied over thirty people and thousands of outside toilets had to be
emptied every day, resulting in streets full of human waste attracting vermin. In

total over half a million people had barely 300 acres of open space.[3] By contrast, Neville Chamberlain grew up on an estate with 18 acres of grounds.[4]

Neville was the only son of Joseph Chamberlain (1836–1914), known affectionately as Joe, and his second wife, Florence Kenrick. Joseph Chamberlain's first wife, Harriet Kenrick, Florence's first cousin, had died giving birth to Neville's half-brother, Austen, in 1863. The previous year she had given birth to Joseph's first child, Beatrice. His second wife, Florence, was to give him four more children. In 1870, a year after Neville was born, she gave birth to Ida, then another girl, Hilda in 1872 and the following year, in 1873, a third daughter, Ethel. On 13 February 1875 a fifth child was born but complications set in and the next day tragedy struck for a second time when Florence and the child died.

Joseph was a wealthy, self-made businessman who, at the age of 18, had joined his uncle in law's screw-making business, Nettlefolds of Birmingham. Joseph's father, also called Joseph, was a shoe manufacturer who had invested in the business, and he worked his way up, eventually becoming a partner, after which the company was known as Nettlefold and Chamberlain. The business was hugely successful and at its height produced two-thirds of all the screws made in England, exporting them throughout the world. Its virtual monopoly on screws meant that it literally held the British Empire together.

By the time of Neville's birth in 1869 Joseph had already became involved in Liberal politics, influenced by the strong radical traditions among Birmingham shoemakers, and his Unitarian church. Joseph's religion was a very important part of his life. As a Unitarian he believed that God was one entity as opposed to the mainstream Christian belief of the Trinity of Father, Son and Holy Spirit. More controversially, Unitarians also believed that Jesus was a saviour but was not the son of God. However, the deaths of both his wives in childbirth had a profound effect on Joseph and his young family. Up to that point, as well as being an aspiring politician, he had been a devout and regular churchgoer, attending the Church of the Messiah on Broad Street in Birmingham.[5] The Minister of the chapel, John Henry Crosskey, was a progressive and radical reformer, championing the rights of the poor, and a leading advocate of women's equality, proclaiming 'ye are all one in Christ Jesus'.[6]

Joseph was a familiar figure at the church and, like many other prominent local men, led Sunday School classes on his free Sunday afternoons. But the death of Florence caused him to question his faith for the first time and some of Neville's earliest memories as a 6-year-old boy would have been of his father grieving and crying out to God. As a result of his suffering, Joseph renounced his personal faith but he did not relinquish his long-held Unitarian principles. This theological compromise of having a lapsed faith but still respecting what

Christianity stood for was a position that his son Neville would later adopt, applying the Unitarian principles he had grown up with to tackling poverty in the slums.

At a young age Joseph instilled in Neville a concern for the poor, borne out of a moral conscience rather than a religious conviction. So Neville did not follow in his father's footsteps by telling Bible stories, but he was still a regular church member, joining in the singing of vigorous Unitarian hymns such as *'Nearer My God, to thee'* and *'City of God, how broad and far'*.[7] As a result, Neville became an agnostic, believing that if there was a God he was a good and kind one, not one who judged people as being bound for heaven or hell. His cousin, Norman, who was later to play a pivotal part in his life, said, 'We always understood as children that, as our lives had fallen in pleasant places, it behoved us the more to do what we could to improve the lot of those less happily placed.'

Instead of a religious faith, Joseph encouraged his children to be strongly independent and to challenge authority, even if this meant taking an anti-establishment stance on political issues. To instil his values he taught his children to tell the truth, to do what they were told, but to question afterwards if necessary, and, whatever they did in life, to do it well. However, there was one aspect of the church that Joseph embraced all his life. Reflecting the mores of Victorian Britain, Unitarians were encouraged not to show emotion in public and so all Joseph's children were raised with no outward displays of affection. This was reflected in the family motto *je tiens ferme*, or 'I hold fast'. It aptly summed up Joseph's personal belief, that you kept your problems to yourself and did not show emotion in public or private because it meant that you were weak. So Joseph never told his children about the death of their own mother and Neville only remembered being told about it by Florence's twin sister, Louisa. As a result of having no mother and an austere father who was always away on business, Joseph's children grew up forming very strong bonds with each other and with the wider Chamberlain clan. This closeness, relying on each other for emotional support, was to become a hallmark of all the Chamberlain children throughout their lives.[8]

After the death of their mother, Neville and his three sisters were brought up by their Aunt Caroline (known as Lina) while Beatrice and Austen were sent away to boarding school. Holidays together were one of the few shared family times, visiting Scotland or heading to the seaside. Despite Joseph's absence, Southbourne was an idyllic place to grow up. It boasted a large garden and it was here that Neville Chamberlain's lifelong interest in natural history first started. His father, who would go on to become one of the world's experts on breeding orchids, had installed a greenhouse with heating to grow his exotic plants and Neville enjoyed nothing better than playing in it with his sisters. There he became captivated by the beauty and diversity of orchids, which his father had collected from all over the world.

The children also had their own gardens where they were taught to grow a wide variety of plants, a hobby he and Ida enthusiastically embraced. Joseph also encouraged his children to have pets and, in a field at the bottom of the garden, they kept a Shetland pony called Tom Thumb. Neville cared little for the horse, preferring instead to identify insects, plants and birds he found while out rambling. To amuse themselves, the Chamberlain children invented a game called 'sparrowhawks and eagles'. The birds represented two warring tribes of Indians: the sparrowhawks, who were good, and the eagles, who were evil, and for fun they would stage mock battles between the two. In 1877, their Aunt Lina married and was replaced by her sister, Aunt Clara, who actively encouraged Neville's fledgling interest in natural history, helping him to identify the wildlife he found in the garden.[9]

A passion for natural history ran in Neville's family. His uncle, Walter Chamberlain (1847-1920), who also worked in the family business, was an avid ornithologist who amassed a huge collection of birds during his lifetime. The youngest brother of Joseph, Walter's collection consisted of some 300 British birds and over 200 foreign ones, many new to science. From 1875, Walter spent a decade travelling the world with his brother, Herbert, to some of the most remote locations on earth in search of exotic species to add to his collection. During these epic adventures, Walter would firstly identify 'target birds' using the limited bird books available and then track them down using specialist local guides. To 'preserve them for science' he would first shoot them, then carefully skin them and boil down the remains, adding the skins, skull and bones to his collection. When he showed his collection to the young Neville, his nephew was so enthralled that he started his own (Walter left his impressive bird collection to the Birmingham Museum but sadly many skulls and skins had to be destroyed in 1946 as they were in poor condition). After returning from his travels, the eccentric Walter lived at Harborne Hall in Birmingham where, in keeping with his interests, he maintained a small private zoo. Neville was a regular visitor and his favourite activity was helping to feed the penguins.[10]

Another uncle on his mother's side, George Kenrick (1850-1939) was a prominent entomologist who specialised in lepidoptera (butterflies and moths) and travelled widely in his youth, visiting New Guinea on several expeditions. He began writing about tropical butterflies in journals, especially the prestigious *Proceedings of the Zoological Society of London*. From 1902 to 1903 he supported the renowned Victorian naturalist Antwerp Edgar Pratt and his two sons, Carl

Brenders Pratt and Felix Biet Pratt, on an expedition to the British part of New Guinea, and from 1909 to 1910 on another expedition to the Arfak Mountains in Dutch New Guinea. Both expeditions were very successful, discovering hundreds of new species of butterfly, including the endemic Rothschild birdwing *Ornithoptera rothschildi*. To the young Neville his lepidoptera-loving uncle was fondly known simply as Uncle George and he was to have a huge influence on him growing up.

As well as being an idyllic playground, Southbourne, as the home of an up-and-coming Member of Parliament, acted as a magnet for politicians and celebrities. Neville would have seen and met many of the leading politicians of the day, including the Prime Minister William Gladstone (1809-1898), who arrived in an open carriage with four horses and a police escort. Joseph actively encouraged his children to debate the issues of the day and to practise public speaking. On one memorable occasion this included a debate about whether it was right to execute Charles I, Neville being profoundly shocked when his father said that Oliver Cromwell had been well within his rights to chop off his head as King Charles had abused his position.[11]

In 1877, at the age of 8, Neville was sent away to boarding school at Southport, an experience he did not enjoy as it separated him from his beloved sisters. However, it was during this time that they first started writing letters to each other, a practice that would continue throughout their entire lives. These letters, sent each weekend from alternate sisters, were to be a lifeline to the young Neville and, as an adult, allowed him to share his innermost thoughts and fears with people he trusted implicitly. In this way Ida, Hilda and Ethel became more than just sisters, they became his best friends and closest confidants.

In 1878, Joseph, as befitted a wealthy man rapidly climbing up the political ladder, commissioned the building of his own home, Highbury Hall in Birmingham, known by the family simply as Highbury. It had fifty rooms and was located in the district of Moseley, three miles south of the city centre, where his favourite brother resided. Highbury was named after the eponymous district in north London, where Joseph lived as a child. It was designed in a 'roomy Venetian-Gothic style',[12] by the architect John Henry Chamberlain (no relation) who incorporated a distinctive terracotta decoration into the façade, while the grounds were landscaped by Edward Milner, who designed 'a circuit path that ran around the periphery of the estate leading from the drive to points of interest, including a pond and a lake'. The hall also boasted a palm house and thirteen glass houses for Joseph's burgeoning orchid collection. In front of the hall was a terrace leading to a semi-circular parterre from which there were magnificent views over the Worcestershire countryside.[13] By 1880, when the family moved in, Joseph had already been Mayor of Birmingham and elected as an MP had entered the Cabinet as the President of the Board of Trade.

Highbury had thirty acres of grounds and Neville loved nothing more than exploring and playing in them with his sisters and cousins. In his holidays he built wigwams in nearby Moor Green bluebell wood, climbed trees and spent his time birdwatching. He began identifying the many different species occurring there, from the more common ones like the robin *Erithacus rubecula* and blackbird *Turdus merula* to the rarer ones such as the nightjar *Caprimulgus europaeus* and barn owl *Tyto alba*. Yet it was insects that became Neville's real passion, encouraged by his Uncle George who was a Fellow of the Royal Entomological Society and a leading member of the Birmingham Entomological Society. An Alderman and a major benefactor to the city, Kenrick was a bachelor and Neville was his favourite nephew. In Joseph's absence he took the boy under his wing, teaching him everything he knew about insects and nature as well as how to shoot and fish.

At the age of 11 Neville started to record the common butterflies and moths he saw in the garden and at nearby local sites in two old, black, leather-bound address books, writing on the front *'Where is it?'*. He recorded his first sighting of an orange-tip butterfly *Anthocharis cardamines* on 29 May 1880 and a buff ermine moth *Spilosoma lutea* on 28 May 1881.[14] These happy years came to an abrupt end when, in April 1882, at the age of 13 and after a short period at preparatory school, Neville was sent to Rugby School where his brother Austen had already made a name for himself. Austen was in his final term before going on to Cambridge and was renowned for political speeches, which he notoriously practised on his dormitory as well as in the debating society.

The motto of Rugby School is *Orando Laborando* or 'prayer and work' but it seems that Neville didn't care for either. In church services he turned away from the altar during the reading of the creed while his academic record was distinctly average. He was also bullied by a boy who disliked his brother and as a result became shy and introverted, traits that would stay with him for life, despite in adulthood learning to hide them. While at Rugby, Neville was encouraged by a friend to take part in the debating society like his brother but he refused, reportedly stating, 'No, I don't take any interest in politics, and never shall.' When asked why, he replied, 'You don't know what our house is like for days before my father makes one of his big speeches. Everybody has to be quiet, and even at the meal the conversation is subdued.'

What did excite Neville was his passion for natural history. At Rugby he was co-curator of the vivarium, or animal house, and was put in charge of the insect collection. In a journal entitled *'Entomology 1886'*, with his initials ANC on the cover, he kept detailed notes of the moths and butterflies he bred there, including the development of the pupae and chrysalids. He also recorded moths and butterflies from around Rugby and in nearby Brandon and Frankton woods. Although introverted at school, Neville made some lifelong friends, including Leslie Scott, who would go on to become the Lord Justice, and Whitmore Lionel Richards, who was to marry his sister, Ethel. Just like when he lived at Southbourne, the summer holidays were by far his happiest times. Leslie Scott wrote of him, 'He seemed to know by instinct just which bush on a woodland path we ought to beat to make a rare moth fly out.' When he left, in the summer of 1886, the annual report of the Rugby Natural History Society praised 'a very good worker'. Yet, natural history apart, it was not a period in his life that Neville enjoyed or looked back on fondly. Unlike his brother Austen, who loved the school and later became chairman of the governors, Neville never returned.

By the time Neville left Rugby School it was very clear that Austen was being lined up to follow in his father's political footsteps. In 1886, Austen helped out his father in the general election, six years later entering Parliament beside him. In contrast, Neville's destiny would be to take over the family business. At the age of 17 he was taken away from Rugby by his father and sent to study science, metallurgy and engineering at Mason College in Birmingham. At the same time, a young Stanley Baldwin, the future Prime Minister who would go on to mentor Neville, was also studying there. Mason's was founded by the great philanthropist Sir Josiah Mason (1811-1881) and it taught pupils all the skills they needed to get ahead in Birmingham's burgeoning new industries. However, Neville again struggled academically and did not do well at any subject, coming bottom of the class. It was another difficult period in his life and one which, like Rugby, left him feeling deeply demoralised. Worse still, Neville's father had ordered him to teach at their church Sunday School, as he had done previously, believing it would do him good. Lacking any real faith, Neville became bored and instead spent his time studying the works of the great naturalists like Charles Darwin (1809-1882), Thomas Henry Huxley (1825-1895) and Alfred Russell Wallace (1823-1913), all of whom were proponents of the theory of evolution through natural selection. It was a subject that fascinated him and he would study it long into the night.

In 1888, in Washington DC, Joseph was married for a third time to Mary Crowninshield Endicott (1864-1957), the 24-year-old daughter of the extremely wealthy US politician, and later Secretary of War, William Crowninshield Endicott (1826-1900). Joseph was over twice her age and the marriage attracted a lot of press attention.[15] After returning from their honeymoon on the French Riviera, Mary became an ever-present counsel at his side. It was a happy marriage, albeit childless, and she threw herself into organising social events at Highbury and moving in ever more celebrated circles.

Mary was only five years older than Neville, but found him very shy and immature. Neville and his sisters saw little of their new stepmother as both she and Joseph were in London when Parliament was in session, returning to Highbury only once a month for a few days, although they spent longer periods there at Easter and in the summer. However, over time, Mary became very fond of Neville and his sisters. Highbury's sheer size and design lent itself to large social gatherings and Mary hosted many of these 'At Homes', which could be attended by up to 500 guests, as well as many smaller, more intimate dinners.

Whenever possible, Neville absented himself from these large social gatherings, instead continuing his studies of the natural world, enjoying botany, birdwatching, horse riding and taking long walks with his faithful retriever, Crusoe. It was also at this time that Neville developed a passion for his father's orchids and they would tend them together on Sundays. The family also enjoyed travelling, visiting Paris and Venice as well as taking a memorable trip to Egypt, then a British puppet state, in the winter of 1889-90. While there, Neville was engrossed in the art, history, architecture, wildlife, landscape and people of the country, all of which he faithfully recorded in his diary. However, he found travelling with his illustrious father irksome because of the constant officialdom with 'sheiks salaaming respectfully', dinner guests who 'stayed a great deal longer than was necessary' and the continual 'review of garrisons'. In Cairo, Joseph dined with the Prime Minister, Riyad Pasha, and Neville sat next to Colonel Herbert Kitchener (1850-1916) who had just been appointed Inspector General of the Egyptian police. Kitchener would later become famous as a recruiting sergeant for the First World War, but Neville found that he was 'fond of flowers, so we talked a good deal about them'.[16]

Yet it was his hobby of entomology, and in particular moth collecting, which really excited Neville, spurred on by his Uncle George, who had risen to be vice president of the Birmingham Entomological Society. The monthly meetings of the society, which were held at Avebury House in Newall Street, were well attended and consisted of talks, peer reviews of scientific papers and the showing of specimens collected on field visits. The minutes of the society in 1890 show a passionate 21-year-old Neville debating and engaging with experts many years his senior. Together with his uncle, Neville made a special study of the camouflage of pug moths, a species that blends in with its background as a defence mechanism against daytime predators. He also showed his extensive collection of geometer moths, a species whose caterpillars are well known for moving in a very distinctive looping way.[17] Neville caught them, using light traps and by a method known as 'treacling' or 'sugaring', which consisted of making up a mixture of treacle and sugar mixed with alcohol. He daubed this on walls, fences and tree trunks around the family home at night, coming back an hour or so later with a torch to see what he had caught.

In the autumn of 1890, Joseph met the Governor of the Bahamas on a visit to his wife's family in Canada. Sir Ambrose Shea, an Irishman with the gift of the gab and an eye for a profit, convinced Joseph that a fortune could be made by planting sisal which grew in the islands like 'a weed' and from which, he insisted, hemp of the best quality could be made. By this time Joseph was in desperate need of money, having paid for the building of Highbury and losing much of his remaining savings on some bad investments in South America. Convinced by Shea, he reserved 20,000 acres and sent Austen and Neville to investigate which of the islands would be most suitable to plant the crop. They arrived in the capital Nassau in December 1890, travelling on the weekly mailboat, and from there explored the exotic islands by launch.

Neville was in ecstasy over the wildlife, writing home enthusiastically about the herons on the southernmost islands of Inagua. Then, as now, the islands were a mecca for wealthy birdwatchers, supporting over 80,000 flamingos as well as parrots, pelicans, ducks and hummingbirds found nowhere else in the Bahamas. The two islands of Inagua supported no fewer than five species of heron: the black-crowned night heron *Nycticorax nycticorax*, yellow-crowned night heron *Nyctanassa violacea*, green heron *Butorides virescens*, tricolored heron *Egretta tricolor* and the little blue heron *Egretta caerulea*. For a birdwatcher like Neville coming from Britain, which only supports one species, the grey heron *Ardea cinerea*, it was paradise. He also saw a vast colony of roseate, or West Indian, flamingos *Phoenicopterus rube* on the island of Mayaguana 'swimming about like pink swans', and on Long Island he saw a huge diversity of striking butterflies. Here he chased about the island with his net in hand in 'hot chase after the most magnificent Papilio I have ever seen; after running about a mile at full speed I lost him.' The *Papilio* in question was the Bahaman swallowtail *Papilio andraemon*, a majestic butterfly with a four-inch wingspan, its name being derived from the tail-like extension on its hind wings which resembles a swallow. Lastly, on their island recce they visited the island of Andros, which was so wild Neville had to make his way through swamps and drag their launch off sandbanks. However, the land was cheap and it was here that Austen and Neville thought would be the best location to grow sisal.

In February 1891, they returned home with their report, giving a very favourable account of the potential for growing sisal, estimating that profits of 30 per cent could be expected on their investment. Moving quickly, Joseph decided to take a huge financial risk and duly dispatched Neville in April to make the family fortune while Austen stayed at home and was lined up for a parliamentary career. Neville promptly bought up land on Andros, the largest of the twenty-six inhabited Bahamian islands with a population of 6,000. Together with his team of 'four Europeans and 800 negro workers' he built a home and then burnt, cleared and planted around 10,000 acres. To transport the sisal he built roads and a wharf. To service the plantation he built a store and, to show he was willing to do his share of all the jobs, served behind the counter. It was lonely and exhausting work, even for a fit 22-year-old in his prime. What made it worse was the relentless heat; by day it reached up to 85°F, while at night he was devoured by mosquitos.

Over the next six years, with only occasional trips home and to the capital, Nassau, Neville threw himself into the task, even building a school and a bank for the locals, but the sisal simply would not grow well enough in the thin, arid soil. Isolated and missing home, he spent long periods reading, studying the wildlife and writing lengthy letters to his sisters. Despite the conditions, he remained ever the Englishman abroad, wearing a frock coat and top hat to government receptions in the capital, despite the extreme heat. Back on Andros he kept a small menagerie at his home, Mastic Hall, including a praying mantis and two iguanas. His Uncle George sent out the only known book about the birds of the Bahamas and he set about enthusiastically ticking them off, soon identifying most of the birds on the island. As at Highbury, he got to know many of them not just by sight but by their call. Encouraged by his other uncle, Walter, he trapped and killed some of the more unusual birds so that he could collect their skins and in the process he identified many rare species. As a result he became a good amateur taxidermist and on his return to Britain donated the skins to the British Museum. To impress his Uncle George, he also collected many butterflies and other insects, informing the Birmingham Entomological Society about his collection when he returned home and again donating them to the museum. Studying these a year after he got back, the British Museum's chief taxonomist, Arthur Gardiner Butler, identified a new butterfly species to science and named it Chamberlain's Yellow *Terias chamberlaini* after its collector.[18] (The male butterfly is orange with black wing tips while the female is a brilliant yellow. Neville Chamberlain remains the only British Prime Minister to have discovered a new species and had it named after him. The butterfly has subsequently been reassigned to a different genus and is now called *Pyrisitia chamberlaini*).

On his rare visits home for holidays, Neville did not take a well-earned break as most people would have done, but instead went on trips to study lepidoptera. On one such expedition, to the Norfolk Broads in July 1895, he and his Uncle George identified eighty-five species of butterfly and moth, including the only British *Papilio*, the strikingly beautiful swallowtail butterfly *Papilio machaon*.

After staying in Britain for a couple of weeks, he would then dutifully return to the Bahamas, continuing the unceasing task of trying get the sisal crop to grow. Eventually, in the winter of 1896, Neville had to admit defeat and sold off the machinery before leaving for good in March 1897. In abandoning the enterprise, his father Joseph had lost in excess of £50,000, equivalent to half a million pounds today. Neville was 28 years old and felt he had failed himself and, more importantly, his father. All that was left was the land, which was 'worthless', eventually being sold in 1921 for just £200. When he got back to England, Queen Victoria's Diamond Jubilee was being celebrated in style and he commented to a friend that December, 'How far away the Bahamas seem already ... yet I often think of it, and with very grateful recollections, for in spite of all the disappointments it was a great experience and I know I am much the better and stronger for it.'[19]

Upon his return from the Bahamas, Neville returned to Highbury with few qualifications and few prospects. He may have felt a failure but he soon found his feet again, thanks to his extensive family connections and the family name. Neville became head of Elliott's Metal Company and director of the famous Birmingham Small Arms Company. He also became director of Hoskins, a business employing seventy men, who fitted out berths on Admiralty and private boats. Just like on Andros, Neville threw himself into the work, his driving motivation to recoup his father's investment and at the same time to make his own fortune. When Parliament was sitting, he was the only member of the family living at Highbury so all the rooms except those he used were closed. He spent what little spare time he had absorbed in his studies of Darwin and tending his father's tropical orchids. His only holidays were expeditions in search of rare moths. From 1896 until 1910 these took him all over England and up to Scotland. Chamberlain's notebooks are full of detailed field trips and at each location he would meticulously record every species. Entries in his notebook include species lists from trips to the Sussex Downs, Wyre Forest in Gloucestershire, Brandon Woods in Warwickshire, Cannock Chase in Staffordshire, Oundle in Northamptonshire and the Scottish borders.

As well as entomology, Chamberlain continued to develop his skills as an ornithologist. Having Highbury to himself meant that he had time to record all the species he found in the grounds and the surrounding area, much of which was farmland. The landscape of tree-lined lanes, pasture, heath, hedgerows, open watercourses and flood meadows was rich in bird life. By now Neville was an expert ornithologist who could identify many species just by their calls and he regularly sent details of his sightings to the local natural history society. He also undertook a bird survey of the grounds and from his observations and other local records submitted a species list for Highbury and the surrounding area to the society.[20]

The list ranged from common garden, woodland and farmland birds like tits, woodpeckers and thrushes to far rarer species such as the red-backed shrike *Lanius collurio* – known as the butcher bird because of its habit of impaling its prey on spines – and the nightjar *Caprimulgus europaeus*, which hunted the grounds at night in search of Neville's favourite insects, moths. It also included unusual birds like the wryneck *Jynx torquilla*, which can twist its neck through nearly 360°, as well as real rarities like the grey phalarope *Phalaropus fulicarius*, an elusive wading bird which breeds in the Arctic and is rarely, if ever, encountered inland. Also present were secretive species like the corncrake *Crex crex*, whose rasping call was rapidly disappearing from the English countryside. In total, the surveys identified over eighty species for the grounds and surrounding area, an impressive list by any standards for a suburban area, even in Victorian times.

Birds were not the only visitors to Highbury. When Parliament was not sitting, Joseph would return home and the hall then became the focus of his political life outside Westminster. Neville always received his father's guests with great courtesy, but still felt public life was not for him. Now he was not only living in the shadow of his father, but also his brother Austen who was, by this time, a junior minister and being openly talked about as a future leader. Instead of debating, Neville preferred to spend time studying orchids with his father, and it was botany, not politics, that they discussed long into the night. It was at this time that Neville was also introduced to shooting and fishing by his Uncle George on trips to Scotland. Like entomology and birdwatching, fishing would become a lifelong passion. (Between 1921 and 1934 he fished the river Dee for salmon every Easter with his friend Arthur Wood. Each Christmas Chamberlain would present Wood with a signed wildife book in appreciation of their friendship. A.H.E. Wood is now credited with developing the 'greased line' method of salmon fishing. Chamberlain also kept a fishing diary detailing weather, water current, fishing equipment and his catches, right up to 22 June 1940, five months before he died).

Chapter 3

Love, children and the Council Chamber

'Let all that you do be done in love.' 1 Corinthians 16:14

On 25 January 1902 Neville wrote to his friend F. B. Matthews (the Rector on Andros), 'My time is divided between business and local work ... with now and then a short holiday, and then business again. I haven't quite found my mission yet and feel a bit dissatisfied about it.'[1] Neville's answer to that dissatisfaction was to develop the family businesses, in particular improving the working conditions at the companies where he was a director. He also became heavily involved in his father's campaign to develop a university for the Midlands, which by royal charter became the University of Birmingham in 1900. This was the first civic or 'redbrick' university in the country that welcomed students from all religions and backgrounds on an equal basis.

Neville also travelled extensively, visiting Italy, Croatia, Algiers, Holland, Switzerland and, in the winter of 1904-5, Burma and India. While on a steamer going down the Irawaddy river (noting with satisfaction that his berth had been kitted out by his firm Hoskins), he wrote in his diary, 'Far away on the other bank some little spots of white, pink and yellow show where a party of Burmese are poling along by the sandbank in a long, narrow dugout. Behind them is a broad patch of yellow sand crowded with cormorants, terns, fish eagles, and enormous black and white storks standing on one leg or lazily passing their wing feathers through their long black bills.' The tour of Burma and India, however, was marred when he was told, while visiting the Punjab, that his youngest sister, Ethel, had died. Ethel had suffered from poor health for most of her adult life, especially after the birth of her daughter, Hilda Mary, in 1901. She developed tuberculosis, and died in Switzerland on 15 January 1905. Being so far away made the loss even greater to bear but he consoled himself that 'at any rate she has come into the great peace'.

The following year was to bring further tragedy. The Liberal Unionists, of which Joseph was now the leading member following a split with the Liberals over tariff reform, were trounced in the general election of 1906 by their former partners. On 8 July Joseph celebrated his seventieth birthday, receiving thousands of congratulatory telegrams. He celebrated in style with days of official luncheons, public addresses, parades and bands. On 10 July tens of thousands of people crowded into the centre of Birmingham to hear him make a passionate speech promoting the virtues of tariff reform. Three days later Joseph collapsed while dressing for dinner in the bathroom of his London house at Prince's Gardens. He had suffered a stroke that paralysed his right side. Although unaffected mentally, the stroke resulted in his sight and speech deteriorating and he lost the ability to write. After a month, Joseph was still only able to walk a few steps and was never to recover his health or his political career.[2]

Now 37, Neville was devastated by his father's stroke but at his behest carried on managing the family businesses. The only consolations for the family were Austen's marriage to Ivy Muriel Dundas that year and Neville becoming chairman of Birmingham General Hospital where he immediately started fundraising for a new, larger building. The campaign was to go on for most of his life and, though building did eventually start in 1934, Neville was still fundraising for it when he became Prime Minister.

When he wasn't running the family businesses, Neville was investing in his rapidly expanding collection of moths. In January 1909, he visited the home of Ernest Swinhoe, at 6 Gunterstone Gardens, West Kensington. Ernest was the son of the famous naturalist Charles Swinhoe and was a dealer in 'exotic lepidotera'. His catalogue boasted over eighty different specimens from South America, South Africa and India which provided 'an excellent reference for museums and collectors'. Chamberlain carefully wrote down every species in each of the cabinets in his notebook and invested in over forty specimens, with prices ranging from 1 shilling to over £1, over £100 in today prices. To please his father he also became a member of the Birmingham and Edgbaston Debating Society, later becoming president, like Joseph. However, he was not an enthusiastic member and when he came to give his retiring address, in September 1910, it was to Darwinism that he turned, not politics.

Neville's address to the society was on the subject of 'human development under natural selection'. He concluded that man's progress was 'extinguishing species, just as drainage of the fens had killed the large copper butterfly'. The spectacular large copper butterfly *Lycaena dispar* was first discovered near Spalding in Lincolnshire in 1749 but had become extinct in the British Isles by 1851, the last recorded sighting being in Bottisham Fen in Cambridgeshire. For lepidopterists, the butterfly had become a totemic species and summed up the effect man was having on the natural world. Neville, by highlighting its cause, made a passionate case for the conservation of all species. He also mused over the role of war in human development, presciently stating '....it is natural to suppose that this disinclination to set in motion the machinery of war will grow stronger'.[3]

Despite being incredibly busy, there was still one vital part of his life missing: love. There had been fleeting romances, and in 1903 he thought he had found the right woman, but the relationship didn't work out. So, at 40 years of age, Neville found himself still single and resigned to remaining a bachelor. Then, in 1910, he met Miss Anne de Vere Cole (1883-1967, also known as Annie), the daughter of William Cole, a Major in the 3rd Dragoon Guards, and his wife Mary de Vere, who hailed from Curragh Chase, County Limerick, in Ireland. On first meeting Anne, in the Whitsun holiday, Neville 'fell head over heels in love with her from the first moment.' She was 29, beautiful and the niece by marriage of his aunt, Lilian Cole. According to society reports, 'She had the blue eyes, racy manners and the humour that goes with Irish blood.'

Humour of a sort certainly ran in Anne's family as her brother was the celebrated prankster and hoaxer, Horace de Vere Cole (1881-1936).[4] According to legend one of his more adolescent pranks was hosting a party at which the guests discovered that they all had the word 'bottom' in their surnames. He also bought tickets for a row of seats at a theatre performance and gave them to eight bald men if they would paint a letter on the top of their heads. When seen from the circle and boxes above the letters spelled out the word 'B-O-L-L-O-C-K-S'. Cole would also wander the streets with a cow's udder bursting through the fly of his trousers causing public outrage, after which he would cut off the offending teats with a pair of scissors. With his thick mane of black hair and bushy moustache, he regularly pretended to be the Labour politician Ramsay MacDonald and at public meetings would relish attacking Labour Party policy. (It clearly did MacDonald no harm as he later went on to become the first Labour Prime Minister).

Cole's best known trick was performed on 7 February 1910 when he fooled the Admiralty into believing he and a group of friends, including the writer Virginia Woolf, were the Emperor of Abyssinia and his entourage. Cole and friends, disguised in heavy black make up, were treated to a full civic reception at Weymouth followed by an inspection of the Royal Navy warship HMS *Dreadnought*. When asked about the *Dreadnought*'s awesome firepower, the Emperor reportedly gesticulated wildly and shouted, 'Bunga! Bunga!' A few weeks later when the hoax was finally made public the Admiralty became a laughing stock and were furious. When the real Emperor of Abyssinia arrived in Britain shortly afterwards crowds shouted 'Bunga! Bunga!' at him and the phrase became a running music hall joke. Asked by Anne what Neville thought of him, he replied, 'I was obliged to say what I did think, but fortunately it appeared that was her opinion too and she was not all inclined to be proud of her brother's exploit. It appears that he is 28. I think he must be a little mad.'

Her eccentric brother apart, Anne was a perfect match for Neville. In his diary he wrote: 'Everything that went before seems only to have been an introduction to this absolute contentment for I no longer have a care in the world.' For Neville, she completed his life and he was devoted to her. She encouraged many of his interests and while not an entomologist, ornithologist or a fisherman, she could talk insects, birds and fish and would often look on with wry amusement as Neville would 'scramble about for an hour over rough ground after two little birds – stonechats I think they were.'[5] If his sisters, Ida and Hilda, who up to that point had been the centre of his devotion, were in any way jealous they didn't show it and Anne, realising the very intimate relationship they shared, never sought to exclude them.

They decided to marry the year after, in 1911, and for their wedding the happy couple compiled a list of essential items that they would need to set up home. The gift list, as well as the usual domestic items, also reflected Neville's interests. It included a moth which he had long cherished for his collection, *Phyllodesma ilicifolia*, or the small lappet moth. The species, one of the rarest in Britain, was duly collected and presented to an overjoyed Neville by the Birmingham Entomological Society.[6] (Now almost certainly extinct in the British Isles, the small lappet moth was formerly found in moorland and woodland habitat in the Midlands and the south-west). Anne, Neville and his moth collection then set up home at Westbourne, a large house in Edgbaston. Two children quickly followed, Dorothy, on Christmas Day 1911, and Frank, on 23 January 1914.

The arrival of the children delighted Neville who had been 'miserable at the thought of a childless old age'. He dedicated himself to fatherhood, determined to give his children the love and emotional support he had not received growing up due to the early death of his mother. One of the first things he did was to encourage his children to take an interest in nature. He read to both of them from the 'animal book' and there were frequent trips to the zoo and to the countryside where he identified plants, moths and birds.

The year before his marriage, Neville had taken the big decision to stand for election to Birmingham City Council. Living in the shadow of his famous brother, and with multiple businesses to manage, Neville had been reluctant to run, fearing the political backlash. However, it was his wife Anne who changed his mind. Within a couple of months of meeting her, she had persuaded him to drop some of his less high-profile causes and instead encouraged him to do 'as much as I like in Birmingham and in politics generally. The fact is she thinks politics great fun and can't have too much of them.' Anne not only loved entertaining, she also revelled in moving in the sort of circles associated with the Chamberlain dynasty. Setting aside his previous reservations, and with Anne's active encouragement, he finally decided to throw his hat into the political ring.

Neville was duly elected in the local election of November 1911, the second of three councillors to represent All Saints ward in the Birmingham constituency of Ladywood. His acceptance speech focused on the need for better town planning, more open spaces, better technical education and the redevelopment of canals, all pet subjects. But to the reporters who questioned him afterwards about his ambition, he was quick to quell any rumours that he planned to enter national politics, replying, 'I fully expect the council chamber to not only be the beginning but the end of my public career.'[7]

In the spring of 1912, the Chamberlain family was busy supporting Joseph while also pursuing their own careers; Neville balancing business and politics with his burgeoning interest in natural history. On 16 May 1912 Charles Rothschild, a rich banker and avid naturalist, called a meeting in London with the radical idea of identifying and protecting Britain's best places for wildlife.[8] To do this he formed the Society for the Promotion of Nature Reserves, or SPNR, which held its first meeting in the boardroom at the Natural History Museum on 26 July. A large number of eminent people joined, including the Foreign Secretary, Sir Edward Grey (1862-1933), the 1st Viscount Grey of Fallodon, a talented ornithologist (still best remembered for his quote 'The lamps are going out all over Europe, we shall not see them lit again in our life-time' on the eve of the First World War). In all, fifty Fellows of the prestigious scientific academy, The Royal Society, joined the SPNR and so did Neville as an associate member. (The SPNR would eventually become The Wildlife Trusts, today one of the largest and most influential nature conservation organisations in Britain).

At the same time Neville's sisters Ida and Hilda, both accomplished botanists in their own right, decided to write a book about the wildlife of the French Riviera. All the Chamberlains had spent some very happy childhood summer holidays there and the sisters decided to write about the species they had found in the Côte d'Azur. Hilda wrote the text while Ida, who was a gifted amateur artist, did the illustrations, producing a wonderful set of miniature paintings of the plants. Neville, ever supportive of his beloved sisters, contributed financially, as did Austen, and the book was published in 1913 with the less than catchy title *Common Objects of the Riviera*.[9]

Ida and Hilda dedicated the book to their father 'J.C. whose never-failing interest in their expeditions and discoveries has been a constant source of pleasure and encouragement to the authors.' Chapter eleven was entitled 'Birds, Beasts and Insects' and bemoaned the lack of birds in the area, stating:

> There is no denying the fact that in comparison with England birds are very scarce on the Riviera, and the reason is not far to seek in a country where, on every high day and holiday, every man not engaged in playing bowls is amusing himself by roaming through the fields and along the hedge, a gun in his hands and a dog at his heels. To such a one all is fish that comes into his net, and he shoots indiscriminately at every feathered creature that he meets, from a thrush to an ant-eater [a green woodpecker].

The fishing analogy cannot have been lost on Neville who enjoyed shooting but generally confined himself to grouse and pheasants. In contrast, Hilda and Ida in their book made the case for conservation, which was then in its infancy but beginning to win public support. This was being led by the Royal Society for the Protection of Birds, which was campaigning vigorously to ban the trade in importing bird feathers to adorn women's hats and was encouraging members instead to 'discourage the wanton destruction of birds and interest themselves generally in their protection.'[10]

After Neville's election, his rise was rapid, even for someone from a family steeped in politics. Shortly after the election, the City Council had formed a Town Planning subcommittee and Neville became its first chairman. At home, Joseph took great delight in his new grandchildren, but his health continued to deteriorate. To help his recovery Joseph was packed off to the French Riviera where the Chamberlain clan took their summer break. However, there his condition worsened and he lost his sight, which made him even more depressed. Joe's illness was hard on the whole family but particularly his wife Mary, who then fell ill herself with appendicitis. Renouncing his seat in Parliament, Joseph returned home in the autumn of 1913 a gravely ill man.

Neville, meanwhile, had made a good impression on his fellow councillors and in July 1913 became chairman of another committee, this time a special one investigating the state of Birmingham's housing, particularly the slums. Believing that private landlords had failed Birmingham's poor, he advocated the creation of a Birmingham Corporation that could help rebuild the city based on a planned approach with separate zones for housing, business and open spaces. It was a vision of Birmingham's future championed by his father, but the intervention of the Great War meant his bold initiative had to be put on hold.

The year 1914, a fateful one in history, started off quietly enough for the Chamberlain family, but then, on 12 February, a home-made bomb was found at Moor Green Hall, the home of the late Arthur Chamberlain (1842-1913), one of Neville's uncles. Arthur, an industrialist, had died the previous year and was the third of Joseph senior's six sons. Luckily, the bomb failed to explode but suffragette leaflets were found in the vicinity. Like Neville's plans for a Birmingham Corporation, their campaign for universal suffrage had to be put on hold with the onset of war, but the bomb clearly showed that the Chamberlain family was now on their target list. Further bad news followed when Neville was told by doctors that his father only had weeks to live. In June 1914, Joseph was driven from his convalescent home in London to Birmingham one last time to bid farewell to his friends and constituents. Cheering crowds gathered in the grounds of Highbury and he was pushed up and down in a wheelchair, waving weakly at the onlookers. He then returned to London and died there on 2 July, surrounded by his whole family, except Anne who had stayed in Edgbaston to look after baby Frank. Austen, writing to her immediately afterwards, said, 'The end was peaceful. The heart just failed and there was no suffering. Father was interested in politics this morning and early this afternoon spoke of you as he did of us all. Then he slept and passed away.'[11]

The death of Joseph devastated his children. While his politics continued to influence them for the rest of their lives, financially he left them with huge debts and they had no choice but to dispose of the cherished family home (with the outbreak of war, Highbury was turned into a convalescent home. In 1932 it was given in trust to the City Council and in 2016 The Chamberlain Highbury Trust was established to restore the property). Birmingham now remained only a base for Neville, his sisters Ida and Hilda buying a new home together in Odiham, a village near Basingstoke in Hampshire, while Austen returned to London to resume his political career. However, Neville, after serving three years on the council with distinction, was now being openly talked about as the next mayor.

Chapter 4

The war to end all wars

'Proclaim this among the nations: Prepare for war! Rouse the warriors!
Let all the fighting men draw near and attack.' Joel 3:9

The opening salvos of the First World War in August 1914 meant the Chamberlain family had to set aside their grieving for Joseph and help with the war effort. Birmingham life was turned upside down. Elections were suspended, the new university was turned into a military hospital and the gas department was converted into making explosives. Neville, at 45, was too old to serve King and Country but nevertheless did everything he could to support the troops, both on the council and in his business life (the Birmingham Small Arms company, of which he was a director, doing particularly well out of big new government contracts). Two months later he became an alderman, a co-opted member next in status to the mayor. In May 1915 he was asked to become the next Lord Mayor, a notable achievement after just four years of service.

He wrote to Hilda on 2 August 1915:

I am glad that you approve of my decision about the Lord Mayoralty although indeed I felt that all my womenfolk would do so and the only person who would be doubtful would be Austen. It is a fact that he is the only one who has not congratulated me ... The sacrifice which I mind the most is the fact that both of us will see but little of our children. In my case it may not make so much difference but Dorothy is just getting to the age when I should have liked her to be under her mother's eye a bit more.

Well aware that he was stepping into his father's shoes, he also wrote to his stepmother Mary, 'At the moment of putting on my armour I feel how far short of what Father's son should be.'[1]

Neville became mayor in the second year of the war when the horrific death toll was mounting abroad, while at home more and more severely injured servicemen were being seen on the streets. Initially he was sanguine about the war, stating to Hilda on 14 March 1915, 'I'm afraid we must look for a long list of casualties after the heavy fighting of the last two days, but you cannot make an omelette without breaking eggs and if we can obtain a substantial success we shall bear the losses without flinching.'[2]

As a civic leader he championed the war effort, ensuring that the town's munition firms had the electricity they needed and that there were sufficient coal and milk supplies. He even tried to control the flow of liquor into the factories to stop women drinking too much. To set an example to the population about the need for self-sacrifice during a time of war, he voluntarily halved his salary from £1,000 to £500 as an 'example of economy and because the expenses are really much less than in normal times when social functions are necessary.' He also put in place a scheme for women to work the land to help boost food production and became a vocal proponent of national service as a way of ensuring there were enough troops going the front.

While the job of mayor was all consuming, Neville continued to make time to study nature, and to fish and shoot. Through his work promoting the SPNR he became firm friends with Charles Rothschild who, like his Uncle George, was a gifted entomologist who specialised in fleas. Rothschild had made his name as the first entomologist to identify the Oriental rat flea *Xenosylia cheopsis* as being the vector of the great plague (his collection of fleas now resides in the Natural History Museum in London). Neville frequently visited Ashton Wold, Rothschild's home, in Northamptonshire, where he enjoyed collecting butterflies and was photographed with Charles and his friends. In 1910, Charles had bought Woodwalton Fen, one of the last remaining fragments of fenland in Eastern England, to protect it from drainage, in the process creating one of Britain's earliest nature reserves. After Charles formed the SPNR in 1912, the society put out press releases asking the public to send in suggestions of sites 'worthy of preservation' and in the summer of 1915 it submitted a list of 284 nature reserves to the government. Neville enthusiastically supported the idea of what became known as the 'Rothschild Reserves'. Among them were stretches of the Cornish coast, Scottish mountains, Irish bogs, shingle beaches, ancient woodlands, marshes and wetlands.

On 4 September 1915 Neville left behind his mayoral duties and headed to Scotland for a holiday, writing to Hilda, 'Though the war cloud hung over us all the time, there were spells during which one really did forget it … My shooting was on the whole satisfactory.'[3] Not long after returning to London, he saw the devastating effect of the Zeppelin raids for the first time. 'I was in the Strand on Thursday,' he wrote to Hilda, on 17 October 1915, 'and saw some of the damage, which was considerable, and I then heard that the casualties were far higher than appeared from the premature statement issued by the Home Office.' On the subject of war, he added, 'The only clear proper course is to adopt National Service ... It is maddening to think that all the time good lives are being thrown away. I hear that in the big offensive we had 81,000 casualties and 1,400 officers whilst the French lost 130,000, but that the Germans lost probably more on both fronts, while in their last offensive they were simply mown down by our machine guns.'[4]

As Lady Mayoress, Annie proved extremely skillful at convincing Birmingham's women to give generously to the war effort by buying war bonds. However, when it came to the men, Neville had the opposite problem. By the end of 1915 many working men simply didn't trust the Post Office savings banks and so were not investing in bonds, despite many firms paying higher wages than normal to meet the insatiable demand for munitions, guns and artillery. Neville's answer was to create 'a municipal savings association', with the City Council guaranteeing the interest rate to lend the scheme 'the prestige and weight of the local authorities.' The idea of a savings bank was to become a great personal crusade for Neville, who invested a lot of time and energy into it. His letters to his two sisters during this period reflect the many struggles he had getting it off the ground. Despite his best efforts, the Treasury vetoed his idea, feeling that any new bank would compete with the Exchequer.

On the last day of January 1916, Neville got caught in the first air raid on Birmingham by German Zeppelins. Although he was unhurt, the nearby Mayoress of Walsall was severely injured. Neville was appalled at the lack of air defences, there being only four guns, 'each in close proximity to a munition works. They have no proper searchlights and no interconnecting telephones. Their observers have to signal to them with red lamps! Their crews have never fired a shot.' To prevent the situation recurring he came up with a detailed plan and submitted it to the Home Secretary and senior military personnel. It included the use of observers, a warning system to alert the public, simultaneous signals between guns and a complete blackout within the vicinity of the raid. (Chamberlain's proposals were, to all intents and purposes, the forerunner of the Air Raid Precautions organisation, which became Britain's first line of defence during the Blitz, over twenty years later).

A big part of Neville's motivation for an effective air raid warning system was to keep his family safe. He wrote to Ida on 19 February 1916 that the 'children are flourishing. Dorothy is much taken up with fairies since she saw some at the pantomime and has hopes that somehow or other she will be able to fly one of these days. Frank and she play together a lot with the result that she is more childlike and less precocious than she was.'[5] He also added, breaking every rule that a parent should not favour one child over another, 'But I fear he will never have her brains. When I give wrong names to the animals in the scrap book he says "Yes" whereas she used to catch me up at once. But when he comes up in the morning and seizes my hand shouting "come along Papa p'ay toys" he is irresistible.'

One of Neville's other great loves was music. On 26 March 1916 he wrote to his sister Beatrice, 'A.[nnie] and I went to a concert in the town hall, and in the interval I addressed the multitude on the future of orchestral music in Birmingham ... I dropped a little bombshell by suggesting that we should have a first-class orchestra, and contribute to its support out of the rates.'[6] Over the next few years he would go on to champion the city having its own orchestra, until eventually, in 1919, an annual grant from the rates made it a reality.

By Easter 1916 Neville's plan for women to help work the land had not been universally welcomed by either farmers or the press. He wrote to Hilda on 15 April 1916 that, 'They [farmers] are a queer suspicious race and desperately cautious but circumstances are too strong for them this time and they will have to take on the women or seed down their arable.'[7] As usual, Neville put everything he had into making the scheme work while actively promoting national service as a way of getting more troops to the front. But at times the continual criticism and harping from his opponents caused him to question why he was doing it. He wrote to Hilda on 14 May 1916, 'Being Lord Mayor is dust and ashes and I should like to resign and return to obscurity. But I suppose I shall have to face it out and pretend I don't care. I'm beat and the Savings Bank is dead!'[8] But face them down he did and Neville's scheme for getting women to work the land would result in a quarter of a million women volunteering to work in the fields. (This would lead to the formation of the Women's Land Army which would be resurrected again in 1939). He also stoically continued to push his plans for a municipal savings bank. In June 1916 the Treasury finally gave way and a few months later the Birmingham Corporation Savings Bank was created by an Act of Parliament (the bank later became the Birmingham Municipal Bank and in 1976 became part of the Trustee Savings Bank). Writing to Hilda on 2 September 1916 he said with great pride, 'As for me I have started work on the Bank.'[9]

Being Lord Mayor during wartime was stressful and too often all consuming. As a break from thinking about the war, Neville played with his children, tended his garden and, when time allowed, loved nothing more than getting out into the countryside and birdwatching. 'To my great joy I have got a blackcap this year and he sings much of the day in the trees by the Botanical Gardens,' he wrote to Ida on 16 July 1916, adding, 'yesterday I saw a hawfinch – the first I have seen here.'[10] On 18 October he told Hilda, 'The "large green caterpillar" is really a common one although unfamiliar to people who are not entomologists.

I found a number recently when weeding my dell. Its name is *Mamestra Persicaria* (the dot moth). Its wings are nearly black with a very conspicuous white mark on each.'[11]

As the war dragged on, Neville, who had thought the casualties a year earlier a price worth paying, became far more critical as the death toll mounted and the list of the 'glorious dead' became personal. On 8 July 1916 he wrote to Hilda about the Battle of the Somme: 'But in spite of all this I feel rather depressed. Birmingham has been hit with a vengeance this time and both City Batts [battalions] and the Territorials have been terribly cut up. There is an awful and constantly lengthening list of casualties among officers and as I have undertaken to write a personal letter to the relatives of all who are killed it comes home to me very forcibly … That is the worst of local battalions, it does hit the district when they get cut up and a great part of Birmingham is in mourning today.'[12]

On the first day alone of the Battle of the Somme, Birmingham lost over a thousand men. Eight days later, on 16 July 1916, he wrote to Ida, 'The 6th and 8th Warwicks, two of our Territorial Batts, have been wiped out. They went in with 44 officers and 1350 men and came out with 4 officers and 240 men.'[13] The dead of the First World War would haunt Neville for the rest of his life, but up to that point the conflict had not affected his family. Then, on 10 December 1916, the war came very close to home when his favourite cousin, Norman, who had served with him on the council, left for the trenches.

The job of looking after the Birmingham troops at the front was given to a Depot Committee and his wife Anne became its president. The scale of the logistical challenge was huge. In the early summer of 1916 it was decided that the committee would take on the entire responsibility for providing the extra clothing and comforts for all the Birmingham units serving abroad. In May that amounted to thirteen units and some 8,000 men, but by the following April it had increased to twenty-three units composed of 13-14,000 men. The report of the committee noted that they 'viewed with some apprehension the very large increase in the number of troops for whom they had undertaken responsibility.'

Anne took on the considerable task of again galvanizing the good women of Birmingham to get knitting in support of their men at the front. As a result of their efforts, the total number of garments and other home-made clothes increased from 113,773 in May 1916 to a colossal 173,636 the following April, an average of 1,336 per week. However, during the winter of 1916-17 the demand for extra winter clothing was so great that the committee could not cope and was compelled to purchase considerable quantities of shirts, pants, socks and other items from private firms. The committee noted it was 'with regret that they had to recourse to machine-knit socks, as they are admittedly inferior to the hand-made article, and the Committee hope that this intimation will make the effect of stimulating the efforts of the ladies so as to meet the full demands.'[14] By April 1917 the Depot Committee had spent over £5,000 on clothing and 'amusements', over £10,000 on supplying prisoners of war, over £1,200 on medical equipment and over £2,800 on emergency measures that, when combined with working expenses, amounted to over £20,000.

By November 1916, Neville had made a real impact as Lord Mayor and had considerably honed his political skills. No longer the son who would go into business, he was now a rising political star in his own right. However, just when his career was going well, tragedy struck again when, in early December, Anne had a miscarriage and, being anaemic, had to undergo surgery. One of the side effects of the operation was that she could have no more children. He wrote to Hilda on 3 December 1916: 'We were keeping a little bit of news as a surprise for you at Christmas ... but last Tuesday things went wrong and our hopes are at an end. Poor Annie has had a perfectly beastly time as, in addition to the disappointment, she has had to undergo an operation which was carried out last Thursday ... It's a bitter disappointment but I remember Father's favourite maxim "It's of no use to kick against the pricks". We must regard it as our "bit", one of the sacrifices you have to make if you do public service.'[15]

Chamberlain's success in designing an air raid precaution scheme, getting women to work the land, creating a savings bank and, above all, promoting national service brought him to the attention of the Prime Minister, David Lloyd George (1863-1945). On 19 November 1916, while on a train home, he was summoned by Lloyd George, who offered him the directorship of a new Department of National Service. Recommended by Austen for the new role, he was flattered but still felt he had work to do as mayor:

> We saw LL.G. in his room and he at once asked if I would accept. I painted the picture of Birmingham sans Town Clerk [he had resigned the previous month much to Neville's disappointment] and sans Lord Mayor and he replied "But the Empire". I said it wasn't decent to leave them without a word to anyone. He replied "But this is wartime". Finally he said "Think it over for ten minutes and send word by Austen. It would make all the difference if I could announce it now". I said several damns and thought for two minutes and then sent Austen to say yes.[16]

Throughout the war, Neville continued his love affair with nature. In the spring of 1917 he wrote, 'At last the blackcap has arrived. His song always makes a peculiar appeal to me, not only for the beauty of the notes, but because it carries a sort of pot-pourri of old associations, in which youth, Highbury and Cannes are all mixed up together.' He also tended his garden and was particularly proud of his flowers and trees, drawing inspiration from them. Nature was his release from politics and its solace was needed more than ever when, on 8 August 1917, he resigned from his new role in a storm of acrimony. His first foray into national politics had ended just nine months later in failure.

In defining Chamberlain's role, Lloyd George, fearful of the public reaction to national service, declared compulsion out of the question and instead wanted volunteers from industry. However, he didn't give Chamberlain control of military recruiting, or any civil servants or a seat at the Cabinet table. On 12 August 1917 he wrote to Hilda that Lloyd George 'really is quite impossible to work with and I am convinced that sooner or later he will come to grief.'[17] Convinced the Prime Minister had handed him a poisoned chalice, the disagreement would make him a lifelong enemy of the 'Welsh Wizard'. Chamberlain memorably said he was 'without instructions, without powers, without a staff and without an office.' In his war memoirs, Lloyd George gave his version of events, saying the role called for 'a great breadth and boldness of conception, a remorseless energy and thorough execution, and for the exercise of supreme tact' by a 'man of exceptional talents.' But he went on, 'Mr Neville Chamberlain is a man of rigid competency', and was of a type 'lost in an emergency or in creative tasks at any time', with 'a vein of self-sufficient obstinacy.'[18]

Unable to go back to the council and without a prominent role in public life, Neville fell back on his business interests, his love of wildlife and, like politicians through the ages who have fallen from grace, spent more time with family. In October 1917 that included catching up with his cousin Norman who had returned on leave from the front. The son of Joseph's brother, Herbert, and his wife, Lilian, he had joined Birmingham City Council in 1911, where he had served as chair of the parks committee. He joined the Grenadier Guards in 1914 and a year later, at the age of 31, was promoted to captain.

While serving at the front line, Norman had become severely depressed (suffering from what we know today as post-traumatic stress disorder) and, following an operation that had gone wrong, he had been stripped of his captaincy. Then tragedy struck when he was reported missing in action and later declared dead. Norman's death, at the Battle of Cambrai in December 1917, hit Neville incredibly hard and resulted in the only book he ever wrote.[19] Entitled *Norman Chamberlain, A Memoir*, it was intended for future generations to realise 'how greatly Norman had contributed to the family fame'. After his death Neville eulogized Norman, stating on 10 February 1918, 'Somehow I had always associated Norman with anything I might do in the future. He was like a younger brother to me.' To help manage his grief, Neville immediately set about collecting material for his book, though it would take him five years to get it published (Following the Second World War, a former gravel works in Shard End, Birmingham was landscaped and named the Norman Chamberlain Playing Fields after him).

In July 1918, Highbury became a home for disabled soldiers, Neville preferring this to the 'only other fate for it namely to be pulled down'. Then, on 11 November, the Germans and the Allies finally signed the armistice following four years of war and the greatest slaughter of young men the country had ever seen. Yet any rejoicing for Neville was to be short lived as further family tragedy struck when his half sister Beatrice died, aged just 56. During the war she had worked tirelessly for the Red Cross treating wounded soldiers, but soon after had contracted influenza, becoming a victim of the 'Spanish flu' pandemic then sweeping the country. It was another blow to the family and, like Norman, another Chamberlain who had gone too soon.

Neville was still grieving when a general election was called in December 1918. He stood for the Conservative and Unionist party in the constituency of Ladywood. At one of the hustings he made it clear why he had at last decided to throw his hat into the national ring: 'To show gratitude to those who have fought and died for England by making it a better place to live in. My sole reason for wishing to enter Parliament is my desire to assist in bringing about this transformation.'

Chapter 5

Horrors, atrocities and monstrosities

'Even the stork in the sky knows her appointed seasons, and the dove, the swift and the thrush observe the time of their migration.' Jeremiah 8:7

The 1918 general election was the first election in which women over the age of 30 could both vote and stand as candidates. In Ladywood, Mrs Margery Corbett Ashby (1882-1981), a leading suffragette, stood against Chamberlain as the Liberal candidate. Greeted by the men in her family with 'hoots of laughter', she later admitted that she didn't have 'the faintest idea of getting in – which would have been very inconvenient – but did so in order to get people used to the idea of a woman standing.'[1] Before the war, Birmingham had become known as the 'Mecca of the anti-suffragists' and, as a consequence, the movement had been particularly active there. Joseph had been adamantly against women getting the vote, declaring it 'an entire mistake.' Both he and Austen were members of the National Anti-Suffrage League and Beatrice served on its executive committee. Neville was also against women getting the vote.[2]

Chamberlain's Labour opponent was John William Kneeshaw, a pacifist who stood on a truly radical socialist manifesto of nationalisation and the redistribution of wealth to pay for the war. Chamberlain stood on a platform of a progressive state pension for the elderly and a minimum wage for the poor, with shorter working hours, greater protection for key industries and more money for health and welfare. But his main motivation was to tackle the slum housing in Birmingham and, to begin this massive task, he advocated the state building of homes fit for heroes. In the heady, victorious and patriotic climate that followed the war, the result on 14 December 1918 was never in doubt; Chamberlain secured nearly 70 per cent of the vote with a comfortable majority of over 6,000. Kneeshaw received just over 2,500 votes but Ashby, with over 1,500 votes, did as well as any male Liberal candidate in the Birmingham area. Her candidature had been greeted with surprise rather than contempt by the electorate but it would be another nine years before all women finally got the right to vote. However, tired of the war and cynical about politicians, only 40 per cent of the electorate in the chronically poor neighbourhood of

Ladywood had turned out to vote. Despite this, Chamberlain was delighted at the result. At nearly 50 years old, he was finally following in the footsteps of his father and brother.

A new coalition government of Conservative Unionists and Liberals under Prime Minister David Lloyd George set about making a new world after the war to end all wars. Yet, during the next six years, there would be unprecedented political turmoil and no fewer than three general elections, after which the Liberals, so beloved of his late father Joseph, would not hold power again until 2010. However, Lloyd George was in a very vulnerable position as the Conservatives – under their leader, Andrew Bonar Law (1858-1923) – held the vast majority of the seats in the new coalition. While in theory Chamberlain was just another backbencher trying to make a name for himself, in reality he stood out from the pack because of his age, his family name and his political record. In the new Parliament he made his maiden speech on rent restrictions, focusing on the slums in his home town of Birmingham, and served on various committees, scrutinising bills on transport and electricity.

In the summer of 1919, Chamberlain went to France on holiday to see for himself the scenes of such carnage and, in particular, the place where Norman had fallen. He spent four days touring the battlefields, visiting Rheims, the Somme and Ypres. He described the Somme as 'Nothing but weeds, shell holes, graves and dead stumps of trees', and Ypres as 'Tracts of immense thistles, the down flying in all directions'. He also saw some German prisoners of war 'herded into their barbed-wire cages in the evening ... a humiliating spectacle for humanity, they looked like slaves, but I felt no sympathy for them.' Seeing the devastation they had wrought made him 'savage ... that their own country is untouched.' He also visited Haweswater in the Lake District where he enjoyed long walks up the becks and birdwatched, noting, 'Wheatears nest just over the water as if the bird liked to sit on eggs where it could hear the tinkling of the little stream all day.' He also recorded how juniper flourished in the rock crevasses and watched red deer on the hills while the majestic raven soared overhead, its deep croaking call echoing down the valley.[3]

With his usual energy, Chamberlain applied himself to the job of being an obscure backbencher. It was a role that, at times, bored him and often left him feeling deeply depressed about his future. However, a stroke of luck in the Private Members' ballot (whereby a backbencher can introduce a bill to the House of Commons though it rarely becomes law) enabled him to introduce the incongruously named 'Bastardy Bill', which was designed to give unmarried mothers the right to legitimise their children if they married again, and to get some support out of absent fathers. Despite later being renamed the less pejorative

'Children of Unmarried Parents Bill', it was blocked in 1920 and 1921, though it did become law the following year, a significant achievement that enhanced his reputation in the House. He was also offered a junior ministerial post as Under Secretary of State (the lowest rung on the political ladder) by an embarrassed Bonar Law who was well aware of his former position as Birmingham's Lord Mayor and his age. He turned it down, citing his bad experiences with the national service job. His loathing of Lloyd George meant that any major roles were out of the question, a position made even more difficult by his brother Austen becoming leader of the Conservative Unionists in the Commons.

Then, in October 1922, the government fell after the Conservatives voted to end the coalition, leading to Lloyd George and most of the Unionist leadership resigning. Chamberlain's brother Austen also resigned after he lost the leadership to Andrew Bonar Law who, on the back of the Conservative vote, became party leader and Prime Minister, winning the election on 15 November. Chamberlain, in a rare act of citing God, offered 'profound thanks to Providence for delivering us from the Goat' (his nickname for Lloyd George). The tectonic plates had finally shifted and the way was now open for him to climb the political ladder.

Natural history, in particular birdwatching, continued to be his release from the stresses of political life. On 26 March 1922, he wrote to Hilda about his 'great excitement' at the repeated visits of a greater spotted woodpecker *Dendrocopos major* to a coconut outside his dining room window. 'This is a bird which I was never able to record even at Highbury thou' once I saw a bird high in an ash tree that I thought might be one … I have written to the Birm. Mail about it as it really seems to me a very remarkable occurrence. The G.S. Woodpecker is not a common bird anywhere and his haunts are generally forests not gardens.'[4] Today, the species is commonly found in woods, parks and gardens, the population having increased rapidly over recent decades. In Chamberlain's time the greater spotted woodpecker was far rarer and probably the only place in Birmingham where it would have been common would have been the green oasis of Edgbaston. Although a forest bird, he was mistaken about their haunts as they will come into gardens if food is provided. However, in the 1920s far fewer people fed birds so garden sightings would have been much less common.

In the spring, Chamberlain was never happier than when the migrant birds arrived back at his Westbourne home after wintering in southern Africa. On 7 May 1922 he wrote to Hilda, 'The garden is heavenly today. All the migrants have arrived with a rush and the air is full of the songs and calls of cuckoos, willow wrens [willow warblers], chiff-chaffs, greenfinches, chaffinches and turtle doves beside the common thrushes, tits, robins, hedge sparrows and wrens. Overhead the swifts are circling and I saw a kestrel pass over this morning. The daffodils are still very brilliant and the saxifrages are just opening. The early rhododendron is a blaze of scarlet and in 10 days the cherries should be at their best.'

Politically, new opportunities also alighted on his doorstep. As none of the previous administration's Conservative Unionists would serve in his government, Bonar Law needed experienced politicians to give the impression of stability and to help heal the rift in his own party. He fell back on what was cruelly referred to by those refusing to serve as the 'second eleven' or reserve team. This included Chamberlain who he appointed as Postmaster General outside the Cabinet in October 1922. Within ten months Chamberlain had risen to become Chancellor of the Exchequer, following a brief spell at the Ministry of Health. His tenure at the Treasury would only last five months, until the general election of 1923, and he never got the opportunity to deliver a budget. Despite this, it was a meteoric rise, almost unparalleled in modern political history, and he would stay at the forefront of national and Conservative politics until his death in 1940. It took Lloyd George and Winston Churchill eighteen years to rise to the front bench and Stanley Baldwin fourteen years. Neville Chamberlain reached this position in less than five years.

The general election on 6 December 1923 saw the first ever minority Labour government, under its leader, James Ramsay MacDonald (1886-1937) who governed with the tacit support of the Liberals. Although short-lived, lasting barely ten months, it represented a turning point in British politics. However, following a vote of no confidence in 1924, there was a third general election in less than three years. At the previous election, Chamberlain's seat of Ladywood, a very poor neighbourhood, was successfully targeted by the Labour Party and his majority had been drastically reduced to under 2,000. In response, Chamberlain complained that they 'exploited the sufferings of the poor, setting class against class and particularly appealed to the out-of-works who were in such a hopeless state that they were ready to believe that their sufferings were due to political causes.'[5] This time, though, his Labour opponent was not a communist sympathiser but the far more formidable Oswald Mosley who had recently defected to the party following a stint as MP for Harrow, first as a Conservative then as an independent.

Mosley, the future leader of the British Union of Fascists, was by this time an accomplished orator, rabble-rouser and a cad. In his memoir he wrote: 'Six weeks before the election in November [sic] 1924 I entered the fight in Birmingham ... The Chamberlains and their machine had ruled Birmingham for sixty years, first as Liberal Radicals and then as Conservative Unionists. Their party machine was at the time probably the strongest in the country. We had six weeks in which to smash it. I chose to fight Neville Chamberlain, who sat for the working-class constituency of Ladywood in the centre of the city; his brother Austen was the neighbouring MP and their names and abilities made them a formidable combination.'

Mosley threw everything he had at the campaign but felt let down by his fellow Labour candidates, describing them as a motley crew:

> My colleagues among the candidates we found on the spot were a rather simple lot. A grand old pioneer of religious bent called Frank Smith was fighting the neighbouring constituency against Austen Chamberlain. We held a meeting with Frank in the chair, packed with our working-class constituents but with the front row occupied by prominent businessmen who had come to see the new freak. The chairman began with what seemed an interminable oration about his own particular brand of meta-physics and just as I was entertaining some transient hope of its conclusion, pulled out a football referee's whistle, blew it and shouted "Half time". He then called for prayers, flopped down on his knees and said them. Soon he got up, blew his whistle again and said "Half time is over" and continued his speech. After 30 minutes of the best, he called on me. It was an inauspicious start.[6]

To unseat Chamberlain, Mosley ran a particularly dirty campaign, accusing him of being a 'landlord's hireling', a barbed insult that stuck, putting Chamberlain at odds with his working-class voters who mainly rented. Mosley noted:

> My raging speaking campaign, both indoor and outdoor, and the superb work done by Cimmis in leading the canvassing team, eventually turned the scales. It was a joyous day when, in the courtyards running back from the streets in Birmingham slums, we saw the blue window cards coming down and the red going up. The court leaders of some hundred people were usually dominant old women, and when mother turned they all turned. Mrs Chamberlain worked magnificently on the other side in street canvass, but when it came to demagogy Neville was not in the ring. An able administrator – despite F.E.'s [Frederick Edwin Smith, 1st Earl of Birkenhead, 1872-1930], jibe that he was an adequate Mayor of Birmingham in a lean year – he had no great appeal to the masses.

Chamberlain sensed the tide of public opinion turning against him and on the night of the count, Wednesday, 29 October 1924, said he hated the thought of being beaten by that 'viper'. Mosley recalled: 'During the count he sat huddled in a corner, either exercising an iron self-control or in a state of near collapse; his agents did everything and he never moved.' At the result there two recounts which, according to Mosley, first gave Chamberlain victory by seven votes and then declared he had won by two. 'It was alleged by some of our people that votes had disappeared and uproar broke out with men fighting in the crowded public gallery and people pointing to the floor as they bellowed, "That one's got 'em in his pocket!"'

In a letter to Ida on 1 November, Chamberlain gave his version of events: 'The galleries of the Town Hall were filled with Socialists who booed at us and shouted directions to the counters in the most scandalous fashion. They even invaded the floor and yelled insults which our feeble Lord Mayor pretended not to hear. Annie was splendid. She and I sat calmly by, not interfering with the proceedings but waiting for whatever the decision may be.'[7] According to Chamberlain there were five recounts, the first giving him a majority of thirty, then fifteen, then seven and then it was declared for Mosley by two. Finally, among scenes of near pandemonium after a fifth count at 4.30am, Chamberlain was declared the eventual winner by just seventy-seven votes.

If Chamberlain had hung on by the slimmest margin, the result nationally was a triumph for the Conservative Party who won decisively with a majority of 209. Their new leader, Stanley Baldwin (1867-1947), whom Chamberlain had studied with at Masons, became Prime Minister (Bonar Law having died of throat cancer the previous year). When the new Conservative government took office, Baldwin again offered Chamberlain his old post as Chancellor of the Exchequer, but Chamberlain refused, instead asking for the Ministry of Health. He wrote to Baldwin on 7 November 1924, 'I believe I may do something to improve the condition for the less fortunate classes – and that's after all what we are in politics for.'

The Ministry of Health suited Chamberlain down to the ground because its remit included housing. It gave him the opportunity to bring in policies that provided an alternative to the socialist ideals of the Labour Party, which he so disliked. The role was also significant because, for the first time, Chamberlain sat around the Cabinet table with his high-flying brother, Austen, who had been appointed Foreign Secretary and would, the following year, be awarded the Nobel Peace Prize for his work in creating the Locarno Pact. (The Locarno Treaties were seven agreements negotiated at Locarno, Switzerland, on 5-16 October 1925 and formally signed in London on 1 December 1925, in which the Allies sought to secure the post-war territories with a defeated Germany). The younger brother, who had been destined for the family business and had only been in national politics for six years, had caught up with his older brother, who had first entered Parliament thirty-two years previously.

On 15 November 1924 Chamberlain wrote to Ida, 'Of course the public thinks of nothing but Housing, but … I want to take the opportunity of dealing with the big questions of rating and valuation, Poor Law, Pensions and Health Insurance and the re-organisation of the medical services.'[8] Chamberlain instantly set his office to work on a four-year plan and on 19 November laid before the Cabinet a list of twenty-five measures he wanted to pass into law. Of these, twenty-one had become law by the time he left the Ministry in 1929, an impressive record. On housing he decided to continue with the Wheatley Housing Act of 1924, passed by the previous, short-lived Labour administration. This resulted in over half a million council homes being built in Britain by 1933, a massive achievement. It was the one really influential legacy of the first ever Labour administration, and one for which Chamberlain, wrongly, got most of the credit.[9]

Throughout his time at the Ministry of Health, Chamberlain was only too aware of his age, and that time was not on his side. He wrote to Ida on 23 May 1925, 'Though I shouldn't be a favourite with the press like Father was or Winston is, yet, if I have have 4 or 5 years of office I may leave behind as … great a reputation as Minister of Health as Father did as Colonial Secretary. Only it will probably take longer for the public to find it out and it will only be after I am dead that my administration will be talked of as the Golden Age of the Ministry!'[10] That year he introduced the De-Rating Act 'to simplify and amend the law with respect to the making and collection of rates.'[11] The act was a detailed and highly technical piece of legislation that aimed to reduce the tax burden on industry so that more companies would be encouraged to invest in poor areas. Chamberlain won plaudits in the House of Commons for piloting the bill through each of the various legislative stages, staying up late night after night working on its complicated clauses. Dressed immaculately in black when attending the House, his attention to detail and cold manner also attracted critics who gave him the unflattering nickname 'the Coroner'.

Chamberlain cared little for his critics and was determined to use the Ministry of Health to make a difference to poor people's lives, especially women. He championed the introduction of the first comprehensive widows' pensions in the 'Widows, Orphans and Old Age Pensions Act 1925' based on compulsory contributions by both employers and employees. The Act also piloted health insurance which was extended the following year so that 'no person genuinely seeking work was to be penalised in respect of arrears of health insurance contributions'. Chamberlain also set up committees to look at midwifery services and to tackle the higher maternity mortality rate among poor women, particularly those living in the slums. On introducing the measure during a speech in Leeds, he asked the audience, 'What happens to the family when the mother is taken away and there are young children left who never can have the care and influence which a mother alone can exercise over them?' Pausing at the end of the speech he then ad-libbed in a low voice, 'My own mother died in childbirth.' It was an uncharacteristic show of emotion from a man who rarely expressed his feelings in public.[12]

To deliver his vision for health and to reform the poor laws, Chamberlain had to work for the first time with Winston Churchill (1874–1965), who was then Chancellor, and from the beginning it was a strained relationship. Where Churchill was impulsive and relied very much on his instincts, Chamberlain was utterly methodical and much more consensual in his approach. But whilst Churchill, over time, learnt to respect his Cabinet colleague's approach, the same was not true of Chamberlain. 'The fault with which he is generally credited,' wrote Chamberlain to Hilda on 1 November 1925, 'is lack of judgement and there public opinion seems to me to be absolutely right. And with his courage and strong will and power of oratory he is a very dangerous man to have in the Govt.'[13]

In January 1926, Chamberlain was approached by the President of the Royal Institute of British Architects, Guy Dawber, and invited to a preliminary meeting to be held in March to discuss the organisation and aims of a proposed new Society for the Preservation of Rural England. Although its wide-ranging remit was outside of his brief, it was a cause that was close to Chamberlain's heart. Unable to attend in person due to a prior commitment, he instead sent the following message, which was read out at the meeting: 'I sympathise very strongly with your endeavour to awaken public opinion of the importance of preserving rural amenities though, as I am sure your committee will realise, it will be necessary for them to be careful to advocate measures in consonance with modern requirements. I wish every success to the movement.'

The year 1926 was also marked by trouble in Chamberlain's personal life, and strife in the country at large. Anne, who had seen little of her husband since he was appointed to the Ministry of Health, fell into a deep depression and had to be packed off to Biarritz in the south of France to convalesce. In May there was a general strike by over a million miners which paralysed the country. Organised by the Trade Union Congress, nearly two million workers in heavy industry and transport came out in support of the miners who were demanding better working conditions. In response, Winston Churchill wanted to send in the army.

Widespread conflict and loss of life was only avoided by Prime Minister Stanley Baldwin insisting that the soldiers remain unarmed and negotiating a compromise. But the threat of sending in the army caused emotions to run very high and resulted in deep divisions in the country. Clifford Sharp, the editor of *New Statesman*, wrote, 'For having so notably helped to teach us all this, ought we to thank Mr Churchill or ought we to hang him on a lamp-post for the incorrigible "blood-letter" that he is? We are really not quite sure what is the proper answer to that question; but probably – to be on the safe side – it would be best that he should be hanged.'[14] Chamberlain supported Churchill but remained out of the spotlight, instead continuing to work on housing and undertaking a tour of the country to see for himself what local authorities were doing. He also received representation from the two great Birmingham hospitals, The General and The Queens, for more money, which he rejected, instead encouraging them to merge. This resulted in the Birmingham United Hospital in Edgbaston.

Chamberlain's support for the Society for the Preservation of Rural England was picked up in a *Manchester Guardian* article dated 3 September, written by its 'London staff'. In strident tones, it called for the imposition of order in the countryside, 'It is certain that there is a widespread alarm about the steady spoiling of rural England, and one hopes that this new movement will catch on and be effective.'[15] The article was followed at the end of 1926 by Chamberlain speaking at the inaugural meeting of the new campaigning body, later to be called the Council for the Preservation of Rural England (today the Campaign to Protect Rural England or CPRE). The CPRE, however, caused Chamberlain a dilemma: it pitched his love of countryside against his desire to build affordable housing for the poor.

The meeting on 7 December began with the chairman of the newly formed CPRE using his speaker's privilege to whip up the audience into a frenzy of environmental indignation. He lamented the British countryside disappearing at an alarming rate under bricks, mortar and concrete, and in particular singled out the government's road-building programme as being the greatest single threat to England's green and pleasant land. To describe this wanton destruction he deployed colourful language, stating that the government had inflicted on the countryside a succession of 'horrors, atrocities and monstrosities'.

Listening intently, Chamberlain decided to diffuse the tension when he addressed the meeting by starting with a *mea culpa*, followed by a joke: 'I cannot disguise from myself that, unconsciously, and indeed, unwillingly, my department has been responsible for some of those horrors, atrocities and monstrosities to which the chairman has referred, and as I watched the state of indignation into which the chairman was working up this audience as a preparation for their acceptance of his resolution, I could not help wishing that that great bridge-builder, my colleague the Minister of Transport, was here, that I might offer him up as an acceptable sacrifice before I myself embarked upon my address.'[16] The idea of stringing up the Minister of Transport, Wilfrid Ashley, clearly appealed to the audience who roared with approval, although history does not record what Ashley thought of the idea.

To protect the character of villages and improve the design of rural buildings, the next year Chamberlain gave statutory powers of rejection to local authorities, backed up by an advisory panel of architects. The same year he was made an honorary member of the Birmingham Natural History and Philosophical Society, to add to his memberships of the Royal Entomological Society, the Birmingham Entomological Society, the Society for the Promotion of Nature Reserves and the CPRE. By championing the countryside, Chamberlain became an early leader in the fledgling environmental movement and his changes paved the way for the 1947 Town and Country Planning Act, the foundation of our modern planning system.

Chapter 6

Churchill, Kenya and the Great Depression

'We also glory in our sufferings, because we know that suffering
produces perseverance; perseverance, character; and character, hope.'
Romans 5: 3-5

The next year, 1927, saw Chamberlain do battle, not just with the horrors of
rural development, but with the intransigent Chancellor Winston Churchill
over his Poor Law reforms. The Poor Laws dated back to the 1880s and stated
that each parish had to look after the poor in its area, the parish later being
replaced by 'Boards of Guardians'. By the mid-1920s, the boards had declined
in importance due to other forms of financial help becoming available, but they
were still the primary means by which the destitute received help from the state.
Many of the boards were controlled by Labour officials who openly defied the
government by distributing relief funds to the able-bodied unemployed as well
as the non-able bodied living in the workhouses and other institutions. Churchill
wanted to reform all local government finance and he continually clashed with
Chamberlain over the nature and scale of his reforms.

In 1929, Chamberlain introduced legislation to abolish the boards entirely
and transfer their powers to local authorities. On the second reading of the Local
Government Bill, he spoke in the chamber for two-and-a-half hours, one of his
longest ever Parliamentary speeches. Chamberlain devoted an immense amount
of time to each clause of the bill, highlighting the appalling conditions of those
living in Birmingham's slums. This 'personal touch' was Annie's idea and, as a
result, the speech was listened to in near silence by those in the chamber. When
he finally sat down, there was rapturous applause from both sides of the House
of Commons. The bill was passed with a large majority on 27 March 1929.

Chamberlain's tenure at the Ministry of Health also resulted in marked
improvements in both ante-natal and post-natal care. (These, like his changes
to the planning system, paved the way for more radical reforms such as the
Midwives Act of 1936, which introduced a national salaried midwifery service).[1]
Chamberlain was immensely proud of these reforms, stating that they will 'prove
to have been my magnum opus when my obituary is written.' As befitted a man
celebrating his '*magnum opus*' in 1929, he commissioned the artist William Orpen

to paint his portrait. The painting was critically well received when it was shown at the Royal Academy later that year. Orpen had previously painted Winston Churchill, who counted it as his favourite portrait, and Chamberlain had a similar high regard for his own painting, which was hung in his dining room.

Following the passage of the Local Government Act, the country went to the polls in a general election on 30 May 1929. Only too aware of how close the contest had been last time in Ladywood, Chamberlain had by this time secured for himself the safe seat of Edgbaston. Expecting a comfortable majority for the Conservatives, he was extremely shocked at the result. The Labour Party of Ramsay MacDonald won the largest number of seats, though they failed to win enough to form a majority. Worse still, Labour had broken the monopoly that the Chamberlains had enjoyed in Birmingham for more than half a century by gaining four of the twelve Parliamentary seats. While Neville easily won Edgbaston, Austen clung on by the skin of his teeth in neighbouring West Birmingham, winning by just forty-three votes. The only consolation from Chamberlain's perspective was that the Liberals under Lloyd George also did badly. MacDonald then put together a minority Labour administration and, for the first time in years, both Neville and Austen found themselves without jobs in government.

Writing in his diary on 8 June 1929, Chamberlain said, 'The election has come and gone in disaster.' He then went on to denigrate the surprise Labour victory saying the result was due to the 'ceaseless propaganda that has been going on for years among the working classes, to the effect that things would never be right for them till a "Labour" government came in … There is no conversion to Socialism. It is merely the present discontents showing themselves in a desire for change.'[2] Fearing he could be out of office for seven years – by which time he would be 67 – he wrote: 'I dare say politics will have ceased to interest me. On the other hand, the new government may make such blunders that, before two years are up, the country will be glad to be rid of them.' It was another prescient remark, but at the time he despaired. Writing to Ida on 2 June 1929 he said, 'My pleasure is in administration rather than in the game of politics … To me it makes all the difference to be in office. If I were told that I could never hold office again I should prefer to go out now.'[3]

His answer to being out of government was not to concentrate on his constituency but to again look to the future by creating the Conservative Research Department, a small devoted group of people who could progress radical Conservative ideas with him at its helm. It was the first right-wing think-tank and for fifty years it occupied its own premises in Old Queen Street, overlooking St James's Park, Chamberlain's favourite birdwatching haunt.[4] He also decided to take a long break away from the front line of politics on the basis that the rest and change of scene would do him good, Anne in particular welcoming the opportunity for 'quality family time'.

On 30 December 1929 he departed on a two-month trip to Kenya and Tanganyika (now Tanzania), taking Anne and his daughter, Dorothy, with him. As an avid ornithologist, he had always wanted to see Africa's exotic birds and its other magnificent wildlife, but ever the politician he also thought the trip might benefit his career if the job of Colonial Secretary ever became available. (The position which his father had made his own). Recording his trip in two diaries, he devoted pages to discussing the problems of the region, from the historical slave trade to the future of 'native' reserves, and from the state of soil erosion to the value of cash crops. While there, he asked to see a sisal plantation, which he toured in near silence, his mind clearly going back to the difficult days on Andros. As the trip neared its end he became depressed again at the thought of returning to England, and this only worsened on reaching Suez where he found many letters waiting, informing him of a political situation that he found 'detestable'.

By 1930 the Great Depression had gripped America, with over five million people unemployed, and its economic impact was being felt in Britain and around the world. In response, the Labour government borrowed more money to pay off the increasing national debt but could not push through more radical measures, only legislating with the help of the Liberal party. Within the Conservative ranks there was now increasing talk of replacing Baldwin, who many MPs saw as too weak to unite a divided party. In June, in another act of providence that was to define his career, Chamberlain was voted party chairman after Baldwin's first choice, Viscount Bridgeman (1865-1935), who had retired from the House of Commons the year before as MP for Oswestry, refused to run. While Chamberlain was always careful to be publicly loyal to Baldwin, many backbench MPs despaired of his leadership and now talked openly about Chamberlain as the next leader of the party.

That summer, Chamberlain went on another family holiday, to the Low Countries, and, with his cousin Norman in mind, visited Ypres again, over a decade since his first visit in 1919. He was delighted to see that nature had reclaimed what was once 'a blasted, derelict desert, full of tanks, barbed wire, pill boxes and shell holes full of stagnant water,' and was now 'a smiling landscape dotted with villages and bearing abundant crops.' After France, he went on to Germany, visiting Baden and then the Black Forest, greatly enjoying the opportunities its lakes and hills afforded for fishing and birdwatching, but not taking to its people, noting in his diary, 'On the whole I loathe Germans.'[5] Two months later, on 30 September 1930, the German federal election took place.

It was won by the Social Democratic Party, who remained the largest party in the Reichstag, winning 143 of the 577 seats. However, the National Socialist German Workers' Party, or Nazi party, dramatically increased its number of seats from 12 to 107. Overnight, the Nazis had gone from the smallest to the second largest political party in the country.

The year 1931 saw the economic situation worsening further with the Bank of England losing its gold reserve at the rate of £2.5 million a day and a budget deficit of £120 million. In response, the Committee on National Expenditure, chaired by Sir George May, recommended extensive public sector spending cuts, reducing the rate of unemployment benefit and increasing taxation. Then, on 31 August, the Labour Cabinet resigned as a result of being unable to agree on how to tackle the deficit. Prime Minister Ramsay MacDonald, at the prompting of King George V, proposed the formation of a National Government composed of all three major parties, Conservative, Liberal and 'National Labour', and went to the country with this coalition on 27 October. However, the Labour Party refused to join the coalition and expelled MacDonald, arguing that it was a cynical move to rescue his career while also causing a major rift in the party. In contrast, Chamberlain was a keen supporter of the new National Government, stating to Hilda on 24 October 1931, 'I hope we may presently develop into a National Party and get rid of that odious title of Conservative which has kept so many from joining us in the past.'[6] The general election resulted in a landslide victory for the new National Government under Ramsay MacDonald, but it was the Conservatives who were the real winners with an outright majority of 470 seats. Labour lost 80 per cent of the seats it had won in 1929 and the Liberal party, although winning more seats than Labour, saw its vote split between three different party factions.

The Labour Party were routed in Birmingham, with all twelve seats being won by the Conservatives. Chamberlain easily held on to his own seat in Edgbaston and on the hustings blamed 'socialist ministers' who, 'after agreeing cuts, which in several cases were considerably larger than those now in operation, ran away from their responsibilities.' His answer to the country's economic woes was to restore the trade balance and, while recognising that the situation was complex, he believed 'a tariff levied on imported foreign goods will be found to be indispensable … The ultimate destiny of this country is bound up with the Empire. I hope to take my part in forwarding a policy which was the main subject of my father's last great political campaign.'

In the new National Government he was offered the role of Chancellor of the Exchequer while his brother Austen was offered First Lord of the Admiralty but after a few months retired. Churchill was also out. Chamberlain was 62 years old. In a letter to Hilda, dated 7 November 1931, he reflected on the changing fortunes which had befallen both brothers: 'I rather doubt by the way whether you are right in supposing that my family connections have stood in my way on this occasion. In fact, I always feel that in my political life I have to a large extent escaped the handicap which certainly afflicted Austen in being his father's son. The fact that they were for a long time actually in the House together made comparison inevitable. On the other hand, to my contemporaries in the House, Father is a name only and they judge me on my own record.'[7]

Upon Neville becoming Chancellor, his brother Austen was one of the first people to congratulate him, stating that it gave him 'The deepest satisfaction. I was the first Chancellor to introduce, in a humble way, Imperial Preference into the Budget. You will be the Chancellor to complete the building for which I laid the first brick in 1919. Father's great work will be completed by his children.'[8] In recognition of his achievement he was also awarded the Freedom of the City of Birmingham, the third Chamberlain to be given the honour and a unique achievement in the history of the city.

On 4 February 1932 Neville Chamberlain laid his first bill as Chancellor before the House of Commons with Austen looking on. As Austen had predicted, Neville proposed a ten per cent tariff on foreign goods and a lower or no tariff at all on goods from the Empire, in recognition of their father Joseph Chamberlain's famous policy of 'Imperial Preference'. For a man not known for expressing his personal feelings in public, he for once became quite sentimental, 'More than seventeen years have gone by since he [Joseph] died … I believe he would have found consolation for the bitterness of his disappointment if he could have foreseen that these proposals … would be laid before the House of Commons, which he loved, in the presence of one, and by the lips of the other, of the two immediate successors to his name and blood.'[9] At the end of the speech, Austen walked down from the back benches and shook his brother's hand. The Import Duties Act 1932 was Neville's triumph but Joseph's legacy.

Later in February, Chamberlain attended the World Disarmament Conference in Geneva, but it made little progress, with the German delegation insisting that no deal could be done until the Treaty of Versailles was ripped up. It was his first experience of dealing at a very senior level with a German government who, even before the Nazis got into power, blamed the Allies for the economic depression that had gripped their country. The Treaty, signed at the French Palace of Versailles on 28 June 1919, brought the First World War to an end but made Germany accept responsibility, forcing them to disarm and to make substantial territorial concessions and pay huge reparations. As a news item, however, the stalling of the disarmament conference was overshadowed by other

news, principally the Manchurian crisis in China and the presidential elections
in Germany. The German elections had returned President Hindenburg but
Hitler polled thirteen and a half million votes. In the federal elections that
followed, the Nazis won 230 seats in the Reichstag, becoming the largest party.

In April 1932, Chamberlain brought his first budget before the House and
maintained the severe cuts that had been agreed at the inception of the National
Government. The year before, Philip Snowden, Chamberlain's predecessor as
Chancellor, had abandoned the gold standard (which pegged sterling to bullion
so that it was worth a fixed amount in comparison to other currencies). He had
little alternative.[10] Britain's foreign exchange reserves were being drained at an
alarming rate as a result of the political and economic turmoil that was engulfing
the country. By sticking with the policy of his predecessor, Chamberlain did little
to ease the country's woes, but he had more success in renegotiating the interest
on the country's massive war loan. This was a cool £2 billion and he negotiated
a reduction in interest payments from five per cent to three-and-a-half per cent,
a notable achievement. Chamberlain also put before the Cabinet his plans to
tackle the growing crisis of unemployment. He proposed introducing a new
commission to oversee relief or unemployment benefit, stating 'It is nothing
less than taking the whole relief of the able-bodied away from local authorities
and ministers, and putting it outside party politics by entrusting it to a statutory
commission.' The year 1932 ended with a small glimmer of light at the end of a
very dark tunnel when Theodore Roosevelt was elected in the US, promising a
better relationship with Europe, and in Germany when the federal elections in
November saw a significant drop in votes for the Nazis.

The year 1933, which proved to be a turning point in twentieth-century
history, started off with Chamberlain grappling with war debts and wagtails. On
24 January, while taking one of his early morning walks in his beloved St James's
Park, he spotted a grey wagtail *Motacilla cinerea* by the dam on the lake. On
returning to his private office at No 11, he fired off a letter to *The Times*:

January 24, 1933

Sir,
It may be of interest to record that in walking through St James's Park
today, I noticed a grey wagtail running about on the now temporarily dry
bed of the lake, near the dam below the bridge, and occasionally picking
small insects out of the cracks in the dam. Probably the occurrence of
this bird in the heart of London has been recorded before, but I have
not myself noted it in the Park.

I am your obedient servant,
Neville Chamberlain
P.S. For the purpose of removing doubts, as we say in the House of
Commons, I should perhaps add that I mean a grey wagtail and not a pied.[11]

The grey wagtail is more colourful than its name suggests, with slate-grey upper
parts and distinctive lemon yellow under its tail. While common today on rivers
and streams, in Chamberlain's day they were still increasing their range into
southern England from their upland strongholds in the north and west of the
country. In 1933, a sighting of a grey wagtail in central London would have
indeed been rare and worthy of mention. The letter was widely picked up in the
rest of the media, provoking the ire of some commentators who questioned why
the Chancellor had time to stroll around St James's Park 'birdwatching' when
the country's finances were in such dire straits. To others, though, it showed a
more interesting, if slightly eccentric, side to Chamberlain's personality than had
hitherto been known. Despite the novelty, Chamberlain had in fact been firing
off letters to the press about wildlife since he was growing up in Highbury, but
until this point no one had taken much notice.

In his letter to Hilda on 29 January 1933, Chamberlain robustly defended
himself against the attacks and seemed to revel in the controversy that his
sighting had caused. He wrote:

> I enclose a cutting from the Yorkshire Post which may amuse you.
> It is extraordinary what interest my letter about the Wagtail caused.
> Buckmaster [Stanely Buckmaster, 1861-1934, Liberal MP and
> Viscount] wrote that it had given him more pleasure than all the
> rest of The Times put together (not surprising perhaps!). Another
> man spoke of his delight in reading it and declared that it was "like
> a gleam of warm, bright sunshine coming through the murky gloom
> of politics". S.B. [Stanley Baldwin] says that it has firmly established
> my popularity in the great heart of the nation and then and there (in
> Cabinet) composed a letter announcing the discovery of a Pelican in
> St James's Park![12]

This showed Baldwin's jocular side and was designed to raise a smirk in Cabinet
as the pelicans had been resident in St James's Park for well over 250 years, having
been presented as a gift from the Russian Ambassador to King Charles II in 1664.
Chamberlain concluded, 'The fact is that we are an intensely sentimental people,
and while my interest was prompted by my inborn love of Natural History, the

public loves to hear about "dear little birds" and to believe that generally callous statesmen have a "yuman" soft spot about them somewhere.'

A day after his letter to Hilda, the 'murky gloom of politics' became Germany's darkest hour when, on 30 January 1933, Hitler was appointed Chancellor. A prophetic Pathé newsreel playing in British cinemas at the time showed Hitler giving the thumbs up and stated, 'Berlin ... Adolf Hitler assumes Bismarck's mantle as Germany's Chancellor. He is now master of his adopted country's destiny and a wondering world awaits ... what?' Yet the comparison with Otto von Bismarck (1815-1898) was wide of the mark: while the latter, as the first German Chancellor, was reported to be demonic, he was also widely credited with unifying Germany, whereas Hitler was seen from the outset as a very divisive politician.[13]

By this time, Chamberlain was busy working hard on his second budget. Again, he would not borrow to reduce taxation and instead made swingeing cuts across the board, including to Britain's beleaguered air force, while warning the country that it could expect a decade of high unemployment. His only concession to the working man was to reduce beer duty, presumably so the unemployed could drown their sorrows. To raise revenue he decided to tax Co-operative Societies who had over 1500 stores and over five million members. These, unlike private shops and businesses, did not pay tax on their profits because they gave a bonus back to their members in the form of a dividend – or 'divi' – which could be spent in the store. The Co-op was founded in 1844 and the divi was paid to members as a share of the profits depending on the amount of goods they bought. People took great pride in keeping books recording what they had spent at their local Co-op and members found it an ideal way to save, particularly those too poor to have bank accounts. However, small private shopkeepers hated and feared Co-ops for taking away their trade while the working classes and those living in the slums felt a great sense of loyalty towards them.

Chamberlain had wanted to introduce the measure in his first budget but had postponed doing so because the Prime Minster, Ramsay MacDonald, demanded an inquiry into the subject. For MacDonald the subject was politically very sensitive because, along with other Labour MPs, he had campaigned in the 1931 general election that he would resign if the government taxed Co-ops. The resulting Raeburn Committee concluded that the divi was, in fact, a trade discount rather than a real share of the profits and therefore should be taxed. This created an acute dilemma for MacDonald and Labour Ministers serving in the National Government about whether should they support the government or stay true to their word.

Outside of Parliament the Co-operative movement had run a very successful campaign in support of not taxing Co-ops, getting over a million people to sign a petition in support of the status quo. The campaign was led by Samuel Perry (1877-1954), father of tennis legend, Fred, who had been the Co-operative Party's first general secretary and formerly Labour and Co-operative MP for Kettering (The Co-operative Party was set up in 1917 and in 1927 entered into an electoral pact with Labour which continues to this day). Letters in support of not changing the taxation rules flooded into the Cabinet and it soon became an electoral issue, resulting in Labour winning several by-elections. The Inland Revenue was so furious with the campaign that they seriously considered mounting a smear campaign against the Co-ops.

Chamberlain was sensitive to how the issue looked, particularly to those on low incomes, but was also aware that the Conservative Party relied on donations from businesses large and small. With the inquiry backing him up, he pushed through the measure, against the wishes of MacDonald and Labour MPs who had asked him to think again. While Chamberlain won the day with the overwhelming support of his Conservative peers, MacDonald and many Labour MPs never forgave him. MacDonald afterwards blamed himself for not forcing Chamberlain's resignation on the issue.[14]

Reflecting on the slings and arrows of office, Chamberlain wrote in a letter to Hilda on 29 April 1933: 'It is a depressing business to be in politics at present and I get very weary of it sometimes, seeing nothing ahead to look forward to, but only long struggles against a gradually more and more disgruntled public opinion. I wonder whether it will seem worthwhile to go after the next Election.'[15] However, there were compensations. In June, Chamberlain went to Oxford to receive an honorary degree in the lavish Sheldonian Theatre, designed by the architect Christopher Wren, as reward for his political achievements. He had come a long way from the young man who had left Rugby with few qualifications.

In the same month of June, to tackle the global depression, sixty-six nations from around the world came together at the Economic Conference, held at the Geological Museum in London. All eyes were on the Americans, the rest of the delegates looking to them to provide leadership in reviving the world economy. Attending the talks was President Roosevelt who had just passed the New Deal and, as a result, had accumulated the largest deficit in the world. In his negotiations with Chamberlain and other world leaders he was therefore in no mood to compromise on war debt repayments or currency stabilisation with thirteen million unemployed at home. Chamberlain was quietly appalled at the behaviour of the brash American President and after the conference was over he escaped to Tarland in Aberdeenshire, on a grouse shooting holiday. In a letter to Ida on 27 August 1933, he described it as the best holiday in many years and he would 'look back upon it with satisfaction for the rest of my life,' as his shooting party had bagged 'immense quantities of grouse'.

Following the Conservative conference in October, which he told his sister Ida 'does not go on long but is strenuous while it lasts,' Chamberlain opened the 40,000th house built by the Birmingham Corporation, which he had helped to found. It was a proud moment. Writing on 28 October 1933, he said, 'They have built a number of "maisonettes" on the site of the old cavalry barracks ... You can imagine what a change this is from the old filthy back-to-back dens.'[16] To further help the poor in Parliament, he had introduced the Unemployment Bill, which sought to reduce the age a person could enter the national insurance scheme to 14 and the age they could claim benefit to 16. Furthermore, for the first time it set up an Unemployment Assistance Board to provide means-tested payments to those not entitled to benefits.

On 11 November 1933 he wrote to Ida, 'I rather thought our Unempl etc Bill would have had a good reception but it has been better than I thought ... Our people in the House are very pleased and the Local Authorities though anxious to get the best possible financial terms are pleased to be relieved of the Means Test.' Despite his heavy workload, Chamberlain still found the time to teach his children about animals and the natural world. He wrote, 'Tomorrow we are going to visit the Zoo where I want particularly to see the humming birds feeding and the Birds of Paradise in their nuptial display.'[17]

Chapter 7

Great Expectations

'For You have been a defence for the helpless, A defence for the needy in his distress, A refuge from the storm.' Isaiah 25:4

The next two years marked a turning point in Chamberlain's Chancellorship as the economy made a remarkable recovery for which he was able to claim much of the credit. In his eyes it vindicated the tough decisions he had taken over the previous four years, particularly not going down the path of borrowing and spending on great programmes of public works, such as Roosevelt had in America with his New Deal, a policy also championed by Lloyd George. As the economy improved, so Chamberlain began to believe that it was his unique brand of personal politics and hard work that had made the difference. 'In my office the amount of work you have to do largely depends on what you make for yourself. Unhappily it is part of my nature that I cannot contemplate any problem without trying to find a solution to it,' he wrote to Ida on 12 May 1934. He also added, 'And so I have practically taken charge now of the Defence requirements of the country.'[1] Though widely accepted at the time, this was to have far-reaching consequences for the country in the run up to war.

The year 1934 started with a hearty dinner on 2 January with the 'bush beaters union' which was a 'full-blooded meal beginning with a fat meaty soup and going on with pork and beef and mutton and plum pudding. After that come speeches of interminable length.'[2] Five days later he solved an avian mystery at home that had been puzzling him for months: 'We have solved the problem of the pecked rotten posts. A pair of nuthatches have appeared at our bird table and devoured coconuts, filberts and bird seed. I am very delighted as I have never seen nuthatches in Birmingham before.'[3]

As well as being passionate about nature, Chamberlain was also a great music lover, with a deep appreciation of Beethoven. Although he couldn't play an instrument, his daughter, Dorothy, was an accomplished pianist.[4] On 27 January 1934 he wrote to Ida, stating that he much preferred the German conductor Bruno Walter (1876-1962) over his fellow countryman Wilhelm Furtwängler (1886-1954), both at the time being popular with audiences across Europe. His personal taste was vindicated by subsequent events: Walter, a Jew, was the chief conductor of the Berlin Philharmonic and would go on to settle in the USA after fleeing the Nazis while Furtwängler was the principal of the Berlin Philharmonic and would controversially serve under the Nazi regime.

Natural history, though, was Neville's first love and on 25 February 1934 he wrote to Hilda, telling her he had reacquainted himself with Charles Darwin by reading a new book published that year, *Life of Darwin*, by the naturalist Richard Hingston, 'Whatever new discoveries and rediscoveries may have done to throw doubts on the effects of natural selection as pictured by Darwin there is nothing which has established itself in its place,' he told her. 'But one has to re-read the old letters to recollect the prodigious change effected from the dogmatic assertions of creation which held the field when the Origin appeared. The whole of Botany, Zoology, Geology, Distribution, Classification, Embryology, Paleontology, Homology, in fact the whole study of the animal and vegetable kingdoms has been revolutionised and almost begun again; and all this owing to this lifelong invalid who was sick almost every day of his life and could never forget that he had a stomach except when he was completely absorbed in his work.' Yet to make such amazing discoveries, Chamberlain believed you had to be wealthy. In a final sentence, which revealed a lot about himself and his attitude to money, he stated, 'If he had not been a rich man of course he never could have achieved what he did.'[5]

Another one of Chamberlain's recurring preoccupations was his age and the day before his sixty-fifth birthday, on 17 March 1934, he wrote to Ida, thanking her for her birthday good wishes and stating that he had just been looking at a 'list of the Government with their ages and I see that only the P.M. [Ramsay MacDonald, 1866-1937] and S.B. [Stanley Baldwin 1867-1947] are older than I. However, it isn't a question of years but how you feel and even if my body is not as active as it was I don't seem to be aware of any decline in mental powers just yet.'[6]

The next few years certainly saw no let up in Chamberlain's frenetic work rate. In his 1934 budget he began the process of reversing the deep cuts he had made in 1931. A recovering economy also allowed him to focus on housing and he made it a statutory duty of all local authorities to examine 'all houses unfit, or likely to become unfit' in order to tackle slum housing. During the ensuing debate he memorably told the Commons, 'We have now finished the story of *Bleak House* and are sitting down this afternoon to enjoy the first chapter of *Great Expectations*.' It was a good line that pleased his MPs and as a result he was able to write to Hilda on 21 April 1934, 'No Budget in recollection had so good a reception both in the House and in the country.'

The budget was followed by Chamberlain getting three acts on the statute book in just two years: the Unemployment Act, 1934, which established the

Unemployment Assistance Board; the Special Areas Act, 1934, which established four trial areas where funds for tackling high unemployment were targeted; and, a year later, the Housing Act, 1935, which required local authorities to identify unfit homes and build replacements. This was another notable accomplishment, but the measures, while radical in vision, were only experimental in nature and they made little real impact on unemployment or slum housing. As a result, throughout 1934 and 1935 he faced criticism of his policies, not just from his usual critics like Lloyd George, but also Conservative backbenchers who felt that his measured approach and rigid sticking to the financial rules showed the National Government had no real plan for dealing with unemployment.

The year 1934 also marked the time when Chamberlain began to spend far more time on foreign affairs, and in particular the defence of the country in the face of the escalating threat from Nazi Germany. On 9 June 1934, he wrote to Hilda, 'I have saddled myself with a big job over Defence. The proposals at present being considered are not satisfactory to my mind and when I have finished this letter I must begin consideration of a very important State paper which will put forward an alternative.'[7] The obstacles that he faced in doing this were considerable, not least because the Empire at that time still accounted for nearly a quarter of the globe and Britain's obligations far outweighed its defensive capabilities.

On 28 July 1934, just after the Nazis had murdered the Austrian Chancellor, Dr Dollfuss, in a failed coup, he wrote to Hilda, 'That those beasts should have got him at last and that they should have treated him with such callous brutality makes me hate Nazi-ism and all its works with a greater loathing than ever.'[8] In response, Chamberlain tried to negotiate a marked increase in the defence budget, but was stuck between a rock and a hard place. Winston Churchill, and many other Tory MPs, wanted him to go further, and faster, while the Labour leader, Clement Attlee, and the Liberal leader, Herbert Samuel, were far more cautionary. He told Hilda that he wanted 'to convince the country as a whole that the Government is right in restoring our defences. It was lucky that our statement on the Air Force was made before the coup and not after so that there was no appearance of panic. I anticipate that the vote of censure debate will show a stronger feeling for the suggestion that we are doing too little and Attlee or Herbert Samuel can bring out their exclamations of horror that we should be doing so much.' Chamberlain went on to outline his proposals for the Royal Air Force, Britain's first line of defence, 'The amusing thing is that the original proposals of the Air Force only showed 52 squadrons available for Home Defence. As an alternative my plans for the defence services showed 80 squadrons and the proposal finally adopted is 75. I am on the whole well satisfied.'[9]

When it came to the threat from Nazi Germany, time was not on his side. Writing to Hilda on 4 August, while on holiday at Kinloch Rannoch in Perthshire, he said, 'Our information shows that she is arming and training as fast as she can and my next budget wears no rosy aspect to me. Whatever happens we have to spend large sums on defence and all the cranks and "experts" are merrily at work doling out subsidies in every direction. As long as I am at the Treasury we shall do nothing rash.'[10]

While Chamberlain could be charming and courteous, he could also be judgmental and snobbish, particularly about the working classes, whom he was, in theory, championing. 'We attended the annual Ball of our Edgbaston Unionist Association,' he wrote to Ida on 24 November. 'It is a sad fact that the presentable specimens there might have been counted on the fingers of one hand. It was not only that the great majority were either dowdily or vulgarly dressed, it was the astonishing plainness of their features that impressed me so forcibly. I am afraid our native city, though it has grown and prospered abundantly, has not become more refined than it was a generation ago.'[11]

The following year, 1935, started with a happy event, the wedding of his favourite niece, Diane Chamberlain to Mr Terence Maxwell, which he attended with his daughter, Dorothy. On 16 March, foreign affairs again came to the top of his in-tray when Hitler announced conscription and the creation of an army of half a million men bearing arms, in flagrant breach of the Treaty of Versailles. 'Hitler's Germany is the bully of Europe,' wrote Chamberlain to Hilda two days later, 'Yet I don't despair. I had a lot of trouble in persuading my colleagues this morning to put the question: Was Germany still prepared to discuss all the questions agreed upon before? [negotiations had been ongoing about limiting the size of their armed forces]. They declared we should get no answer or a negative one. I declared my confidence that we should get a reply in the affirmative. And we got it in about ten minutes.'[12]

Chamberlain 'persuading his colleagues' that he could get an answer out of Germany when others couldn't was the start of his belief that he had a special relationship with the 'bully of Europe'. Around the Cabinet table, Prime Minister Ramsay MacDonald cut an increasingly isolated and forlorn figure, treated with contempt by many in the Conservative Party and hated by his former Labour MPs for propping up the National Government. Buoyed by the recovering economy and a passionate believer in his own abilities, Chamberlain was now being seen as the natural successor to MacDonald who was increasingly absent due to stress-related illness. Chamberlain reported to Hilda on 23 March 1935 that he had now become 'a sort of Acting P.M. – only without the actual power of the P.M. I have to say "Have you thought" or "What would you say" when it would be quicker to say "This is what you must do".'[13]

For the 1935 budget he recorded a 'talkie' which was shown in cinema vans around the country. His Private Secretary had given him a draft but he had rewritten it so it was more 'homely', stating, 'Sound finance has established confidence in industry. Confidence has begotten enterprise and enterprise has increased employment and profits, so that revenue has increased faster than expenditure.' Not known for his modesty, he added afterwards, 'I am sure that it was because it was my own thought and not someone else's that it made such an impression. I was quite amazed at its effect. Two quite different people, who are regular listeners, were reported to me by friends as having said it was the best speech they had ever heard on the wireless. The press in the Lobby who listened to it said the Government ought in future to not let any other Minister do their broadcasting.'[14]

Chamberlain had a surplus in his finances thanks to 'mistakes by departments, better trade, and unexpected discoveries, principally a raid on the Road Fund [set up by the Road Act 1920 it was a tax on each vehicle, which had to be displayed in the form of a disc; by 1935 it amounted to almost £4.5 million].' This allowed him to reverse many of the cuts he had made during the depression, including restoring unemployment benefit in full and cutting taxes for those who earned over £135 per annum and had 'born the greatest burden'. 'In the end it proves much the most popular of my budgets,' he told Ida on 21 April 1935, 'and it is generally agreed by the pundits that it will be very helpful to the Government's prestige.'

Worn out by the budget, he left for his Easter holidays and went salmon fishing on the River Dee in Aberdeenshire. He wrote, 'I saw one decent fish rise at a natural. I cast my dry fly over him and he took it at once. He weighed 1lb 2oz and was a source of much joy.' Politically, the continuing issue of Ramsay MacDonald's health and his absence for prolonged periods from the Commons had now become acute and, in May 1935, he agreed to stand down as Prime Minister with Stanley Baldwin taking over after King George V's Silver Jubilee celebrations.

In July, Chamberlain had the great honour of giving away his only daughter, Dorothy, who married Stephen Lloyd on 24 July 1935 at Old Church, Chelsea. While domestically he was excelling as Chancellor and personally he was happy, storm clouds continued to gather overseas and in September, Hitler passed the Nuremberg Race Laws, depriving Jews of German citizenship and outlawing them from marrying Aryans. This was followed in October by a crisis in East Africa when Mussolini invaded Abyssinia (now Ethiopia) over a disputed border area. In response, the League of Nations voted for sanctions against Italy as the aggressor but received little support. Instead, Britain and France, fearful this would push Italy ever closer to an alliance with Nazi Germany, appeased Italy and recognised her sovereignty, despite widespread public and international criticism.

In November 1935 there was a general election and the National Government again won with a comfortable majority of 255, though with fewer seats than in 1931. Chamberlain's handling of the economy was generally credited with being the National Government's greatest asset on the doorstep. The Liberal National vote held up but the National Labour vote collapsed and Ramsay MacDonald lost his seat. The real winners, however, were the Labour Party who, under Clement Attlee (1883-1967), registered their largest ever share of the vote with 154 seats. On the upside for Chamberlain all twelve seats in Birmingham again returned Conservative Unionist MPs, the only city in the country to go completely blue in both elections. They included Ronald Cartland, the brother of the acclaimed novelist Barbara, who won in Kings Norton. The election was to mark a watershed in British history, for although no one knew it at the time, the rise of Nazi Germany would mean it was the last election for a decade. The year finished with Chamberlain and his family finally moving into 11 Downing Street just before Christmas, following MacDonald's resignation. 'We moved into Downing Street on Monday,' he wrote to Hilda on 15 December, 'and have already gone a good way towards getting it straight.'

The start of 1936 saw Chamberlain, in his first letter of the year, waxing lyrical about *Hamlet* after reading it during his Christmas break, proclaiming himself free of gout (Chamberlain suffered periodically throughout his adult life from the condition) and reflecting on the passing of both King George V (1865-1936) and Rudyard Kipling (1865-1936). Just before Christmas, Chamberlain had been at a dinner with Kipling, but clearly didn't rate the journalist and author too highly, 'I could never see him as a great poet but he certainly had a great influence in his day both on other literary men and on political thought. He had always had a good deal of the school boy in him.'[15]

George V's death on 20 January 1936 attracted great media attention, as did his successor, King Edward VIII, due to his dalliance with the American society hostess and divorcee Wallis Simpson, but abroad it was Germany that continued to dominate the headlines. On 17 January Joseph Goebbels, Hitler's 'Minister of Enlightenment and Propaganda', said in a speech in Berlin that Germany's colonies lost in the Treaty of Versailles must be returned to the Reich, infamously adding, 'We can manage without butter but not, for example, without guns. If we are attacked we can only defend ourselves with guns, not with butter.' Chamberlain read about Goebbels' speech in *The Times* and said in a letter to

Ida the next day, 'I wonder if you have read the deplorable speech by Goebbels reported in the Times today. It seems extraordinary that such a vulgar common little mind should have been able to preserve his position so long and it has an ominous look as though the fustian he pours out found a ready response among the German people.'[16]

The beginning of February saw Chamberlain again indulging his love of culture by going to see *Romeo and Juliet*, which he described as 'an admirable performance. I do not like Geilgud, but Peggy Ashcroft was charming and the actor who plays Mercutio is very good.' Unusually for such a refined connoisseur, Chamberlain also made a visit to the cinema to see the film *The Ghost goes West*, a British romantic comedy starring Robert Donat about a Scottish ghost who goes to live in Florida and has to deal with American 'vulgarity'. 'We laughed consumedly,' he mused, 'What Americans think of it I don't know.'[17]

By contrast, Chamberlain's sisters, Ida and Hilda, were not having such a good time and were thinking of leaving their idyllic home, Bury House, in Oliham, Hampshire, because of aircraft noise from the recently built RAF base. RAF Oliham had been officially opened in October 1937, ironically by Erhard Milch, then Chief of Staff for the Luftwaffe. (Despite the noise, both spinsters lived out their lives there, Ida dying in 1943 and Hilda in 1967). Chamberlain sympathised with their predicament stating, 'It is really dreadful to think of you pulling up all your roots at your age to start again, and yet I feel with you that much of what you have loved in the place will probably be destroyed by those beastly aeroplanes. It is the same everywhere … and here I am spending the taxpayer's money on more and more planes merely for the purpose of frightening the Germans into keeping the peace. It is a sad, mad world.'[18]

As well as defence, Chamberlain was also busy putting together bills covering the cotton and sugar industries, agricultural insurance and education, but complained to his sisters that his MPs showed no interest in them. Despite his heavy workload, he still found time to quiz his sister Hilda over some birds – reed buntings – that she had seen flocking in a field near her home, 'Are you quite sure that what you saw were black-headed (=reed) buntings? I thought they kept pretty well to the wetland and didn't go in flocks,' he told her on 9 February 1936, 'I can't help wondering whether your birds were not bramblings which do go in flocks and also have black or blackish heads. My P.S. [Private Secretary] tells me that in his neighbourhood (near London) there is a large flock of crossbills. I should think they might easily appear near you among the Scotch firs.'

Despite being a gifted ornithologist, Chamberlain was wrong to suggest that reed buntings *Emberiza schoeniclus* do not flock. While in summer they are a wetland bird, in winter they join in with mixed-species flocks of buntings, finches and sparrows to feed on seed in farmland. This was well known at the time – for example *British Birds* magazine reported on it in 1922.[19] So Hilda's initial identification was probably right. However, Chamberlain was correct in saying that bramblings flock and she could see crossbills near her home. In the same letter he also stated that he had put up a bird box in the garden at No 11, 'I have put up a nesting box in the garden here (much to the amusement of Treasury staff), and have got a table being made, but I don't know whether I shall get anything but pigeons and sparrows, I have seen a pied wagtail round the lake several times lately and a thrush sings merrily in the early morning either in the garden or one of the trees nearby.'

He returned to the mistaken bird identification on 16 February when writing to Ida, 'Hilda misled me about the buntings because she said she saw them "in the fields". If she had reported a pair in the hedgerow as you now say I should not have questioned her identification. I have read of snow buntings in such flocks but never reed buntings.' Chamberlain was right to correct himself in his letter but for the wrong reasons as reed buntings do flock in fields. Snow buntings, in contrast, are a rare breeding bird in Britain, being confined to the Scottish uplands, but they are much commoner in winter and can be found anywhere along the British coastline, where they often occur in small flocks, as Chamberlain pointed out.

He continued, 'For the first time this winter I saw on Thursday and Friday flocks of redwings in St James's Park. Among them were one or two larger birds on Thursday that I thought were fieldfares, but A. [Annie] was with me and had an appointment so I couldn't be quite sure. The next day it was a little warmer and the redwings were much reduced in number while their bigger companions had vanished.' Redwings *Turdus iliacus* and fieldfares *Turdus pilaris* are common winter visitors to the UK from Scandinavia and are very social birds, spending the winter in flocks of anything from a dozen to several hundred strong. They roam the British countryside and are an attractive part of our winter scene. However, they would have been an uncommon sight in St James's Park so, as Chamberlain suggests, their presence would have been noteworthy.

Following his visit to the cinema to see *The Ghost Goes West*, Chamberlain told Ida that his defence White Paper had been well received and that, to celebrate, he and Annie had been to see Charlie Chaplin's latest film, *Modern Times*, with some friends: 'I had never seen him before and we laughed till we ached at his absurdities. The others said that when you have seen him often he palled to some extent because his jokes and mannerisms were always the same but of course it was fresh to me.' Chaplin's film, the last featuring his 'Little Tramp' character, was a social commentary on the aftermath of the Great Depression and how industrial automation had helped to create mass unemployment, both themes Chamberlain had grappled with. By the time Chamberlain finally went to see his first Chaplin movie, 'talkies' had been around for almost a decade and initially Chaplin had intended *Modern Times* to be his first one. He eventually canned the idea, however, and instead used sound effects and background music. (Ironically, Chaplin's first 'talkie' would be *The Great Dictator*, a satire on Hitler and Mussolini, released in Britain in March 1941, four months after Chamberlain's death).

Outside the world of entertainment, in an ominous sign of the real-life modern times, German troops marched into the demilitarised Rhineland on 7 March 1936, in direct violation of the Treaty of Versailles. In response, Chamberlain had created a new role of Minister for Coordination of Defence in his White Paper. With Baldwin's consent, he passed over Churchill for the job, afraid of the message that it would send to Nazi Germany. Instead he offered it to the Conservative Peer Thomas Inskip (1876-1947, 1st Viscount Caldecote). 'I am thankful that in these circumstances we have not got Winston as a colleague,' Chamberlain wrote to Ida on 14 March 1936, 'He is in the usual excited condition that comes on him when he smells war, and if he were in the Cabinet we should be spending all our time in holding him down instead of getting on with our business.'

By this stage in his career, Chamberlain was being privately talked about as the next Prime Minister. Baldwin was feeling the strain of both office and his age, declaring privately that he wanted to retire due to ill health. However, being heir apparent put yet more strain on Chamberlain's relationship with Churchill, who then made disparaging remarks about him when addressing the Jewellers' Dinner in Birmingham. This resulted in a spat over the subject of who knew most about Shakespeare, the nature of which said a lot about the different styles of both men. In a letter to Ida dated 28 March 1936 Chamberlain said of Churchill:

He said "Don't be angry. I called you a packhorse but read the context. It comes out of Henry VI when Clifford is dying". I said to him later on that I was much obliged to him for his generous allusions but that his quotation came from Richard III not Henry VI. "No," he said, "I think I am right; it comes in that speech where the king compares himself to a shepherd." And then, another thought occurring to him, he asked suddenly, "Have you looked it up?" Of course I had, but it was thoroughly characteristic of Winston first that he should have remembered this phrase which is not a familiar quotation then that he should have given it the wrong attribution, and finally that having had his attention called to his error he should not have bothered to look it up.

Chapter 8

Becoming Prime Minister

'For physical training is of some value, but Godliness has value for all
things, holding promise for both the present life and the life to come.'
Timothy 4:8

The spring of 1936 saw Chamberlain working hard on his fifth budget and again
taking his Easter break fishing on the rivers Don and Dee in Aberdeenshire,
where he thoroughly enjoyed himself and reeled in one of the biggest catches of
his life. 'In due course when I had grassed him he was found to scale 2lb 14oz,'
he wrote to Hilda on 19 April, adding, 'I resolutely refused to think of the budget
while I was away but am hard at it now and this morning I spent composing my
broadcast. I still have my "talkie" to do.'[1]

On 21 April Chamberlain brought his budget before the House. It included
a threepence in the pound increase in income tax, as outlined in his Defence
White Paper, to pay for the largest programme of rearmament in Britain's
peacetime history. He received plenty of praise for his budget, but, writing to
Hilda on 2 May, said what gave him most joy was some bird news from the
garden of 11 Downing Street, 'The cuckoo has arrived here!' May was also
Hilda's birthday and Chamberlain sent his best wishes and thanked both sisters
for their continued devotion. 'You and Ida are a great help to me both because
your comments are often illuminating and because I can always count on your
sympathy and understanding.' More good news followed at the end of May
when he caught '9 fish which included ... one 5 ¾ lbs. This last is the record fish
for the water and I was lucky to get him ashore for the weight broke the handle
off my net short just as I was landing him ... I am having my monster set up.'[2]

July was dominated by the start of the Spanish Civil War, an increasingly
strained relationship with Germany and Chamberlain again contemplating how
long Stanley Baldwin would remain in office. But it was the subject of his personal
finances which dominated his weekly letter to his sister. Despite being paid one of
the highest salaries in government, he found himself financially strained following
the breaking down of his car. On 11 July he complained to Ida, 'After spending
£17 on repairs it has broken down completely and we shall have to get a new one

at once; buying it out of my overdraft! My affairs like Austen's go from bad to worse as the country gets back to prosperity.'

The next month, just before his holiday, Chamberlain was again struck down by gout, which had returned with a vengeance despite his gout-free New Year resolution in January. As a result, he had to wear his gout boot to Number 11 which, while inconvenient, he soon accommodated, carefully balancing it on the waste paper basket in his office while giving dictation. His wife Anne was also suffering from her own health problems and was confined to bed with exhaustion. Despite his immobilisation, Chamberlain continued to deal with the work of government, even finding time to fire off an article to *The Daily Telegraph* on 8 August about a mystery bird in the garden at No 11 which had long perplexed him:

> A short time ago people were interested to read of a starling in St James's Park which had learned to imitate the cry of the kestrel, and thereby frightened the sparrows into the bushes. Quite a number of birds occasionally mimic others; this is an account of an instance that came under my notice.
>
> One of the pleasantest features of No. 11 Downing Street is its outlook on the old L-shaped garden that lies between it and the Horse Guards Parade, with its ancient shaded wall, its marvellous turf, and its venerable ilex and hawthorn. When I came to it first, it was mid-winter; the trees, save the ilex, were leafless, the birds silent. Yet it was pleasant to look on, and full of promise.
>
> As, later in the year, the spring brought up the sap, and the green began to show in the tips of the lime-buds, the first sound that came through the open window of my bedroom in the morning was the song of a thrush. "Hey! Ho! Hey! Ho!" He sang so joyously and vigorously that his exuberant spirits were infectious, and I got into the habit of listening for him in the daytime as well as in the early morning.
>
> It was only after a long time that I began to remark to myself that never had I heard a thrush put so little variety into its song. Thrushes generally repeat notes, often many times in succession, but then they will break off and improvise. This fellow seemed to have nothing more to say than his "Hey! Ho! Hey! Ho!" exhilarating as he made them sound.
>
> Could it, I wondered, be a mistle thrush? But no! There was none of that piercing, breathless phrasing of the storm-cock. This was clearly and decidedly a song thrush.

Often, curiously enough, the opening notes were followed by the unmistakable mellow drawling whistle of a blackbird. But it was only gradually that the truth dawned across me.

I had never seen a thrush in the garden, though blackbirds were often on the lawn, and sometimes came to drink at my bird-bath. Could this be a blackbird which had picked up those two notes from a thrush singing in St James's Park? I determined to solve the mystery by observation, but I had to wait long before I could find an opportunity.

At last, one week-end in July, when I had to be in London, I was working in my room when I heard the well-known cry. I ran into the garden: the bird was concealed in the thick foliage of a plane tree by the Foreign Office steps. I waited patiently, motionless, on the lawn, and presently a shadow passed across the trees. "Hey! Ho! Hey! Ho!" came from the interior of the plane opposite, and in another minute the singer emerged at the very top of the tree, shouting out his little song of gladness.

No mistake about it this time – a blackbird imitating the habit as well as the notes of the song thrush, and proud of his accomplishment.

August has come, and the blackbird's song is ended. But I fancy that whenever in future my thoughts turn to the garden of No11 I shall hear again that "Hey! Ho! Hey! Ho!"[3]

During the 1936 summer recess, Chamberlain travelled to Blair Atholl in Perthshire, where he walked, fished and watched birds. On his return in September, he rented out his three bedroom penthouse at Eaton Square to Joachim van Ribbentrop (1863-1946), the German ambassador in London and a man he loathed. Ribbentrop did not take up his post until October but had already developed an extremely poor reputation as a vain bully. Reflecting on the irony of it, he wrote to Hilda on 23 September, 'Did I tell you that we have let Eaton Square to Ribbentrop till the end of the year and possibly longer? I think it is very amusing considering my affection for Germans in general and R. in particular.'[4]

From 5-31 October over 200 unemployed men marched from Jarrow in Tyneside to London in protest against the unemployment and poverty in the town following the closure of its main employers, Palmers shipyard. It was an event which, despite his focus on unemployment, seems largely to have passed Chamberlain by. On 4 November, there was a debate in Parliament about the Jarrow marchers' request to bring their case before the House of Commons, but it was defeated. Chamberlain was annoyed, not because he sympathised with the marchers, but because he had planned to go to see the opera *Figaro* with Annie that evening. Instead, much to his chagrin, he had to sit out the debate on the government benches and wasn't even called to speak.

The Jarrow debate was followed by the Chancellor's traditional annual Mansion House speech to the banking community. Chamberlain confided to his sister, 'I thought it would be so dull,' but in the end he was pleased as it 'put all the stocks up the next day.' He also found time to host a small tea party so his guests could hear some gramophone records of bird songs recorded by the famous German naturalist and author Ludwig Koch (1881-1974), a German he did admire. With great satisfaction he told Ida on 10 October 1936, 'He is the man who wants to record my blackbird if it sings again next spring.'

During the remainder of 1936, Chamberlain, together with the rest of the country, became embroiled in the mounting abdication crisis engulfing Edward VIII and in response he sought to 'regularise the King's relationship'. (Chamberlain's letters from this period were not made public until 2002, following the death of the Queen Mother, due to sensitivities around his references to the King, Wallis Simpson and the fallout from the crisis). The situation was made worse by the return of his gout and, in order to conquer it once and for all, he turned to the bootmakers who had equipped the Everest expedition in April led by the civil servant and mountaineer, Hugh Ruttledge (despite their boots, it had ended in failure). At his request they sent him a 'bulky deerskin cocoon' which, he told Hilda on 31 October, he was delighted with: 'That I am able to travel is entirely due to my new boot ... I am so pleased with the results that I am having an evening shoe made and also a boot that I can put on for shooting purposes. I had almost given up hope of shooting this autumn but I believe now I shall manage it though I daresay my shooting may be affected by bad "footwork".'[5]

Physical fitness was a subject close to Chamberlain's heart and, gout aside, he prided himself on being very fit for his age. To prepare the country for war and ensure that the nation's armed forces were also fighting fit, Chamberlain had come up with his own fitness programme. He was keen that it also covered 'moral training and discipline' and 'health and beauty'. He set up an advisory council consisting of 'Boys Clubs, Boy Scouts, Health and Beauty (women's) organisations, National Playing Fields Assc &c &c.' It would, he noted, advise the Prime Minister 'who as long as he is S.B. will take no active part,' but, 'if it were N.C. would thus have his finger on the whole show.' It was a shrewd move designed to show him as both active and a man of ideas in comparison to the inactive and ill Baldwin.

By mid-November the abdication crisis was reaching a climax with feverish speculation in the US press and public feeling on the issue in Britain running very high, despite a news blackout, all of which manifested itself in hostility towards Wallis Simpson. Chamberlain was also becoming increasingly weary of taking on Stanley Baldwin's responsibilities due to his ill health. The result was that the looming threat from Nazi Germany slipped down the government's list of priorities. 'But the worst of the P.M.'s jobs that I have had to take on,' he wrote to Hilda on 14 November, 'is that which concerns the Monarch. The situation is rapidly becoming worse and at any moment there may be an explosion of feeling. The knowledge of his association with Mrs Simpson is spreading like wildfire and the importation of American papers has enlightened many who have been shocked and humiliated by what they have read. The K[ing] has paid no heed to a warning which prodded on by me, was given him some weeks ago by the P.M.'[6]

On a personal note, November was also tinged with sadness in that Chamberlain decided to give up his precious orchids, the love of which he had shared with his father Joseph. 'I get less and less time to see them,' he ruefully told Hilda, 'and I came to the conclusion that I was not getting enough out of them to justify the continued expense.' Natural history, however, continued to play a pivotal part in his life and he recorded everything he heard or saw in the garden of 11 Downing Street. He finished the letter to Hilda, 'The other night I woke up after I had been asleep some time and heard a brown owl [tawny owl] talking to himself in the garden here, and yesterday after lunch I am almost certain I saw the Kestrel fly across the sky out of the dining room window.'[7]

On 24 November, Germany signed an Anti-Comintern Pact with Japan, stating that in the case of an attack by the Soviet Union they would co-operate 'to safeguard their common interests'. The pact directly threatened British interests in the Far East, in particular the British naval base at Singapore. Commenting on the pact, Chamberlain said to Hilda on 28 November, 'In spite of the gloomy appearance of foreign affairs I think there is just now something of a détente at any rate so far as we are concerned. One result of the German-Jap agreement, which seems to have been badly received everywhere, has been to cause our friends in Japan to make known their anxiety lest anything should be done to jeopardise our good relations.'[8]

On 1 December 1936, Hitler passed a law making it mandatory that all boys in Germany between the ages of 14 and 18 join the paramilitary Hitler Youth movement. In Britain this passed almost unnoticed as, by early December, the abdication crisis had reached breaking point, with Chamberlain acting as a conduit between the Palace and Stanley Baldwin, a role he did not relish and one that caused him many sleepless nights. Writing to Ida on 8 December he said, 'It is difficult to write about anything else and indeed everything else is at a complete standstill, including all Government business. No one is talking or thinking of anything but the King and I can only hope that we shall not have to wait much longer.' More encouragingly, he finished his letter, 'I have seen my doctor or rather he has seen my foot and is astonished at the improvement ... It feels very much better now than it has since the beginning of the summer.'[9]

Chamberlain and the rest of the country did not have much longer to wait. On the morning of 10 December 1936, King Edward VIII abdicated in favour of his brother, the Duke of York, so that he could marry Wallis Simpson. The country was stunned but in government there was a huge sigh of relief that the most damaging episode in recent royal history had finally come to end. The Nazi press, while relishing Britain's predicament, stated that it would take a 'noble stance' and not report on the 'the private affairs of those concerned'. Exhausted, Chamberlain escaped to the French Riviera with his family for his Christmas break. Over the border in Germany, on 21 December 1936, the Junkers Ju88, or *Schnellbomber*, a bomber designed to be so fast that no British fighter could intercept it, had its maiden flight.[10]

The year 1937 started with Chamberlain again trying to predict when Baldwin might stand down so he could measure up Number 10 to move in his furniture, worrying about Germany and complaining about lack of sleep. 'S.B. has not said a word to me about his intentions,' he told Ida on 16 January 1937, 'but he has to other people and I gather that it is his intention to go as soon as the Coronation is over ... One thing that has come to me (but still not from S.B. himself) is that the P.M. would like to remain at No.10 till the end of the summer. This would really suit us very well as it would make it possible to have any desired alterations carried out in the autumn and would avoid the tiresome move in the middle of the session.'[11]

The next month saw Chamberlain being wined and dined by an establishment that was convinced he would become the next Prime Minister. His physical training scheme was well received by the House of Commons, though he noted it had been 'four years now since the idea first occurred to me on reading the letter in the Times from some General about it. I got precious little support from my colleagues for it then and S.B. has never taken the slightest interest in it, but I persevered ... the Sunday Times says the Government have started on a bigger idea than they themselves are aware of!'[12]

On 11 February, Chamberlain presented his third White Paper on defence to the House of Commons, announcing he had borrowed £400 million and it would be 'imprudent' to contemplate expenditure of less than £1,500 million on defence over the next five years. This led to large increases in the amounts available to the army, air force and navy and was well received in Parliament, but it did little to quell Churchill's criticism of the administration. Chamberlain in turn berated the Labour opposition for being more interested in 'malnutrition and the means test for unemployment benefit than defence'. Following his White Paper, he undertook a speaking tour in support of his defence proposals and afterwards took a long weekend fishing trip to the Tweed, where he caught '9 salmon from 7 to 15lbs'. 'The number of fish is incredible,' he told Ida on 7 March. On his return he found time to go with his brother Austen to a concert at which Henry Wood (1869-1944), the co-founder of the Proms concerts, was conducting. Chamberlain was delighted that afterwards Wood wrote to him and expressed 'his pleasure at seeing me in the audience'.

Not long after both brothers had attended the concert together, tragedy struck when, on 16 March, Austen had a massive heart attack and died in his London home at the age of 73. Chamberlain was outwardly grief stricken but took some consolation in that, just days previously, they had spent time together and he had congratulated him on a recent performance in the House of Commons, where he had made 'the most perfect speech I had heard him make'. A side effect of Austen's sudden death was to make Chamberlain once more contemplate his own mortality. 'When my turn comes,' he told Ida, 'I shall have to stand comparison with both Father and Austen. Luckily I shan't care then!'[13]

At Easter, Chamberlain again went fishing in Scotland, but this time came back with only tales of the ones that got away. 'The fishing remained bad to the last as you had anticipated,' he told Hilda on 10 April, 'So ended the worst Easter (for fishing) that I have ever known, for I have never before come away absolutely empty handed.' Afterwards he was 'plunged into a series of the most worrying and apparently insoluble puzzles on the Budget, the Civil List, the Defence Programme and the Imperial Conference.' The Imperial Conference was held in London from 14 May to 24 June 1937, following the coronation of King George VI and Queen Elizabeth on 12 May, and discussed trade and foreign policy (it was the eighth and final conference before the Second World War). As Prime Minister-in-waiting, Chamberlain also found himself being actively lobbied by aspiring MPs who wanted a role in his future Cabinet. 'How curious people are,' he told Hilda, 'Leo Amery [1873-1955, Conservative MP] came to me this week to inform me, quite unasked, which of the great offices of state he would be prepared to accept if it were offered to him … I simply cannot understand how people can be so conceited.'[14] (Amery got no role in Chamberlain's Cabinet and later became an arch-critic).

The centrepiece of Chamberlain's 1937 budget was the National Defence Contribution (NDC), a new graduated tax on the profits of businesses that were awarded government defence work. It was a radical way of redistributing more money into defence, but it proved to be deeply unpopular with big business, the City and his party, although it was broadly welcomed by some in the Labour party. 'I am very glad you approve of the N.D.C.,' he wrote to Hilda on 25 April, 'especially as I flatter myself that your judgement is not in this case warped by some affection for its author. I reckon it to be the bravest thing I have ever done since I have been in public life, for I have risked the Premiership just when it was about to fall into my hands, although I could have easily left the hornet's nest alone.'[15] It was indeed a brave move, if not a politically astute one. Chamberlain belatedly recognised that its deep unpopularity could threaten his ambition to be Prime Minister. In public though he defended the NDC vigorously from the many attacks it received in the House of Commons (the graduated tax was later replaced by his successor with a flat rate five per cent tax).

After finishing the budget, Chamberlain attended a royal party where he rubbed shoulders with the new King and Queen. 'I had a walk with the Archbishop of Canterbury after tea and found a supporter in him and then the King sent for me and I talked to him for nearly an hour, mostly about the troubles with his brother,' he told Hilda on 25 April, clearly proud that he was now included in the royal inner circle. In Chamberlain, King George VI had found a sympathetic ear and a man with whom who he shared much in common when it came to domestic and foreign policy. Where the royals and Chamberlains clearly parted company was in their choice of films. 'After dinner we had a perfectly awful American film,' he told Hilda, 'No one could understand one word in twenty or make out what was going on, but the vulgarity of it was palpable enough and a large number of people were murdered and were always rolling out of hampers or falling out of bed.'

In Spain, hundreds of people were murdered for real the next day when, on 26 April, death rained down from the air on the people of the Basque town of Guernica. Using their aerial power, the Germans and Italians carpet-bombed the town, reducing it to rubble and causing a large number of civilian casualties (the actual number is still disputed by historians, with estimates ranging from over 1,600 to just over 150). The nature of the bombing and the extent of the casualties shocked Chamberlain but also made him more determined than ever to stick doggedly to Baldwin's policy of non-intervention in the Spanish Civil War.

The threat from Nazi Germany and Fascist Italy also hung over the Coronation of George VI, which took place at Westminster Abbey on 12 May. As well as the anointing of the King, the event also had to project the unity and power of the British Empire at a time when both were under considerable strain. As PM-in-waiting, Chamberlain had a front row seat. 'The foreigners simply gaped with astonishment and awe. Since the great day London has been crowded with masses of people all in the highest spirits, determined to see anything there was to be seen and bursting into enthusiastic cheers on the slightest provocation,' he told Hilda on 15 May. Less enthusiastically, but more importantly, he stated, 'I am making progress with my Cabinet'.[16]

On 22 May Chamberlain wrote his final letter to his sister Ida as Chancellor, 'Now it is coming to the end of my term I feel rather unhappy at leaving,' he wrote, 'but I regret nothing I have done while I have been at the Treasury.'[17] On 28 May he was sworn in as Prime Minister, 'kissing hands' with King George VI at Buckingham Palace. A journey that had started nineteen years earlier had, thanks to the family name, hard work and fate, resulted in him gaining the highest office in the land, eclipsing both his father, Joseph and his brother, Austen. It was a remarkable rise for someone who had left Rugby with few qualifications and who had been destined only to enter the family business. He was 68 years old.

Chapter 9

Cabinet, Chequers and 'Musso'

'Let us not become weary in doing good, for at the proper time we will reap a harvest if we do not give up.' Galatians 6:9

Chamberlain's first few days in office were taken up with finalising his Cabinet for his new National Government and filling all the other roles associated with being Prime Minister. 'Well, the changeover has gone like clockwork,' he told Hilda on 30 May 1937, clearly pleased with the smooth handover from Baldwin following months of frustration with his leadership. 'Never has a new Govt been formed complete to the last man, in so short a time,' he told his sister, and he was right on both counts. Among the Cabinet and over a hundred government appointments agreed in record time there was just one woman, Florence Horsbrugh, who was appointed Parliamentary Secretary at the Ministry of Health. (She was later to become the first Conservative female Cabinet member).

    There were four Liberal National members in Chamberlain's Cabinet: Sir John Simon at Treasury, Leslie Hore-Belisha at the War Office, Ernest Brown at Labour and Leslie Burgin at Transport; and two National Labour members, Herbrand Sackville, Lord De La Warr, as Lord Privy Seal and Malcolm MacDonald, who was put in charge of the Dominions. The Cabinet were:

- Neville Chamberlain – Prime Minister and Leader of the House of Commons
- Lord Hailsham – Lord Chancellor
- Lord Halifax – Lord President of the Council and Leader of the House of Lords
- Lord De La Warr – Lord Privy Seal
- Sir John Simon – Chancellor of the Exchequer
- Sir Samuel Hoare – Secretary of State for the Home Department
- Anthony Eden – Secretary of State for Foreign Affairs
- William Ormsby-Gore – Secretary of State for the Colonies
- Malcolm MacDonald – Secretary of State for Dominion Affairs
- Leslie Hore-Belisha – Secretary of State for War
- Lord Zetland – Secretary of State for India and Burma
- Lord Swinton – Secretary of State for Air

- Walter Elliot – Secretary of State for Scotland
- Alfred Duff Cooper – First Lord of the Admiralty
- Oliver Stanley – President of the Board of Trade
- Lord Stanhope – President of the Board of Education
- William Shepherd Morrison – Minister of Agriculture
- Ernest Brown – Minister of Labour
- Sir Kingsley Wood – Minister of Health
- Leslie Burgin – Minister of Transport
- Sir Thomas Inskip – Minister for Co-ordination of Defence

As a result of the international situation, Chamberlain had thought long and hard about his appointment to the War Office. In the end he had decided to move the 'lazy' Duff Cooper (1890-1954), a Conservative MP, diplomat and author, from there to the Admiralty. Cooper greatly resented the move and would soon become a thorn in Chamberlain's side, alongside Winston Churchill, who continued to languish on the backbenches. On the first Friday of his Premiership Chamberlain went to see the King and took the opportunity to ask if he could see him regularly, King George VI replying, 'Yes, because we hardly know each other, do we.'[1] Chamberlain was anxious that the monarch looked on him as a close confidant and not 'an alarming person', and as a result was determined to forge a close relationship. The only black mark on Chamberlain's first few days in office was the continuing controversy over his National Defence Contribution. The City was particularly outraged, but he told Hilda he wouldn't let his government be wrecked by 'pig-headed obstinacy or by too great haste to abandon a threatened position.' Chamberlain was learning early on that it was tough at the top.

Reflecting on taking office, he told Hilda, 'And now you will be wondering what my own feelings are on actually taking up this post which ought to have come to the two senior members of the family and only failed to do so because the luck was against them in forcing them to choose between their natural ambition and their principles. It has come to me without raising a finger to obtain it, because there is no one else and perhaps because I have not made enemies by looking after myself rather than the common cause.'[2] Chamberlain was right that the position had come to him more easily than he could have ever dreamed, but was wrong in his supposition that he had not made enemies on the way up. They were merely biding their time. He added that he should never have been PM without Annie who 'charms everyone with her good humour and makes them think that a man can't be so bad who has a wife like that'. His only major regret was that his father and some close members of his family were not there to see his proudest moment.

The first time Chamberlain was able to escape the frenetic activity associated with No 10 was in early June when he managed to fit in a weekend's fishing on the River Itchen while Annie went home to Birmingham to rest. 'We had a "marvellous" weekend,' he told Ida on 6 June, 'and I caught various trout of most satisfactory size.' There he met the naturalist Tony Buxton, a former soldier and author (who later went on to write the *Fisherman Naturalist* in 1946 and the *Travelling Naturalist* in 1948), describing him as 'A first rate ornithologist and the best trout fisherman I have come across … he gave me some most useful hints besides finding a yellow wagtail's nest.' Following his return, the magazine *Country Life*, not slow to see an opportunity, decided to put Chamberlain on its cover and sent him a complimentary copy. 'I see (since I returned) that he [Tony] has a delightful article in *Country Life* this week on the Water Rail,' Chamberlain told Ida, 'I should never have seen it if C.L. had not sent me a copy with rather a good photo of myself in fishing kit as a frontpiece.'[3]

While being Prime Minister was constantly demanding of Chamberlain's time, it also had its compensations, which he and Annie fully embraced. They attended the Glyndebourne Opera in Sussex and finally got to see *Figaro*, Chamberlain describing it as being 'superb, conductor, producer, artists and orchestra are all the best to be found in Europe.' The week after found them listening to the Italian conductor Toscanini at 'the expense of the BBC'. They also found time to look at redesigning No 10 to meet their needs, 'All depends on whether it is possible to build new bedrooms for us over the present reception rooms,' Chamberlain told Ida on 20 June.

Another big perk of the job was Chequers, the country house bequeathed to serving British Prime Ministers by Lord and Lady Lee of Fareham in 1921.[4] Visiting for first time on 25 June, he wrote to Hilda the day afterwards, 'Annie is greatly delighted with the peace and restfulness of the place and already declares that she will come here in preference to Birmingham.' While his wife enjoyed the tranquility, an excited Chamberlain explored the grounds looking for wildlife. He found a tulip tree in the garden, 'one of the biggest in England,' and 'a yew that might be any age with a number of huge trunks and an elm said to have been planted by King Stephen!' The next morning he walked up the hill behind the house and recorded 'an uncommon plant the Houndstongue *Cynoglossum [officinale]*,' while looking for birds. 'I am sure A. and I will be much more satisfactory occupants than our predecessors who, however much they may have enjoyed the place, don't seem to have taken an intelligent interest in it,' he told Hilda haughtily.[5]

Natural history also featured at 10 Downing Street where a delighted Chamberlain found 'a perfect specimen of the Leopard Moth in the garden'. A distinctive and easily recognised species, the leopard moth *Zeuzera pyrina* has six large black spots on a white body, along with heavy black spotting on white wings. The adults fly during June and July and the larvae feed on the wood of a variety of deciduous trees. Though nocturnal in its habits, the adults can sometimes be found resting conspicuously in the daytime, which is how

Chamberlain happened upon it in the garden. He told Hilda he had 'only twice before seen one alive, but though it is not really very uncommon it is a dark flier and therefore seldom comes under notice.' He was so pleased with the moth that he wrote a short article about it and sent it without delay to *The Countryman* magazine, also including 'some remarks about my tits'. The article read:

> Naturally *The Countryman* is interested first and foremost in the country, but there is a *rus in urbe* where I write, in which sometimes reminders of the country may be visible for those who have eyes to see.
>
> The old garden between Downing Street and the Horse Guards Parade has existed for at least two hundred and fifty years, and perhaps it retains for that reason some traces of more rural surroundings. Only a few days ago, I was delighted to find resting on the trunk of a small hawthorn tree, a specimen of the beautiful, but rarely seen, Leopard Moth, its long, white, blue-black spotted wings folded over its back. The larva of this insect is a wood-borer, and, as far as I know, there is no tree in the garden which would be suitable for its food. Nevertheless, from its perfect condition, I am sure it could not have made any long flight, and it must have passed its earlier stages somewhere in the neighbourhood.
>
> When I first came here in January of 1936, I at once affixed a nesting-box to one of the trees in the garden. Nothing happened for a long time, but last March I saw a pair of blue, or perhaps I should say, black tits, for they were a grimy couple, flitting about the branches of a lime tree. Shortly afterwards they were flying in and out of the box. I did not have time to make any examination till the week-end after I had become Prime Minister, when on looking into the box, I found the nest completed and three eggs in it. Unfortunately, I saw little more movement, and looking again in June, found that the nest was deserted and the three eggs had been reduced to two. Now what is the solution of the mystery of the vanished egg?
>
> Did the tits themselves carry it away, or did some marauder make off with it? I remember, long years ago, my mother's twin sister, a lady much beloved by me for her sweet disposition and keen humour, related a conversation with her venerable gardener. Said my aunt, "John, I see the blackbirds have been busy again with the cherries". "May be, Ma'am," the old man replied, and then with an indescribably sly chuckle, he added, "but I fancy some *two-legged* blackbirds must have been round here". I wonder if some animal of the same species went off with my tits' egg.[6]

The article was promptly published in the October–December 1937 issue of the magazine, along with 'The Labour–Saving Garden', 'A Memorable Walk by Earl Baldwin of Bewdley' and 'More Photographs by Bernard Shaw'. Delighted at their exclusive, *The Countryman* gave his article prominent place on the cover, in large lettering, stating, 'Natural History at Downing Street by the Prime Minister'. They illustrated the piece with Chamberlain planting an oak tree at Fifield, near Idbury, a favourite activity of politicians down the ages who wanted to show they were doing something for the environment. (Chamberlain's description of the blue tits in the garden as black tits was a reference to the 'pea soup fog' which was at its worst in London during the 1920s and 1930s,[7] coating everything from buildings to birds in particles of soot from gas lamps, composed of sea coal mixed with sulphur dioxide. The mother's twin sister he referred to was Louisa Kenrick, who had married his Uncle Arthur in 1870 and who he adored. She had been the one to tell him about the death of his own mother when his father Joseph refused to. Chamberlain's assertion that he suspected that one of his staff went off with his tits' egg reflected the fact that egg collecting was then a popular pastime). The piece was widely quoted in the press and was broadcast by the BBC, with Chamberlain being the first and only serving Prime Minister ever to publish an article about the wildlife of Downing Street.

From the outset of his Premiership, Chamberlain was determined to ensure that all his ministers were singing from the same song sheet. To do this he asked each of them to prepare a two-year plan which he could collate in the autumn into a government programme. But domestic politics were soon overshadowed by foreign affairs. The Spanish Civil War was threatening to draw in other countries and Nazi Germany was becoming yet more menacing. Responding to both, Chamberlain made his first set piece speech on foreign affairs, reinforcing Baldwin's policy of non-intervention in Spain and praising Germany on the 'commendable self restraint' it had shown by not retaliating against the torpedoing of the German cruiser, *Leipzig*, by the Spanish Republicans. 'I saw an opportunity yesterday to say a few kind words about Germany which may have a far reaching effect,' he wrote to Hilda on 26 June. It did have an effect, but not in the way Chamberlain had hoped. Following the incident, Germany and Italy withdrew their ships totally from the non-intervention patrols.

To get on good terms with the King, Chamberlain went to see him again, this time at his own instigation, 'Nominally to tell him about the Imperial conference but really to get on more intimate terms with him. I like him very much and find him easy to talk to.' The King, clearly flattered, returned the compliment, Chamberlain noting with satisfaction, 'He said all the Prime Ministers had expressed great admiration of me to him.' A royal seal of approval and the alleged admiration of Baldwin and MacDonald was music to Chamberlain's ears, even if the King was merely following protocol. At Number 10 he also got his own way with his proposed structural changes, stating, 'The architects say they can make two very good bedrooms and bathrooms for us on the top storey.'[8] Chamberlain had begun to make his mark.

The heavy workload that came with being Prime Minister and the degree of scrutiny it entailed surprised even Chamberlain, who was used to both. 'It is a great relief to be over this week, for 8 speeches in 2 weeks is a bit of an overdose, when every word is scanned,' he wrote to Ida on 4 July. At the beginning of the month there had been a reception for him at the Botanical Gardens in Birmingham, which he described as a 'wonderful affair'. On trying to leave, Chamberlain was mobbed and treated more like a movie star than a politician. 'I refused all the autograph hunters,' he told Ida, 'but neither of us could refuse the hands that were stretched out so eagerly on both sides of the lane which the police strove vainly to keep clear for us.' He went on, 'It was a most touching experience to see all those ugly, honest faces shining with perspiration in the heat but positively beaming with pride and joy and to hear the shouts of Good Old Neville, all the best and (to Annie) Take care of 'im'.[9] It reminded Chamberlain of when crowds used to pursue his father's carriage and cry 'God bless you Joey', though whether they would have shouted quite so loudly if they had known that Chamberlain considered them ugly is a moot point.

When it came to foreign affairs, Chamberlain believed the best way of guaranteeing peace was to mediate with the great dictators, a position that brought him into conflict with his own Foreign Office, and in particular the Foreign Secretary, Anthony Eden. After returning from another big reception in the North of England, attended by 10,000 people, he told Hilda on 18 July, 'I did not want to talk about foreign affairs this time lest I should seem to be encroaching too much on Eden's territory but the debate on Thursday gave me the opportunity of alluding to Spain but turning it into an attack on the Socialists.' Labour had criticised the government for giving equal status to Franco, who they saw as the aggressor, a move condemned by Chamberlain as being a threat to the policy of non-intervention and world peace. Though his political diary continued to be very busy, he still found time for a wide range of social engagements and was pleased with an *Observer* editorial which 'ascribes to the new P.M a firm grip of affairs.' He concluded, 'The Govt's stock has undoubtedly gone up, partly from Opposition weakness, but also because of a feeling we know where we are going.'[10]

Chamberlain's sisters were also politically active in their own local community, and in their weekly letters regularly updated him on what has happening in the Hampshire village of Odiham. On 24 July Chamberlain wrote to Ida, lamenting what would happen to the public bodies on which they sat after their retirement. Hilda was a stalwart of the Women's Institute, serving on both local and national bodies, while Ida was a member of her local Rural District Council and sat on Hampshire County Council. 'I suppose however they will just quietly go to sleep again and that will be that' he concluded. He went on to question the quality of candidates who put themselves forward for public life, stating, 'it is a good thing that there are a few people with initiative and capacity to lead our municipal administration and fortunately it is not necessary to have more than a few.' Warming to his theme of disparaging the masses, he added, 'The majority are not required to do more than get through the routine and follow the leaders when they move forward.'

Chamberlain's desire to take control soon extended to his Cabinet. He wanted to take over what he considered problem areas in his government, noting, 'I have taken the chairmanship of a Cabinet Committee on Agricultural policy as I think it important to hold the balance between the Department and the Treasury and the problems are peculiarly difficult.' As is the lot of a PM, the list of issues and grievances he was expected to solve was long and often bewildering. He had to 'settle a difference between the Chairman and Treasurer of the party, one of S.B.'s [Stanley Baldwin's] legacies, receive a deputation on House of Lords Reform, preserve the peace between the Air Ministry and the Admiralty over the Fleet Air Arm (another legacy) decide what to do over Palestine and engage a number of Welsh bishops and parsons who were raging furiously together over the grievances of South Wales.'[11]

The international situation also continued to give him cause for concern. He was at odds with the Labour Party over Spain, but wanted to keep up 'the facade which at any rate preserves us from a European conflict.' More encouragingly, he had been approached by the Italian ambassador, Count Grandi, who wanted to give him a message from 'Musso' (his nickname for Mussolini). According to the Count the Italian dictator had 'no designs on the Mediterranean nor on Spanish Territory and only wants to be friends again.' To build better relations, Chamberlain agreed to see Grandi so that he could 'find out whether there is any nigger in the woodpile.'[12] (Chamberlain did not intend to use this phrase in a offensive or racist way. Instead it was used to denote that something of considerable importance was hidden. There is no evidence that Chamberlain was racist, indeed when he did work closely with black people growing sisal on Andros in his youth, he thought highly of them). The month finished on a high with Chamberlain stating, 'The Opposition are in trouble again, our people have their tails well up, my colleagues all seem happy and so I hope for an uninterrupted holiday.'

The beginning of August found Chamberlain at Chequers, a godsend to Annie as there were 'no household chores and no one to be responsible to and where she can just sink into bed and into oblivion.' Writing to Hilda on 1 August, he told her that, as well as chairing the Cabinet Committee on agricultural policy and dictating milk policy, he also intended to chair 'all Committees which have made recommendations on matters of major policy.' He also took in hand the army, who had fallen out with the War Office, wanted to get involved in the decision about whether or not to build a new Charing Cross bridge, and even had 'designs on the cotton trade'. No policy stone would be left unturned by the highly controlling new Prime Minister.

After Chamberlain met with Count Grandi he sent a letter to Musso, controversially acknowledging Italian hegemony over Abyssinia (today Ethiopia), which it had invaded that year in flagrant breach of the League of Nations' charter. This delighted the Italian ambassador, who declared that Italy and England had been 'divorced for two years but were now going to be remarried'. It was to be the start of a long personal crusade to win over the Italian dictator. Chamberlain fervently believed that his twin-track policy of rearmament combined with better relations with Germany and Italy would 'carry us safely through the danger period,' but only if 'the F.O. [Foreign Office] will play up'. Yet the cracks were already beginning to show. 'I see indications that they are inclined to be jealous,' he wrote to Hilda, 'but, though it is natural that they should be annoyed at press headlines about the "Chamberlain touch" instead of "the Eden touch" there is no desire on my part to take credit away from the F.S. [Foreign Secretary] and I shall try now to put him in the foreground.'[13] Just over two months after taking office 'the Chamberlain touch' had made its mark across government, but it was not always a deft touch and had raised hackles, particularly in the Foreign Office. However, he had more success in wooing the new King, 'I managed to get in another talk with the King which lasted 1¼ hours,' he proudly told Hilda. 'He is a bit tired but very pleased with the way things are going and is evidently gaining confidence all the time.'

Following his stay at Chequers, Chamberlain departed on his summer holiday to Scotland, staying at Lochmore in Lairg, courtesy of the 2nd Duke of Westminster, Hugh Grosvenor, one of the wealthiest men in the world (1879-1953, the Duke had anti-Semitic and pro-German sympathies, later joining the notorious Right Club). The opulent hunting lodge clearly appealed to Annie's love of high living and Chamberlain wrote to Ida on 8 August, 'There is no doubt that she is a child of luxury by nature and to be the guest of a millionaire, to have all her meals cooked by a first rate artist, to be waited on by three butlers and a footman and have cars and ghillies always at her disposal, all this goes a long way towards making her holiday tolerable.'[14] A diplomatic bag or pouch also arrived from Number 10, which he worked through in between fishing trips. He was particularly pleased that 'Musso' had responded positively to his letter. 'As it is

I can look back with great satisfaction at the extraordinary relaxation of tension in Europe since I first saw Grandi,' he proclaimed grandly. 'Grandi himself says it is 90% due to me and it gives one a sense of the wonderful power that the Premiership gives you.' He then contrasted his ability to influence events in his previous role with his new-found power as Prime Minister, 'As Ch. of Ex [Chancellor of the Exchequer] I could hardly have moved a pebble; now I have only to raise a finger and the whole face of Europe is changed!'[15]

Following his visit to the Duke of Westminster's hunting lodge, Chamberlain went to stay with the King and Queen at Balmoral, but had to break his holiday to return to London and deal with Musso. 'Not unnaturally there is a great deal of suspicion about Mussolini and a certain apprehension about the reception in this country of any proposal to accord formal recognition of the Abyssinian conquest,' he told Hilda on 29 August. Referring to the Labour Party, who opposed the move, he said, 'I must say I am astonished at the lighthearted way in which people who think they are pacifists are yet prepared to advocate measures which would almost certainly bring us into war.' He wanted to believe that his letter had 'made an enormous impression in Italy,' and would go a long way to restoring 'Anglo–Italian relations to what they were before the Abyssinian adventure.'[16] The 'adventure' would go on to claim over 20,000 lives, most of them Abyssinian. However, Chamberlain believed they had 'made a very important step forward towards European appeasement'.

After dealing with Musso, Chamberlain returned to Balmoral to complete his stay, telling Ida on 7 September about a shoot, in which he 'made two especially spectacular shots which excited much "migration".' He went on, 'Of course for a Cabinet Minister to hit anything is considered very extraordinary so one gets more than one's share of credit. But I learned from the household that the King and Queen were very pleased with their P.M.' He had yet to win over 'Musso' but he had certainly ingratiated himself with the royal couple. By early September, Chamberlain was back in Inverness and wrote to Hilda on 12 September, 'Many thanks for your letter which was delivered to me here with every appearance of importance. It is really comical to see how valuable my time has become since I have been called P.M. instead of C. of E. Every time I leave this hotel to drive round to the fishing or vice versa I am preceded by a police car from Inverness while a plain clothes man stands all day in the road to see that no authorised stranger intrudes upon me.'[17]

On his return, the 'Chamberlain touch' continued to be felt across government, particularly at the Foreign Office, which in his opinion had 'no imagination and no courage.' Commenting on his Foreign Secretary, Anthony Eden, Chamberlain told Ida he was 'awfully good in accepting my suggestions without grumbling,' but that it was wearing to 'have always to begin at the beginning again and sometimes even to rewrite their dispatches for them.' He complained that the 'F.O. persist in seeing Musso only as a sort of Machiavelli putting on a false mask of friendship in order to further nefarious ambitions.' He went on, 'If we treat him like that, we shall get nowhere with him and we shall have to pay for our mistrust by appallingly costly defences in the Mediterranean.'[18]

The holiday had been a chance to forget about government and foreign affairs for a while, but on returning to London he feared that he had come back to a 'very troubled world'. In the final weekend of September he stayed at Chequers, where he told Ida that Italy and Spain continued to be a source of great anxiety. To relax, he visited a new sculpture gallery at the Tate and a new gallery at the British Museum to house the Elgin marbles, both donated by the art dealer Lord Duveen (1869-1939). Writing to Ida on 26 September 1937, he noted that the 'vile C[entral] O[ffice] is planning a horrible "Talkie" on the "House of Chamberlain", an odious expression in itself.'

Two days later, on 28 September, Chamberlain received a letter from a Gilbert William Collett that would result in a remarkable friendship that would endure until his death. Collett co-owned a shirt shop at 84, Jermyn Street, not far from Downing Street, where all the best tailors were located and, in his youth, hung out with a fast set of celebrities who included the famous actress Lilli Langtree. One of Collett's hobbies was philately and he was elected to the Royal Philatelic Society in 1927, a year later co-editing a seminal book entitled *Jamaica - Its Postal History, Postage Stamps, and Postmarks*. His other great passion, like Chamberlain's, was ornithology. To escape the hustle and bustle of the capital he would regularly birdwatch in St James's Park, which soon became his 'local patch'. Reading Chamberlain's article on the natural history of Downing Street in the October issue of the *Countryman* magazine, Collett boldly wrote to the Prime Minister, offering to alert him if any interesting birds turned up in the park. Much to Collett's surprise, Chamberlain enthusiastically took up the offer and asked his Principal Private Secretary, Osmund Somers Cleverly (1891-1966) to reply.

10 Downing Street
Whitehall

29 September 1937

Dear Sir
The Prime Minister asks me to thank you for your letter of the 28th September and to say that, if it is not troubling you too much, he would

be glad to take advantage of your offer to let him know when something of interest in the bird-life of St James's Park comes to your notice. If you would ring up me or one of my colleagues, we shall always be ready to pass on your message to the Prime Minister.

Yours truly
O.S. Cleverly[19]

Over the next two years Collett would write or ring Chamberlain's private office on numerous occasions when an interesting bird turned up. Chamberlain, in turn, when time allowed, would write back, sending in total a dozen letters. Most days when he was at Downing Street, and his schedule permitted, Chamberlain would take an early morning walk in St James's Park, accompanied by Annie or one of his private office, and his bodyguard. The letters show that, as well as Cleverly, who was the most senior private secretary directly reporting to the Prime Minister, Chamberlain also relied on two other private secretaries, Miss Campbell and Mr Rucker, to correspond with Collett. In order to check reports he would send some of his staff out searching for birds in the park armed with an identification guide, on one occasion using them to identify a popular tree that a kestrel was using as a hunting perch. Chamberlain's love of birds soon spread throughout the upper echelons of government, and while some undoubtedly disapproved, others who overlooked the garden embraced his pastime and sent him records, which he would pass on to Collett. It was a unique relationship and one that Chamberlain valued so much that he even wrote to Collett after he had resigned as Prime Minister, asking him to continue sending in observations.

The beginning of October saw Chamberlain address his first party conference, held in Scarborough, as Prime Minister. Unfortunately, the conference clashed with the tenth anniversary meeting of the Council for the Preservation of Rural England, a cause close to his heart. Unable to attend, Chamberlain instead sent a message saying, 'For many years I have been a supporter of the Council and have watched their work with keen interest. By their efforts they have, I believe, succeeded in wakening the public conscience to the duty of preserving the beauties of the English countryside, and they already have a considerable measure of achievement to their credit. If their work is to go on and be successful they must be given the support of all lovers of the countryside, countrymen and townsmen alike. I wish the Conference now assembled in Leamington every success.'[20]

Only too aware of how important it was to get his political message across to the public, Chamberlain, spurred on by his staff, visited Denham studios to record his 'House of Chamberlain' talkie, which the 'vile Central Office' had organised. In line with his previous efforts, he deemed it a great success, telling Ida, 'They told me that eminent actors "go all of a tremble" when they get in front of the camera and have to go over their pieces again and again but after I had done a short rehearsal I was informed that my performance was beyond criticism!' Whether the sentiment was sincerely meant or the studio staff felt the need to flatter the Prime Minister is debatable. 'Well I hope it doesn't mean that I shall often be called on for the purpose,' he mused, before adding, 'for to tell the truth I was extremely glad when it was over and I was told that would do.'[21]

The 16 October would have been Austen's seventy-fourth birthday and, writing to Ida on the day, Chamberlain commented he had just finished a book on Lord Halifax (Charles Wood 1839-1934, father of Edward Halifax), who had lived to be 94, and that it would be 'strange to think a man of 74 might have another 20 years before him.' (He was also in discussion with both sisters about who should write Austen's biography). Reflecting on his own fate, he wondered how history might judge him, 'I don't expect that but I hope I may have long enough to leave my mark behind me as P.M.' By this stage foreign affairs and the continuing battles with the Foreign Office were taking up so much of his time that Chamberlain asked his office to start preparing domestic speeches for him, which he could then top and tail. Complaining again to Ida of the workload, he felt that he was coping better than his predecessor, Stanley Baldwin, 'I can't do all the things that S.B. did as well as the things he didn't do and I consider that at present at any rate the latter are more important.' His talkie was to be released at once and was to be used as a trailer, but 'ultimately it will form part of a longer film about the "House of Chamberlain" (like the House of Droge) which is to go round with Conservative talkie vans.'[22]

At the state opening of Parliament on 26 October, Chamberlain clashed with Clement Attlee, the Labour leader, over foreign affairs, but felt he had 'much the best of it and all our people were delighted with my speech.' Towards the end of October he and Annie were meant to hold their first party at Chequers, but he was again struck down by gout and bed ridden so it went ahead without him. However, his Achilles heel, the Foreign Office, continued to be a pain politically. The editor of *The Field* magazine had sent them an invitation to attend an International Shooting Exhibition in Berlin. At first the Foreign Office made light of it, then couldn't decide whether or not to attend. Chamberlain was incensed at what he saw as another opportunity to influence the Nazi leadership being 'thrown way'.

By 6 November he had recovered enough to get his shoe on, but was glad of the rest and awaiting news from Berlin about whether or not Hitler would agree to a meeting with Halifax, his close confidante and the Leader of the House of Lords. Chamberlain had selected him to attend the International Shooting Exhibition in Berlin in his capacity as Master of the Middleton Hunt, bypassing the Foreign

Office. Hermann Göring, the head of the Luftwaffe, who had extended the invitation, was a passionate hunter and gave Halifax the nickname 'Halalifax', after 'Halali!', a German hunting call.[23] Halifax's visit would, Chamberlain thought, be 'the acid test of his [Hitler's] good faith'. Despite being so busy with foreign affairs, he still found time to take in a junket to a Toscanini concert, which he greatly enjoyed, again courtesy of the BBC who had 'sent a list of their remaining concerts and have intimated that I have only to telephone and they will send me [free] tickets for any of them'.[24] While he was enjoying the opera, Italy joined the Anti-Comintern Pact with Germany and Japan.

The middle of November saw Chamberlain back at Downing Street and weighed down by four speeches he had to give: one at the Guildhall on foreign affairs; a tribute to the late Labour leader Ramsay MacDonald, who had died of a heart attack on 9 November; an address to the 1922 Committee of Tory backbench MPs; and a speech in Edinburgh. He continued to have a difficult time with the Foreign Office over the Halifax visit, commenting 'I have had to fight every inch of the way.' The spat soon became public and 'raged round Halifax's instructions'. But he had every faith that Halifax was the right man, stating to Ida on 14 November that, 'He won't spoil the effect of his visit by any tactlessness when it comes to talk with Hitler.' He also added, as if trying to convince himself, 'I am quite sure the country thoroughly approves of what I am doing.'

On 16 November Chamberlain received another letter from his birding correspondent, Gilbert Collett, and replied three days later:

10 Downing Street
Whitehall

19 November, 1937

Dear Sir
The Prime Minister asks me go thank you for your letter of 16 November. He was interested to hear of the redpoll.

With reference to the suggestion that he should become a Vice-President of the British Empire Naturalists Association, Mr. Chamberlain would be glad if he could be excused from accepting this invitation. As you will understand, he has a great many similar suggestions made to him and he feels bound to restrict his acceptances to a minimum.

Yours very truly
O.S. Cleverly[25]

The redpoll *Carduelis cabaret* is a small streaky-brown finch with a white wing bar, but its characteristic feature, as its name suggests, is a small red patch on its forehead or crown. Resident in Britain, the redpoll feeds on seeds from birch, alder and spruce found in woods[26] so its occurrence in St James's Park in the middle of London would have been a notable sighting. As a keen ornithologist and naturalist, Collett was also a member of the British Empire Naturalists Association (today the British Naturalists Association), which had been started in 1905. His attempt to get Chamberlain to become its vice president was his way of getting the fledgling organisation greater profile and recognition, but Chamberlain, by this time, was already heavily involved with both the Council for the Preservation of Rural England and the Society for the Promotion of Nature Reserves. However, the ever-diplomatic Cleverly ensured that Collett was let down lightly.

On Sunday 21 November, Chamberlain was staying at Hackwood Park with the Berry family, the country estate having been purchased the previous year by William Berry (1879-1954), the editor-in-chief of *The Daily Telegraph* and later 1st Viscount Camrose. Here he was photographed planting an oak tree and enjoyed the film *One Hundred Men and a Girl*, which he commented to Hilda was 'so absurd as a story as to be almost farcical but nevertheless made an extremely good evening's entertainment.' To his horror it was preceded by a couple of trailers, one of which was his *House of Chamberlain* film made at the Denham studio. 'I suppose it is a good thing to see oneself as others see us but it is a very painful process. My voice appeared to me so distorted as to be unrecognisable and if I had not previously seen the person who addressed us from the screen I should call him pompous, insufferably slow in diction and unspeakably repellent in person!'[27] It was a rare case of Chamberlain looking in the mirror and being too harsh on the person he saw staring back at him. He was also pleased that Halifax's visit to Hitler had finally gone ahead and turned out well, 'I see it is announced that he has invited Neurath (1873-1956 Konstantin von Neurath, Hitler's Foreign Minister) here and this was my second step if the first came off.'

By the end of November, Chamberlain's confidence of securing peace by appeasing Hitler was growing. He had received Halifax's detailed report of his meeting with him, writing to Hilda on 26 November, 'Both Hitler and Goering said repeatedly and emphatically that they had no desire or intention of making war and I think we may take this as correct at any rate for the present.' Chamberlain commented, 'The atmosphere in Berlin is decidedly clearer and even Goebbels has promised to be a better boy in future.' He had also attended Ramsay MacDonald's funeral, where his superlatives even extended to wreathes.

'The service ... was very appropriate and moving and extremely well attended,' he wrote, continuing, 'Annie was requested to order the wreath for the Cabinet and did it so well that my people said it was the most beautiful Cabinet wreath ever seen.'[28]

The beginning of December found Chamberlain staying with his cousin Arthur Chamberlain at his home, Rackenford Manor, in Tiverton, Devon, while Annie retired to Chequers to recuperate from her exhaustion. Here, writing to Hilda on 5 December, he stated that Anthony Eden would be taking a holiday after Christmas and that he would take over responsibility for the Foreign Office in his absence, something that many senior civil servants believed he had been doing anyway. A week later, on Sunday, 12 December, Chamberlain was shooting at Yatendon Court, a stately home near Newbury in Berkshire, where he had a very successful day 'downing 900 pheasants'. On the same day Mussolini withdrew from the League of Nations. 'Musso's latest outburst,' he told Ida, 'is I think to be attributed to a request from the Germans who appear to be trying to accumulate as many cards as possible for the game they will presently be playing with us.'[29] He also had continued to flex his muscles with the Foreign Office by playing a part in removing the intransigent Robert Vansittart (1881-1957), a senior British civil servant who he considered far too anti-German, and replacing him with Alexander Cadogan (1884-1968), a man he considered better understood German grievances.

Writing to Hilda on 17 December 1937 from his home of Westbourne, where they were braving freezing temperatures, he complained about the weakness of democracies, 'Which requires their Governments always to lay their cards on the table while the dictators can keep theirs in their hands.' The next year would see Hitler and Mussolini revealing their hands to devastating effect while exposing the weakness of Chamberlain's cards. Chamberlain, as ever, was determined to enjoy the moment whatever storm clouds lay ahead, and he spent Christmas 1937 at Chequers, extending an invitation to Hilda and Ida to join him and his family there. It was, he concluded, 'the best Christmas we had had for a long time.'

Chapter 10

The 'Chamberlain touch'

'He who is slow to anger is better than the mighty, And he who rules his spirit, than he who captures a city.' Proverbs 16 : 32

The start of 1938 again found Chamberlain consumed by foreign affairs, this time trying to get more US support for any impending crisis. 'I am trying to jolly them along with a view to making some sort of joint (or at least parallel) naval action,' he told Hilda on 9 January in response to increasing Japanese aggression in their war with China, adding, 'I do wish the Japs would beat up an American or two! But of course the little d-v-ls are too cunning for that and we may eventually have to act alone and hope the Yanks will follow before it's too late.'

Irish politics and the vexed issue of home rule – which had dominated British domestic policy for years – also took up his time. Following the Irish Free State of Eire coming into effect on 29 December 1937, Chamberlain spent three days in January meeting Irish delegates, including the Irish Taoiseach (or Prime Minister) Éamon de Valera, with whom he got on surprisingly well. De Valera had been the political leader of Sinn Féin and had played a key role in the 1916 Easter rising (he would become infamous at the end of the war for being the only statesman to send his condolences on the death of Adolf Hitler). The talks were wide ranging, covering trade and political recognition but no progress was made on the most controversial issue: partition. 'That is a difference that can't be bridged without the assent of Ulster and her assent won't be given unless she has confidence in the Govt of Eire and that cannot be attained except slowly and step by step,' he told Ida on 23 January, adding, 'I am satisfied that, queer creature as he is in many ways, he is sincere and that he is no enemy of this country.' As ever, with an eye on his own legacy, he concluded, 'It would be another strange chapter in our family history if it fell to me to "settle the Irish Question" after the long and repeated efforts made by Father and Austen.'

On dealing with a resurgent Nazi Germany, he revealed to Hilda that he was already thinking of using his own unique brand of personal diplomacy to find common ground with Hitler. This shuttle diplomacy, which was to become such a pivotal moment in twentieth-century politics, was at the time top secret. 'I have got an idea for further conversations with Germany which does seem to me to open up a hopeful prospect. I haven't revealed it to my colleagues yet but I am going to try it on a few of them tomorrow.'[1] What Chamberlain ultimately had in mind would take his policy of appeasement to a new level, stun his Cabinet colleagues and cause an irreconcilable rift with his Foreign Secretary.

The end of January found Chamberlain again at Chequers where 'Annie heaves great sighs of contentment,' and he found 'endless amusement in the garden and park.' The winter flowers in particular impressed him. 'I never saw such drifts of aconites and the house is full of bowls of them,' he told Hilda on 30 January. He and Annie had been making preparations for 'Constituency parties at No 11' (works were continuing at No 10) and had attended a Prokofiev and Beethoven concert, courtesy of free tickets from the ever-generous BBC.

To help foster closer Anglo-German relations, Chamberlain had been approached by the office of Baldur von Schirach, the Head of the Hitler Youth, to write an article for its monthly publication *Wille und Macht* ('Will and Might') for a special issue focusing on England. Seeing it as another opportunity to influence the Nazi leadership, he readily agreed and after consulting with Lord Halifax, penned the following article:

> I welcome the intention of the German Youth Movement to devote a special issue of their Magazine to the subject of England, and I gladly accept the invitation to contribute to a project which I regard as a sign of the growing desire for mutual understanding between our two countries.
>
> In writing to you, the young manhood and young womanhood of Germany, I need to remind you that you are, in the words of the poet Shakespeare, "The expectancy and rose of the fair State". A great responsibility lies upon you – the responsibility for your country's future. All the hopes of Germany are set upon you; to your care is committed your national heritage and traditions, your national honour and your national prosperity. All this is entrusted to you for safe keeping, and I am confident that you will prove worthy of the trust.
>
> But your responsibility does not end there. You have a responsibility for the future of your country: But you have also, in common with the youth of other nations, a joint responsibility for the future of the world. It is already and in the future will be still more the happy fortune of the organisations of youth now flourishing in many lands to foster – by means of mutual interchange of visits and otherwise – that understanding between nations which is so essential to the settlement

of differences and the appeasement of the world. The admirable motto "The Year of Understanding", which you have chosen for the year 1938, shows the part that you are playing in this work.[2]

(Signed) Neville Chamberlain

The letter, written on 10 Downing Street notepaper, was duly published in a special edition dated 15 March 1938, together with a similar message from Lord Halifax. Its contents were typical of Chamberlain, quoting *Hamlet* Act 3 Scene 1 and appealing to the 'young manhood and young womanhood of Germany' to help 'appease the world'. Shakespeare was popular with the Nazis because of the anti-Semitic content of some of his plays and there was a German Shakespeare Appreciation Society which met annually. However, whether or not a youth hardened by ceaseless propaganda to see war as a way of life would really be won over by reference to them as the 'rose of the fair State' is a moot point. The Hitler Youth doctrine certainly didn't see mutual understanding or appeasement as a way of settling differences between nations.

The letter followed on from a number of exchange visits between the Hitler Youth movement and British youth organisations the year before, particularly the Scouts. However, it again put Chamberlain at odds with his own Foreign Office who thought the visits, far from promoting 'understanding', were being used by the Germans for propaganda and to spy on Britain. This was backed up by Sir Vernon Kell, the Director General of MI5, who believed they were being used to recce military and other strategic installations. In response he tasked his organisation with carrying out covert surveillance of many of the Hitler Youth visits, particularly cycling tours around southern England, which became known as 'spycling' tours.[3]

Back in Germany, on 4 February, Hitler, in another move designed to give him yet more power, replaced his Foreign Minister, Konstantin von Neurath, with Ribbentrop, the German ambassador in London, and took over personal control of the Germany military, abolishing the War Ministry and creating the *Oberkommando der Wehrmacht* (High Command of the Armed Forces), while purging a number of senior officers. The changes sent shockwaves around the world, particularly in London, where the British government was caught completely unawares. Chamberlain in particular was concerned about Ribbentrop's promotion as he had 'always professed the strongest desire to come to an understanding with us, but his actions never appeared to be quite in keeping with his professions.' Despite this, he felt optimistic about conversations with the Italians as a result of 'the part played by Ivy while in Rome'. Ivy Chamberlain, Austen's wife, had visited Rome the month before. There she had met Mussolini and read him Chamberlain's letter suggesting joint Anglo-Italian talks. Ivy knew Mussolini, she and Austen having first met him in October 1925 at the Locarno conference, but she had acted in a purely personal capacity, much to the anger of Eden.

On 12 February, at Berchtesgaden, Hitler met with the Austrian Chancellor, Kurt von Schuschnigg, who, under threat of invasion, gave in to German demands for far greater Nazi participation in the Austrian government, effectively making it a puppet state. By this time the increasing tensions between Chamberlain and Eden on foreign policy had become public and there was much talk of a split in the national press. Writing to Hilda, he commented it was 'all untrue in every respect. I saw Anthony on Friday morning and we were in complete agreement, more complete perhaps than we have sometimes been in the past.' Moving on to happier subjects, Chamberlain told her that, like the garden at No 10, he had ordered nest boxes to be put up in the grounds of Chequers: 'I have now got my two groups of trees and my thicket of thorns planted and my latest proceeding is to order a number of nesting boxes. I have included one for the green woodpecker but I feel rather doubtful whether he will occupy it.'[4]

Despite his belief that there was no truth in the press reports of a split, Eden tendered his resignation following two days of fraught discussions on Chamberlain's policy of entering into talks with Mussolini.

Foreign Office, S.W.1.,
20th February, 1938.

My dear Prime Minister,

The events of the last few days have made plain a difference between us on a decision of great importance in itself and far-reaching in its consequences. I cannot recommend to Parliament a policy with which I am not in agreement.

Apart from this, I have become increasingly conscious, as I know you have also, of a difference of outlook between us in respect to the international problems of the day and also as to the methods by which we should seek to resolve them. It cannot be in the country's interest that those who are called upon to direct its affairs should work in an uneasy partnership, fully conscious of differences in outlook yet hoping that they will not recur. This applies with a special force to the relationship between the Prime Minister and the Foreign Secretary. It is for these reasons that with very deep regret I have decided that

I must leave you and your colleagues with whom I have been associated during years of great difficulty and stress.

May I end on a personal note? I can never forget the help and counsel that you have always so readily given to me, both before and since you became Prime Minister. Our differences, whatever they may be, cannot efface that memory nor influence our friendship.[5]

Yours ever,
ANTHONY EDEN.

The next day Chamberlain replaced Eden with Lord Halifax, a man who shared his opinion on appeasing the dictators. In response to Labour criticism that such a senior post should not be given to a peer, Halifax retorted, 'I have had enough obloquy for one lifetime' while Chamberlain commented, 'I thank God for a steady unruffled Foreign Secretary.'[6]

Privately, Chamberlain had initially been stunned by Eden's resignation, claiming to Hilda on 27 February, 'I had no idea till the 18th that it would come to a break.' He also apologised for not writing for so long but that 'she would not have been surprised that I could not write during that last odious weekend.' The blame, Chamberlain insisted, lay with Eden and the 'efforts of the F.O. to stave off conversations [with Italy] and to prevent my seeing Grandi.' After this, Chamberlain had to 'make my final stand and that Anthony must yield or go.' He and Eden differed not on the principle of appeasing the dictators but on how it should be done, by whom and when. Eden felt strongly that Mussolini should offer up some sign of good faith before any talks could commence, whereas Chamberlain, despite describing Italy as behaving like 'a hysterical woman', wanted to show Mussolini 'that he might have other friends beside Herr Hitler'.[7] The split in the end came down to Eden being deeply unhappy about Chamberlain's style of personal diplomacy and his continual circumnavigating of Foreign Office protocol. Chamberlain in turn came to the conclusion that 'at bottom Anthony did not want to talk to either Hitler or Mussolini and as I did he was right to go.'

Following the split, a wounded Chamberlain took refuge in the fact that 'first the Cabinet, then the House of Commons and now the country have rallied to my side.' He wrote that there was 'plenty of trouble ahead but I feel as if a great load was off my mind.' During the episode Chamberlain had endured 'plenty of abuse from ignorant and foolish people', the most notable of whom was his old adversary, Lloyd George. 'I had a terrific duel with Ll.G,' he told Hilda, after Lloyd George described him as an 'unscrupulous little blackguard' who had done something 'dishonourable'. Lloyd George's attack had been directed firstly at Chamberlain, then Grandi, and finally he had concluded the whole business had been badly handled. At this point, according to Chamberlain, 'The House jeered in derision and Ll.G. suffered the worst humiliation of his life. I confess I found it sweet to see him wriggling.'[8]

The sudden increase in expenditure on the armed services, in particular the expansion of the RAF, now threated one of Chamberlain's passions, the preservation of the countryside. As Minister of Health, he had been a keen supporter of the CPRE, speaking at its inauguration and following with interest its campaigning work on issues from ribbon development in the countryside to the creation of national parks. With defence going to the top of the government's priorities, many areas of countryside had been sacrificed for the building of aerodromes and other military establishments. This had brought the defence departments into conflict with many local authorities, who saw themselves as the defenders of England's green and pleasant land.

In 1934–35 the land given over to the Air Ministry was 3,000 acres, but by 1938 this had increased to 24,500 acres.[9] The CPRE, together with the National Trust, had been fighting both individual applications and the wider issue of plans being given the go-ahead 'in the national interest' without prior consultation or local authority approval. In 1937 alone, CPRE had been involved in twenty major cases, of which three had to be dropped due to parliamentary criticism.[10] With a view to the end of the war, they were also concerned about what would happen to the land once the defence departments no longer needed the sites. By the end of 1937 CPRE had an agreed policy that while national defence must take precedence, other national interests such as agriculture, history, culture and wildlife should also be taken into account under section thirty-three of the Town and Country Planning Act of 1932.[11]

One of the counties most affected was Wiltshire, and Lord Herbert, Chair of Wiltshire CPRE, had sent off a letter at the end of 1937 to Chamberlain asking for 'the establishment of inter-consultative machinery between the Defence Departments and other Departments of State representing other national interests.' The letter was signed by a large number of local landowners, including the Lord Lieutenant of the county, the King's representative, and the CPRE's first General Secretary, H. G. Griffin. Chamberlain, who had a lot of sympathy for the CPRE's cause but was under huge pressure to re-arm, responded in January. He stated that, while national defence must take priority and he was against an 'over-elaboration of consultative machinery', he wanted each defence department to establish a procedure 'which will ensure that other interests of national importance shall receive adequate consideration when the selection and development of sites are being carried out and that full consideration shall take place in time to enable due weight to be given to the results by the Departments concerned, before decisions as to acquisitions are taken.'[12]

The Minister for the Coordination of Defence, Sir Thomas Inskip, was charged with putting Chamberlain's wishes into action and asked each defence department to draw up its own procedure. One immediate result was that, on 1 March 1938, Professor Leslie Patrick Abercrombie, a town planner (who was later knighted in 1945), was appointed as consultant to the Secretary of State for Air, Lord Swinton. Abercrombie sat on CPRE's executive as Honorary Secretary and his selection gave the organisation a degree of influence unprecedented in its relatively short life. The work was, according to Abercrombie, 'troublesome and upsetting' as he had to 'attempt, in a report, to decide what weight to attach to objections by Local Authorities, the local branch of the CPRE, the Farmers' Union, the landowner or villagers affected: on the other hand to consider whether the Ministry were justified, whether speed ... must prevail or whether a rash and unconsidered choice should be abandoned – these attempts were no light tasks ... I don't think I have once been thanked for saving a man from having an aerodrome on the other side of his garden fence.'[13]

Abercrombie may have found the work thankless, but it was the first time that environmental organisations had been formally recognised as statutory consultees on planning development proposals. (The academic Gary Willis, who has researched the relationship, contends, 'Chamberlain's concession to organisations concerned with the environment represented a quite exceptional demonstration of support by a Prime Minister who, whilst investing considerably more hope in efforts for peace than some of his fellow politicians, was nevertheless at the time presiding over a government that was slowly and steadily preparing for war).'[14]

Internationally, negotiations with Italy and Germany continued but at the beginning of March Chamberlain's hope of securing peace was dealt a shattering blow. In response to a German ultimatum on 9 March, the Austrian president, Kurt Schuschnigg, announced a plebiscite about the proposed *Anschluss*, or union, with Germany. This so enraged Hitler that two days later he occupied the country and replaced him as Chancellor with the pro-German Arthur von Seyss-Inquart (1892-1946), an Austrian lawyer and Nazi leader, completing the *Anschluss* on 13 March. As the troops marched into Vienna, Chamberlain was enjoying lunch with the new German Foreign Minister, von Ribbentrop. 'It seemed ironic,' he told Hilda on 13 March, that having 'spent 20 minutes after lunch talking earnestly to Ribbentrop about a better understanding and mutual contributions to peace by Germany and ourselves I went into the drawing [room] and immediately had put into my hands telegrams relating to the successive ultimatums to Schuschnigg.'

Chamberlain read that the Germans were 'in the process of swallowing Austria'. He tried to negotiate with Ribbentrop, but felt it was hopeless, 'He is so stupid, so shallow, so self centred and self satisfied and so totally devoid of intellectual capacity that he never seems to take in what is said to him.' It was a brutal, if accurate, character assassination based on years of knowing him as the German ambassador. Continuing in the same vein, he wrote to Hilda, 'He had much to say about Schuschnigg's "breach of faith" and folly in holding a plebiscite (and in this latter point I don't disagree) but appeared totally unable to comprehend our objection to German methods. Indeed he professed complete disbelief in any ultimatum or even threats from German sources. I gather he considered Hitler had merely given wise advice to good Austrians like Seyss-Inquart [sic] who had themselves "liberated" their country.'[15]

While Chamberlain found the *Anschluss* 'disheartening and discouraging', he was at least relieved it had been achieved without bloodshed. Hitler had shown his hand and again proved that he was prepared to use the threat of force to get his own way even if he was in breach of international law. Chamberlain acknowledged this, stating, 'It is perfectly evident surely now that force is the only argument Germany understands and that "collective security" cannot offer any prospect of preventing such events until it can show a visible force of overwhelming strength backed by determination to use it.'

Yet, despite the dawning realisation that Hitler was now a man who could only be stopped by force, Chamberlain still clung to the vain hope that his personal mission to win over Mussolini might result in a different outcome: 'It is tragic to think that very possibly this might have been prevented if I had had Halifax at the F.O. instead of Anthony at the time I wrote my letter to Mussolini.' Looking ahead, he said, 'If we can avoid another violent coup in Czecho-Slovakia, which ought to be feasible, it may be possible for Europe to settle down again and some day for us to start peace talks again with the Germans.'[16] Chamberlain would go to extraordinary lengths to prevent another setback and a 'violent coup' in Czechoslovakia, while the British public began slowly to think the unthinkable; that the outcome may be a second war with Germany.

To add to Chamberlain's troubles, the trade talks with Ireland had reached deadlock and the government had to make further concessions to get an agreement. However, he felt it was a price worth paying to end a long quarrel and foster better relations, adding that foreign affairs might bring people to their senses. 'It is possible that the Austrian incident may help in bringing home to people here and Ulster that this is no time for keeping open old sores.' In

Chamberlain's opinion, however, it was not the concessions that had made the difference but once again, the fabled 'Chamberlain touch', telling Hilda, 'I must say to you that if this agreement comes off it will be due to the influence I have established over De Valera in our private talks.' The Irish Prime Minister had, according to Chamberlain, been searching in vain for a sympathetic British Prime Minister, 'Now he had found one not only sympathetic but energetic enough to put through any arrangement which he was convinced was right.'

The 20 March again found Chamberlain at Chequers, thanking Ida for her sixty-ninth birthday wishes but reeling from the criticism he had received in the House of Commons following the debate on the *Anschluss*. 'Foreign affairs are as rough as March and our Oppositions are as mad as hares in that month. I did indeed have a grim week,' he told her. Chamberlain claimed it was not the opposition brickbats that he feared but the tangled web of European politics, which was leading the continent inextricably towards war, 'With Franco winning in Spain by the aid of German guns and Italian planes, with a French Government in which one cannot have the slightest confidence and which I suspect to be in closish touch with our opposition, with the Russians stealthily and cunningly pulling all the strings behind the scenes to get us involved with war with Germany (our secret service doesn't spend all its time looking out of windows) and finally with a Germany flushed with triumph and all too conscious of her power the prospect looks black indeed.' Yet it was the opposition, and Churchill in particular, who had really got to him, 'In the face of such problems to be badgered and pressed to come out and give a clear, decided, bold, unmistakable lead, to show "ordinary courage" and all the rest of the twaddle is calculated to vex the man who has to take responsibility for the consequences.'

Chamberlain consoled himself with the many birthday wishes he had received, including from the King and Queen, and the fact that his supporters had sent a 'round robin … expressing their confidence and loyalty.' Annie, who had been dispatched to Belfast to show solidarity with the Unionists during the Irish talks, had 'quite captured the hearts of those dour but sentimental Ulstermen.' With an eye for the luxuries of life, she had returned home with a diamond bracelet as an expensive token of their appreciation. During these testing times it was again the peace and tranquility of Chequers, and in particular its flora and fauna, which brought him solace. 'I can't tell you what a joy and relief it is to get down here. The woods and hedges are full of white and purple violets, primroses and daffodils coming into flower and everything growing. The rooks keep up a gentle cawing (we have 24 nests) and I found a thrush's nest yesterday with 4 eggs.'[17]

The end of March saw Chamberlain at Chequers having had another 'heavy week'. On 24 March he and Halifax had addressed the House of Commons on foreign policy and rearmament, calling into question the value of the League of Nations while reaffirming Britain's military commitments to its allies, including France. It was a major speech, which was generally applauded, but despite being pressed, he wouldn't give any commitment to Czechoslovakia. Realising that this would provide ammunition to his many critics, he added, 'Where peace and war are concerned, legal obligations are not alone involved, and, if war broke out, it would be unlikely to be confined to those who have assumed such obligations. It would be quite impossible to say where it would end and what Governments might become involved.'

But it was Chamberlain's detractor, Churchill, who rallied the House of Commons and the nation when he said, referring to the last war but pointedly contemplating the next:

> Now the victors are the vanquished, and those who threw down their arms in the field and sued for an armistice are striding on to world mastery. That is the position, that is the terrible transformation that has taken place bit by bit. I rejoice to hear from the Prime Minister that a further supreme effort is to be made to place us in a position of security: Now is the time at last to rouse the nation. Perhaps it is the last time it can be roused with a chance of preventing war, or with a chance of coming through to victory should our efforts to prevent war fail. We should lay aside every hindrance to endeavour by uniting the whole force and spirit of our people to raise again a great British nation standing up before all the world, for such a nation, rising in its ancient vigour, can even at this hour save civilisation.[18]

Chamberlain told Hilda that, before his speech, he had held two Cabinet meetings and had a long conversation with Churchill, taking him into his confidence, a policy designed to win over his chief critic and stop him plotting against him. 'But all the same I can't help liking Winston although I think him nearly always wrong and impossible as a colleague. To answer the question in your letter, everyone in the House enjoys listening to him and is ready to cheer and laugh at his sallies but he has no following of any importance.' It was a case of keeping your friends close and your enemies closer. He ended by praising both his sisters for not being 'mere "Yes-women",' adding, 'They have minds and brains of their own and I know that if they approve what I'm doing it is not because it is I who am doing it.'[19] Yet events would soon prove the old adage that, when it came to the 'House of Commons' and the 'House of Chamberlain', blood was certainly thicker than water.

On Sunday, 3 April Chamberlain read his weekly letter from Ida with his morning tea. She was concerned that the regular weekly correspondence with both her and Hilda was taking up too much of his valuable time, but he replied, 'I appreciate your consideration about taking up my "valuable time" but I should be very sorry indeed to break this long established custom which has kept us in close touch for so many years. And now that Austen has gone I am the only link you have with political activities which have been such a lifelong interest to you both. There may occasionally have to be breaks but they will only come if there is no help for it.'

The week had been easier than the previous one and he had twice been able to dine at home and not have to return to Parliament. On one occasion, when Scottish business was on in the House of Commons, he made his excuses and drove to Kew Gardens to see the magnolias with Annie, which cheered him up immensely. On foreign affairs, Chamberlain had made overtures towards France about closer ties with Italy, hoping to strengthen his relationship with Mussolini. Yet the sheer amount of work was clearly beginning to take its toll on him. He described the coming week as a 'real beast'. 'Tomorrow I shall have to speak in the vote of censure,' he told Ida, 'On Tuesday A[nnie] and I are to dine with Liberal Nationals and attend a reception after; on Wednesday I address the National Union Executive; on Thursday I broadcast an address (quite short) in Westminster Hall on the Glasgow Exhibition; on Friday I address the Annual meeting of the Birmingham Unionist Association in the Town Hall followed by an overflow; and on Saturday A. and I return to London and immediately go to Windsor for the week-end! I should think there won't be much left of me by then!'

It was a gruelling schedule for anyone, particularly a 69-year-old man. And while he had received more than his fair share of brickbats over the last week, he consoled himself 'by the number of letters and communications I have had from all over the country, many from M.P.'s who have been addressing their constituents. They all report exceptional interest, record attendances at meetings and enthusiastic support for the P.M.'s policy.' He believed that if a general election was called now 'we should romp in', and in the forthcoming Fulham by-election on 6 April, he estimated the party's chances as 'about 50:50 which is a good deal better than expected when we began.'[20] Yet Chamberlain's optimism was again misplaced, and in a sign of the times the seat went to Labour, having been held by the Conservatives, with only a brief interlude, since the start of the First World War.

On 9 April Chamberlain excitedly wrote about a packed meeting he had attended in Birmingham Town Hall the night before, which showed 'the extraordinary unanimity of the party.' Relieved he had no more speeches until Easter, and no budget to worry about, he was particularly pleased that the debate on the vote of censure was 'disastrous for the Socialists. Greenwood [Arthur, 1880-1954, Labour Deputy Leader] made one of the worst speeches even he has delivered and I had an easy task in replying.' Easter 1938 found Chamberlain at Chequers, enjoying the respite that it offered from the pressures of office. 'It is wonderful and very satisfactory to be able to disengage oneself so quickly,' he told Ida on 16 April, adding that Annie had spent the weekend in bed 'aching all over when she was awake but luckily sleeping a good deal.' The garden and the birdlife gave him particular pleasure and, despite Easter being cold, he wrote that 'two of my new tit boxes have a nest begun in them but I see no sign of the woodpeckers interesting themselves in theirs though I hear their laughing cry all day long.' There was even better news when it came to the birds of No 11, 'Just before I left town I was delighted to see the blue tits going in and out of my box in the Downing St. garden just exactly a month later than they did the same thing last year. I hope they succeed in raising a brood, but it appears that the Office of Works have got £3000 of work to do on No 11 so I am not sure that they won't be disturbed.'

Chamberlain's much vaunted policy of strengthening ties with Italy was formalised when, on 16 April, the government signed the Anglo–Italian agreement, recognising Italy's hegemony over Abyssinia in return for Mussolini ending troop reinforcements to Spain. 'Tomorrow the Italian agreement is to be published together with a fresh interchange of letters between Musso and me,' he told Ida, adding, 'I haven't yet seen Musso's but I hear he was very pleased with mine.' He complained about the first draft he had been offered by his civil servants saying, 'You should have seen the draft put up to me by the F.O. It would have frozen a Polar Bear!' The Foreign Office had been wary as they thought Musso would publish Chamberlain's letter, which simply reinforced his view that 'the F.O. can't get over their old obsession that anything which pleases Musso must be bad for us.'[21]

During Easter, Chamberlain spent a very pleasant week in Sutherland, in northern Scotland, courtesy of Charles Vane-Tempest-Stewart, the 7th Marquess of Londonderry, the former Air Minister and a known Nazi sympathiser. On 24 April Chamberlain wrote to Hilda that he had returned 'with much loot ranging from lengths of tweed to flint and granite arrowheads.' He had also received 'numerous letters of congratulation on the Italian agreement; and De Valera was coming over to sign the Anglo–Irish Treaty.' The French were also arriving, 'Together with a dinner at the Royal Academy of Arts, it promises to be a full week.' His letter to Hilda also coincided with he and Annie finally moving into Number 10 Downing Street following the alterations. 'I can't say I feel at home yet,' he told her, 'but no doubt when I get my pictures up and books in this room will seem more like my own. A. is very delighted with her bedroom and generally very pleased and excited over her new domain though she finds the Office of Works trying.'[22] Number 10 Downing Street had at last become the official residency of the House of Chamberlain.

On 1 May 1938, Chamberlain wrote to Ida that the Anglo-Irish agreement had been signed and that conversations were continuing with the French over Czechoslovakia. The Irish agreement, dated 25 April, stated that Britain would agree to receive a lump sum of £10 million instead of land annuities and 'free trade' would be promoted between the two countries, subject to 'Imperial preferences' or a lower tax rate for goods from the Empire. However, during the negotiations, Chamberlain had, under pressure, agreed to give up the treaty ports, which gave access to the western approaches in the Atlantic. Realising this would make Britain vulnerable, he forewarned his sister that Churchill 'plans to make a great attack,' as he was 'one the authors of the 1921 Treaty' (which established the Irish Free State). In the ensuing debate, Churchill and many other MPs roundly condemned the plan to give up the western ports. Chamberlain admitted that he would have preferred to have retained some control over their defence, but de Valera was very sensitive about potential criticism from his supporters. What he felt was far more important was to have on side 'a friendly Ireland'. Chamberlain complained that 'Winston as usual was backing the wrong horse', but the difference spoke volumes about their respective attitudes to the Irish troubles and the strategic value of the ports in a time of war.

On negotiations with the French about Czechoslovakia, he told Ida that they had come close to breaking down, but that over lunch he had 'mustered what French I could' and had won the confidence of Daladier, the French Prime Minister. As a result, Chamberlain and Annie had got to Chequers in time for dinner on Friday, and 'we had a happy day there yesterday with the gardener in the morning and a stroll through the woods in the afternoon.' Commenting that the grounds looked lovely, he was particularly thrilled by the birds, 'Quantities of blackcaps were singing in the woods with chiff-chaffs and willow wrens, but I haven't yet heard a cuckoo. A tit was sitting in one of my boxes, and another had a nest in it but neither bird nor eggs so I don't yet know if it is deserted.'[23]

In May, Hitler toured Italy to discuss a formal military alliance, but Mussolini had been non-committal, giving Chamberlain hope that his policy of winning him over was working. However, he was having another 'beastly week', telling Hilda on 17 May that he had to sack his Air Minister, Lord Winterton, following a disastrous speech in the House of Commons, and as a result had to carry out a mini reshuffle. By 19 May, German troops were massing on the Czech border, and in response, two days later, the Czechs mobilised their reserve army. Chamberlain was upset, writing writing to Hilda, 'Those d——d Germans have spoiled another weekend for me. I was called to the telephone at 1 o'clock yesterday to hear the latest news from Berlin and Prague.' Following this, he had returned to Downing Street to deal with this latest weekend crisis. He was particularly galled that it had ruined a good weekend's fishing. As a result, for the first time he had questioned whether he wanted to go on, but had come to the conclusion there was no one else to 'hand over to without undermining confidence.'[24]

The final weekend of May saw Chamberlain at Chequers. However, even its wonderful surroundings could not lift his mood as he feared that his visit would be curtailed at any moment due to the worsening situation in Czechoslovakia. In response to his doubts about whether he could go on, Ida had written to her brother, reassuring him how much he was loved by the country. This had boosted his flagging confidence and he responded, 'After gout and cabinet resignations the Czecho crisis was a plateful but I am recovering my spirits.'

The day before had been the nadir when the *Daily Herald* had reminded Chamberlain that he had been in office a year. In commemoration, they had published an article by Professor Laski from the London School of Economics, declaring that 'never had there been such a year of disasters brought about by the weakness vacillation untruthfulness and general wickedness of the Prime Minister.' Rather than depressing him further, he was angry at 'such blatant misrepresentation', and he told Ida he had plenty of evidence to the contrary. He mentioned a long talk with the King, whom Chamberlain had found 'in good form and apparently satisfied with all that the Govt are doing'. A follow-up to the Air debate had also gone 'very well', especially as his arch-critic, Churchill, had 'miscalculated the trend of public opinion and though he amused the House a good many were shocked by his buffoonery on a subject on which he professes to feel so strongly.' He had also won over the Trade Union Congress in a meeting about supply shortages in armament factories. Starting off deeply suspicious of his motives, they had left 'in high good humour, laughing and joking'.[25] Chamberlain had found his touch again.

Chapter 11

The Sudeten crisis

'Peacemakers who sow in peace reap a harvest of righteousness.'
James 3:18

When it came to foreign affairs it was not just Czechoslovakia that Chamberlain now had to contend with but the ongoing civil war in Spain. To bring about a truce there, it was again to the Italians that he turned. Despite the challenges, Chamberlain believed that he could win Mussolini over, 'Seeing how greatly Musso wants our agreement brought into full operation I don't despair of getting him to help. If only we could get an armistice, all this bombing of civilians and ships would cease and what suffering and misery would be saved.' He was also watching for a chance to intervene with his personal touch in the Far East, 'It hasn't quite come yet but it may before the autumn.'

While foreign affairs now dominated Chamberlain's Premiership, he still found time to progress issues close to his heart. As a result of talks during his holidays and lobbying from the Council for the Preservation of Rural England, he told Ida he was keen to set up 'a central authority to act at once as an information bureau with special regard to the location of industry and as a Central Planning body for the country as a whole.' While it would not have executive powers, its plans would, he claimed, 'Profoundly influence development and would focus public opinion. It would do what nobody does now, or in fact has power to do, namely consider the claims of agriculture, which seems to be invariably sacrificed to "development" of whatever character that may be.' He had also found the time to do a survey of his nesting boxes at Chequers and was 'delighted to find that the green woodpecker *has* made use of my nesting box. I hardly thought he would.'[1]

The end of June, following 'a pretty rackety week', found Chamberlain taking a break at Wilton House, near Salisbury in Wiltshire, the ancestral home of the Earl of Pembroke. Annie, meanwhile, recovered her strength by staying at 10 Downing Street. He had also received an honorary doctorate from Reading University and, while there, bumped into the avant-garde artist Walter Sickert (1860-1942), a prominent figure in the transition from Impressionism to Modernism. In receiving their awards the two men couldn't have presented more contrasting images, Chamberlain being bemused at Sickert's sartorial style and his unconventional manners. 'He was absolutely priceless,' he told Hilda, 'with a spade beard and dressed in a beige woven suit of hairy brown tweed. The coat was cut rather like a gamekeeper's with tails and large pockets. He had no collar but a pale shirt and his nether extremities were clothed in thick woollen socks in a large check and a pair of carpet slippers. He drank much too much hock at lunch and was, I understand, very difficult to handle, but in the end they shepherded him on to the dais with someone holding each arm and so all was well.'[2] Sickert's impressions of the elderly Prime Minister in his finest Victorian livery are not recorded.

In Parliament, the government hadn't fared well in a debate on the bombing of British ships in Spanish waters, but Chamberlain consoled himself with the fact that they were batting on a 'sticky wicket'. He noted, 'I am completely convinced that the course I am taking is right and therefore cannot be influenced by the attacks of my critics. I have been through every possible form of retaliation and it is abundantly clear that none of them can be effective unless we are prepared to go to war with Franco, which might quite possibly lead to war with Italy and Germany and in any case would cut right across my policy of general appeasement.'[3]

The beginning of July again saw Chamberlain snowed under with speeches and agitating about Winston. He felt that a Parliamentary row over a question on London's air defences, based on leaked secret information, had been manipulated by Churchill to attack his government, 'Winston was the real mover and he saw or thought he saw an opportunity of giving the Government a good shake,' he wrote to Ida on 4 July. 'People who have spent weekends at country house parties where he has been a guest tell me that he has bored the whole company by monopolising the conversation and denouncing the Government all day long. When I see him in the lobby he seems as friendly as you please and indeed I don't think his enmity is personal to me; it is just his restless ambition that keeps him incessantly criticising any administration of which he is not a member.'[4]

On Saturday 9 July, Chamberlain was enjoying a weekend at Chequers, but had not received his weekly letter from Hilda, which had been 'quite a blow.' That afternoon, he had invited his closest civil servants to join him for a walk in the grounds. The party included the head of the civil service and Permanent Secretary at the Treasury, Warren Fisher, his special advisor Horace Wilson, who he had seconded in 1937 and had his own room at No 10, and his Principal Private Secretary, Osmund Somers Cleverly, plus their respective wives. He had also invited Miss Edith Watson, his Private Secretary responsible for preparing replies to questions in Parliament, and another Private Secretary, Miss Marjorie Leaf. 'Some of them have been to Chequers before,' he told Hilda, 'but never under similar circumstances and I think they will greatly enjoy themselves.'

However, even the genteel delights of a walk in the grounds became political when Chamberlain quizzed them on Ramsay MacDonald, his Labour predecessor. Recalling the conversation, he wrote, 'Miss Watson was once invited to a week end party by Ramsay, but she says he was a most uncomfortable host. On the first evening he announced in a loud voice "I shall go for a walk at 7 o'clock tomorrow morning. Would anyone like to come?". There was dead silence; no one had the courage to volunteer. In the morning R.J.M. [sic], who had got more and more restless, declared that it had become necessary for him to return to London and broke up the party.'

On the morning of 11 July, as Chamberlain was entering the Foreign Office, he saw a kestrel flying overhead and made a mental note of it. After the meeting was over he then added it to his list of birds he had seen since entering Downing Street. Two days later he received a letter from Gilbert Collett, his fellow 'birder', who had first written to Chamberlain the year before, offering to send him any sightings from his regular walks around St James's Park. Collett wrote that he had seen jays in the park that morning, getting a glimpse of their beautiful pink and blue plumage as they flew from a tree. Chamberlain was so pleased that he asked one of his private secretaries, Miss Campbell, to reply. The succinct letter read:

10 Downing Street
Whitehall

13 July 1938

Dear Sir,
I am asked by the Prime Minister to thank you so much for telling him about the jays in St. James's Park this morning.
    Mr Chamberlain thought that you might be interested to know that on Monday morning last, July 11th, he saw a kestrel fly over the Foreign Office at 08.30 a.m.

Yours truly

C.M. Campbell
Private Secretary[5]

Ornithology had now become more than just a hobby or a way of relaxing from the pressures of his Premiership. Watching birds, whether kestrels flying over the Foreign Office or jays foraging in St James's Park, helped him make sense of an increasingly 'sad, mad world', one in which Hitler was brutally demonstrating what his great hero Darwin had termed 'survival of the fittest'.

Three days later, Chamberlain was at home in Westbourne writing his regular weekly letter to Ida. Annie, he reported, was still feeling tired but had thrown 'another party on Monday for Dominions visitors and gave them a talk on the history of No. 10. Of course they are simply thrilled to hear all about it and A. has taken endless trouble reading up every scrap of literature she can find.' Chamberlain was also feeling the pressure associated with high office, telling Ida, 'I am astonished myself at the way I stand the strain, for I don't get much let up.'[6] To his annoyance, an evening listening to Schubert's '*Octet in F Major*' had to be curtailed so he could write a speech for the Birmingham Centenary as it was his 'only chance to find a couple of hours to spare.'

The year 1938 marked the centenary of the City of Birmingham and in July a week-long festival culminated in a huge pageant held in Aston Park. As one of Birmingham's most famous sons, and the Prime Minister, Chamberlain was at the centre of the celebrations. The day before, he had boarded the royal train for the journey, accompanied by the Duke and Duchess of Gloucester, who were standing in for the King and Queen. On arriving, the royal cavalcade made its way around the showground before alighting at a grandstand overlooking the park, where Chamberlain was joined by Annie, their Royal Highnesses, the Lord Mayor, and a large number of local dignitaries, all of whom made speeches. The Editor of the *Birmingham Post* told Chamberlain that his speech was 'astonishing', but Chamberlain, for once picking up on the sycophantic nature of the comment, later called it 'a slightly back-handed compliment I think.' The pageant itself featured a cast of 10,000 performers who re-enacted eight 'episodes' from the city's history. The show was masterminded by the great pageant master Gwen Lally and was captured for posterity on colour film, which was unusual for the time. The historical 'episodes' from the time of the dinosaurs to the Victorians featured huge, lavish sets with hundreds of Brummies dressed in period costume in a truly zany production. Chamberlain and Annie enjoyed the whole bizarre spectacle immensely.[7]

On 24 July, Chamberlain wrote to his sister Hilda about a top secret mission to break the impasse over Czechoslovakia. Hitler had sent over Fritz Wiedemann, his commander during the First World War and a member of his personal staff, and he had met with Halifax on 18 July. Wiedemann had reaffirmed the Führer's desire for friendship with Britain and reiterated that he was not planning to use force over the Sudeten 'problem'. Despite this, Chamberlain told Hilda, 'Reports from Czecho are by no means encouraging and it seems certain that there will soon be a deadlock, the Germans still give no soothing assurances about their intentions.' He particularly hoped that any German moves would not curtail his long-awaited summer holiday.

The beginning of August found Chamberlain staying again at the fifteen-bedroom Highland retreat of Lochmore Lodge in Sutherland, courtesy of the Duke of Westminster. However, plagued by bad luck he found himself suffering from severe sinusitis and reluctantly had to cut short his precious holiday. On his return to Downing Street he was informed that the Germans were carrying out a 'test mobilisation' in early September and, as a result, Halifax had warned Hitler on 11 August that 'the peace of every one of the Great Powers of Europe might be endangered.' Chamberlain was confined to bed and told he had to give up all thought of his planned shooting holiday at the Tillypronie estate in Aberdeenshire. However, this resulted in his depression returning, a condition 'not lightened by the situation in Spain, Paris (another financial crisis) Czecho-Slovakia, Berlin and Tokyo'.

Unable to go game shooting in Scotland, Chamberlain instead opted for the much closer Manor House in Great Dunford, near Salisbury, the home of George Tyron, the Postmaster General. 'I fish in the mornings while A[nnie] stops in bed. After lunch I do a pouch [Prime Ministerial bag] and read or snooze till tea,' he told Hilda, on 27 August, who was herself on holiday in the far more glamorous surroundings of Savoie in the French Alps. On the Czechoslovakian issue he told his sister that there was 'fairly encouraging news' from the Runciman mission. This had started on 3 August, when Chamberlain had sent his friend, the Liberal peer Lord Runciman, to Czechoslovakia to try to mediate a peaceful solution with the Germans, with the mission continuing until 15 September. 'The Germans seem determined to make the worst of everything,' he wrote, 'we are looking forward to Hitler's speech on the Parteitag [Nazi Party Day, which coincided with the annual party rally, the *Reichsparteitag*, at Nurnberg] with some apprehension.' Chamberlain finished the letter, 'Perhaps I may feel able to write more freely when you have returned home. One doesn't like to entrust too much to a foreign letter.'[8]

Following his return from Great Dunford, Chamberlain went back to Downing Street and, feeling better, joined the King and Queen at Balmoral Castle for their annual holiday. From here he wrote to Ida on 3 September that she, like him, 'must now feel a good deal nearer to "the crisis" [over the Sudetenland] than when you were in Savoie.' He then summed up the realpolitik of his dilemma, 'Is it not positively horrible to think that the fate of hundreds of millions depends on one man and he is half mad.' Despite his best endeavours, he couldn't see a way out. 'I keep racking my brains to try and devise some means of averting a catastrophe if it should seem to be upon us. I thought of one so unconventional and daring that it rather took Halifax's breath away. But, since

Henderson [Nevile, British Ambassador] thought it might save the situation at the 11th hour, I haven't abandoned it, though I hope all the time it won't be necessary to try it.'[9] Chamberlain's plan was as unconventional as it was daring; he would offer to fly to Germany to mediate with Hitler in a final attempt to secure peace.

Three days later, on 6 September, Chamberlain was ensconced at Millden Lodge, near Edzell, Forfarshire, where he was staying for a week following his visit to Balmoral. His stay had further 'consolidated my position with the K. and Q. who were both as nice as possible and with whom I can now talk on quite easy and intimate terms. The only downer was that the Duke of Windsor was being a bit troublesome again, wanting to come home.' As a result Chamberlain had sent off 'a very diplomatic letter which I hope will have the desired effect.'

By 11 September the Sudeten crisis had reached breaking point, with Hitler threatening to send in the German army to resolve the impasse. Chamberlain wrote to Hilda, 'Well, it has been a pretty awful week – enough to send most people off their heads, if their heads were not as firmly screwed on as mine.' The febrile atmosphere in Downing Street had begun to take its toll. 'You have no conception what the atmosphere is – every ten minutes someone comes in with a box, bringing some new and disturbing communication, while busybodies of all kinds intrude their advice and the papers do their best to ruin all one's efforts.' He was particularly incensed about a headline in the *Daily Mail*, which was 'splashed even louder in its Paris edition.' It said that the British government had sent Hitler an ultimatum at midnight stating that if he used force they would declare war. It was 'the most gratuitously mischievous of all. I had to send urgent telegrams to Paris, Prague and Berlin to deny it.'[10]

At home, Chamberlain was only too aware of the how the crisis was playing out with his critics, telling Hilda:

> I fully realise that if eventually things go wrong and the aggression takes place there will be many, including Winston, who will say that the British Government must bear the responsibility and that if only they had the courage to tell Hitler now that if he used force we should at once declare war that would have stopped him. By that time it will be impossible to prove the contrary, but I am satisfied that we should be wrong to allow the most vital decision that any country could take, the decision as to peace or war, to pass out of our own hands into those of the ruler of another country and a lunatic at that.

Chamberlain also confided to Hilda that his critics could not know of his daring plan – which he had given the codename 'Plan Z' – adding that, though it was possible that an unexpected attack from Hitler might forestall it, 'That is a risk which we have to take but in the meantime I do not want to do anything which would destroy its chance of success, because, if it came off, it would go far beyond the present crisis and might prove the opportunity for bringing about a complete change in the international situation.' Chamberlain was looking into the abyss, but still believed that his unique brand of personal diplomacy could yet rescue the world from the brink of war. He finished, 'Well, I think I will close now. I wonder what will happen before I write again.' The next week would be a long time in politics.[11]

Neville, Ida, Hilda and Ethel Chamberlain in fancy dress, 1870s. As a result of not having a mother and an austere father who was away all the time Joseph's children formed very strong bonds with each other. (*Cadbury Research Library*)

Chamberlain first recorded the lepidoptera (butterflies and moths) he saw in an old address book entitled 'Where is it?' He recorded his first orange tip butterfly *Anthocharis cardamines* on May 29 1880. He was 11 years old. (*Birmingham Museums*)

Anthocharis cardamines. Orange tip.

May 29/80.

May 28/81 Outside Frankton Woods.

May 9/82. House.

May 24/84. Brandon Woods.

May 29/85. Bilton Road.

Arctia Lubricipeda. Buff Ermine

/80.

May 28/81. At the house.

June 30/82. House. On the Doctor's Wall.

June 10/84. Clifton Canal.

June 25/85. Doctors Wall.
May 31/86. Quad Gates.

A. Menthrasti. White Ermine.

May 22/84. Clifton Canal.

June 6/85. House.

May 29/86. Bilton.

Amphidasis Betularia. Pepper.

April 20/85. Bred.

May 26/81. At the house.

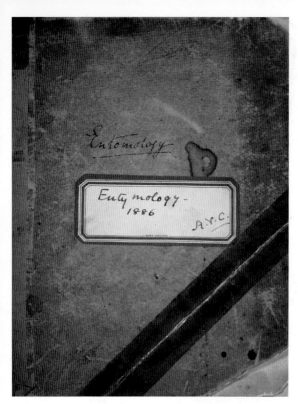

Chamberlain's school entomology book, 1886, with his initials on the cover. The annual report of Rugby School Natural History Society praised the leaving of 'a very good worker'. (*Birmingham Museums*)

Page from Chamberlain's school entomology book listing pupae and chrysalids that he reared in the school's vivarium. (*Birmingham Museums*)

Above: One of thirteen glass houses at Highbury, 1890. Instead of debating, Neville preferred to spend time studying orchids with his father, Joseph. It was botany, not politics, that resulted in them having discussions long into the night. (*Cadbury Research Library*)

Right: Page from Chamberlain's orchid book showing the structure of the flower. Note the design for the bird box bottom right. (*Cadbury Research Library*)

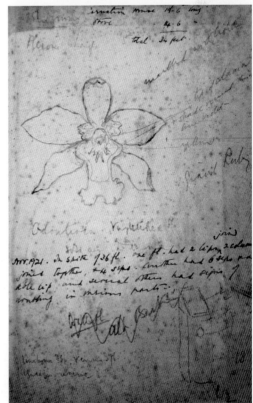

Left: Neville Chamberlain in his 20s. In 1891 he was sent to the Bahamas to make the family fortune growing sisal. It was lonely and exhausting work but the sisal wouldn't grow and he returned home bankrupt, in 1897. (*Bain News Service*)

Below: The Chamberlain family late 1890s. Left to right: Neville, Beatrice, Austen, Mary and Joseph. Neville divided his time between managing the family firms and studying lepidoptera. (*Cadbury Research Library*)

perfectly luxurious. My cabin
is on the upper deck next
Mr Collnip, the others are

to tried the Khedive's Egypt by
De Leon with more success.
After lunch did the same.
Passed Bebbeh the sugar refining
palace & near Beni Suef
got a telegram from uncle William
saying that progress is very
satisfactory. Dined at 7o. Sunset
most beautiful.
Sunday Dec 8
Spent the morning reading
on deck. Lunched at 1.
Caught one of the large wasp
like insects that keep flying
round the boat. Came to
Minieh soon after lunch
where Mr C. B. Milly & I with
the dragoman rowed to
shore to post a letter & see
something of the place. Minieh
is the capital of the province
of that name & has a

town below. Spent the afternoon
on deck watching the banks
& dropped anchor at Bedramays
Saturday Dec 7.
Did not sleep well for the
first night. Was late for breakfast.
After breakfast I got a book
& read on deck till lunch
time. I tried "Warda" by Eber
first but found it too sickly

Above: Travel diary to Egypt in 1889-90. Neville engrossed himself in art, history, architecture, wildlife, landscape and people of the country, all of which he faithfully recorded in his diary. (*Cadbury Research Library*)

Below: Chamberlain's Yellow butterfly. In 1898 the British Museum's chief taxonomist, Arthur Gardiner Butler, identified a new butterfly species to science and named it after its collector Chamberlain's Yellow *Terias chamberlaini*. (*Oxford University Museum of Natural History*)

THE RIGHT HON. THE LORD MAYOR,
ALDERMAN NEVILLE CHAMBERLAIN. J.P.

EDGBASTONIA

CIRCULATING IN EDGBASTON, THE WEST END SUBURB OF BIRMINGHAM.

Vol. XXXV. NOVEMBER, 1915. No. 414.

ALDERMAN ARTHUR NEVILLE CHAMBERLAIN, J.P.

Forty years ago the town of Birmingham elected a Mayor whose unusual qualities raised the scene of his activities to a position of importance it had never previously enjoyed ; whose powers of oratory, political insight and business acumen were to lift the man himself to the high places of national fame. Mr. Joseph Chamberlain never severed his connection with or lost his interest and affection for the town of his adoption, and Birmingham always was proud to shine in the reflected glory of his great career.

To-day, after this long period of years, Birmingham, now a City with enormously widened borders, has again elected a member

Alderman, 1915. The magazine *Edgabastonia* proclaims the second Chamberlain to become Lord Mayor. (*Cadbury Research Library*)

Lord Mayor, 1915. Chamberlain's achievements included designing an air raid protection scheme, enabling women to work the land, creating a savings bank and promoting National Service. This brought him to the attention of the Prime Minister, David Lloyd George. (*Alamy*)

Above left: Chamberlain with his family in 1916. He had been 'miserable at the thought of a childless old age'. He dedicated himself to fatherhood, determined to give his children the love and emotional support he had missed growing up. (*National Library of Australia*)

Above right: Portrait of Norman Chamberlain who was killed in action in 1917. It resulted in the only book Chamberlain ever wrote and made him determined that the horrors of the First World War should never be repeated. (*Cadbury Research Library*)

Right: The new MP for Ladywood, 1921. Chamberlain found being an obscure backbencher tedious at times but stood out from the pack because of his age, his family name and his political record. (*Walter Stoneman*)

Above: As Minister of Health Chamberlain was determined to build better social housing for the poor. Here, visiting slums in Newcastle-upon-Tyne, in the company of John Grantham, Sheriff of Newcastle and minders 16 October 1925. (*Tyne & Wear Archives & Museums*)

Left: Hilda Chamberlain, c1930. As well as writing to Neville every other week, Hilda became National Treasurer of the Women's Institutes. (*Cadbury Research Library*)

Right: Ida Chamberlain, c1929. Like her sister, Ida wrote faithfully to Neville throughout his life and was also a District and County Councillor in Hampshire. (*Cadbury Research Library*)

Below: Chamberlain's Christmas card of 1935 showed the shared garden of Nos 10 and 11 Downing Street. He put up bird boxes in the garden and also found a leopard moth in it, resting on a small hawthorn tree. (*Authors collection*)

Above left: Chancellor of the Exchequer, c1936. Like the rest of the population he became embroiled in the abdication crisis but still found time to write to *The Daily Telegraph* about mimicry in birds. (*Bassano Ltd*)

Above right: Anne Chamberlain. A devoted wife and 'a child of luxury', she enjoyed the trappings of power but often found supporting her husband exhausting. (*Bassano Ltd*)

Left: *The Countryman*, Oct-Nov-Dec 1937. In his article Chamberlain reported on the leopard moth and the mystery of the vanished egg. The magazine was delighted at its exclusive and gave it prominent place on the cover.

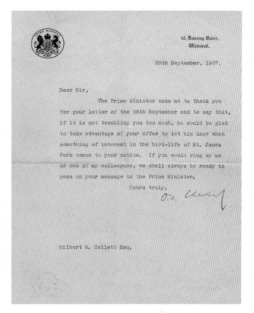

Above left: Gilbert William Collett was a fellow ornithologist who co-owned a shirt shop on Jermyn Street, not far from Downing Street. He corresponded with Chamberlain until his death in 1940 about the birds they found in St James's Park. (*Sarah Kelly*)

Above right: Collett first wrote to Chamberlain following his article in *The Countryman* offering to tell the Prime Minister about any birds that turned up in St James's Park. Birdwatching in the park became Chamberlain's way of coping with the nightmare that was Adolf Hitler. (*Sarah Kelly*)

Below: Chamberlain posing with Hitler following their second meeting at Bad Godesburg, 23 September, 1938. His face betrays the exhaustion caused by Hitler's mood swings and histrionics. Chamberlain believed, 'The Czech problem was the last territorial demand which he had to make in Europe.' (*Alamy*)

Above: Chamberlain greeting the ecstatic crowd at Heston airport waving his 'piece of paper', 30 September 1938. Loud cheering greeted the Prime Minister's theatrics but, in an ominous turn of events, a sudden gust of wind nearly blew the paper away. (*Alamy*)

Below: Following his triumphant return, the Chamberlains visited Buckingham Palace, here flanked by the King and Queen. Afterwards they all appeared on the balcony before a euphoric crowd and then in an unprecedented break with Royal protocol, Neville appeared on his own. (*Alamy*)

PICTURE
POST

"I HAVE DONE ALL ONE MAN CAN DO TO SAVE PEACE"

80 PAGES   HULTON'S NATIONAL WEEKLY   3D

OCTOBER 8, 1938   Vol. 1. No. 2

Christmas
Novelties
and Ideas

To cash in on public opinion J. K. Farnell and Co., Ltd., have just issued this "Chamberlain the Peacemaker" doll. A similar model attired in fishing kit is also available.

See pages 35 to 43

Above left: *Picture Post* magazine, dated 8 October 1938, covers the declaration of peace.

Above right: In the first few days following Chamberlain's declaration of 'peace for our time' over 20,000 letters, telegrams and gifts flooded into Downing Street. Companies rushed to cash in on the Prime Minister's fame, including producing a 'Peacemaker doll' which went down badly with Conservative Central Office. (*Cadbury Research Library*)

Chamberlain with Mussolini. His letters reveal the extraordinary lengths to which Chamberlain went to win over 'Musso' as a way of isolating Hitler. (*Bundesarchiv*)

Chamberlain with Churchill. From the start they had a difficult relationship, Chamberlain remarking, 'His are summer storms, violent but of short duration and often followed by sunshine. But they make him uncommonly difficult to deal with.' (*Alamy*)

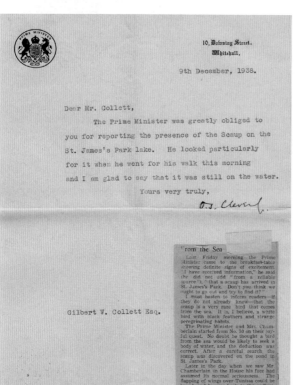

Above and left: Following Collett's tip-off, Chamberlain was delighted to find a rare scaup duck in St James's Park on 9 December 1938, which was reported in *The Times*. (*Sarah Kelly*)

Above: Chamberlain's Christmas card of 1938 featured the Lockheed 14 'machine' he had flown in to see Hitler three months previously. (*Cadbury Research Library*)

Right: *Punch* magazine shows the French Prime Minister, Daladier and Chamberlain as bird watchers spotting a phoenix which has arisen out of the flames of collective security, 19 April 1939.

Above: Chamberlain declaring war on 3 September 1939: 'You can imagine what a bitter blow it is to me that all my long struggle to win peace has failed.' (*Alamy*)

Below left: On the second day of the Commons debate about the Norway debacle which brought about his downfall, Chamberlain was busy trying to find a kestrel's nest in St James's Park. (*Sarah Kelly*)

Below right: Collett wrote to Chamberlain's widow, Anne, on his death. In November 1940, she wrote back saying, 'I knew how interested my husband was in exchanging news of birds with you.' (*Sarah Kelly*)

10, Downing Street,
Whitehall.

8th May, 1940.

Dear Sir,

Some weeks ago you wrote to the Prime Minister about the kestrel in St. James's Park and mentioned that it was fond of perching on the top of a very high tree, rising from the water's edge opposite the incinerator. Mr. Chamberlain has since tried to identify the tree, but without success. Could you therefore give him more particulars? What sort of tree is it, a poplar or a plane? Is it on the island or on the main shore and is it on the North side of the lake or on the South?

Mr. Chamberlain has not himself seen the kestrel again since he wrote to you.

Yours truly,

C. M. Campbell

Private Secretary.

G. M. Collett, Esq.

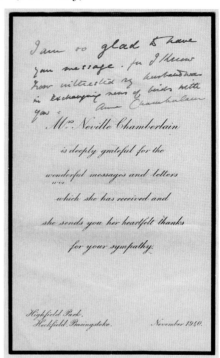

I am so glad to have your message. for I know how interested my husband was in exchanging news of birds with you.

Anne Chamberlain

Mrs. Neville Chamberlain

is deeply grateful for the

wonderful messages and letters

which she has received and

she sends you her heartfelt thanks

for your sympathy.

Highfield Park,
Heckfield, Basingstoke.   November 1940.

Chapter 12

Plan Z

'But whoever keeps his word, in him truly the love of God is perfected.'
1 John 2:5

While most Britons were still eating their breakfast on Thursday, 15 September 1938, Chamberlain was boarding a British Airways twin-engine Lockheed 10 Electra for his first flight to Germany. He was dressed in his characteristic black suit, together with grey overcoat and homburg hat. He also had with him his neatly rolled umbrella, the prop which had come to define his Premiership.

Before Chamberlain's departure that Thursday morning, the country had come to the brink of war over the fate of the three and a half million Sudeten Germans living in Czechoslovakia. In response to the febrile political situation, at 11pm on Tuesday night Chamberlain had cabled Hitler: 'In view of the increasingly critical situation I propose to come over at once to see you with a view to trying to find a peaceful solution. I propose to come across by air and am ready to start tomorrow. Please indicate earliest time at which you can see me and suggest place of meeting. Should be grateful for an early reply – Neville Chamberlain.'

In a letter to his sister Ida four days later, Chamberlain confessed how much he had worried about the fateful telegram:

> I knew the hour must be near, if it was to come at all. Two things were essential, first, that the plan should be tried just when things looked blackest, and second that it should be a complete surprise ... on Tuesday night I saw the moment had come and must be taken, if I was not to be too late. So I sent the fateful telegram and told the Cabinet the next morning what I had done. Of course they did not, for the most part, realise how it would strike the world, but they approved and then followed hours of waiting for the answer, for everything had to be transmitted to Berchtesgaden. At last during the afternoon my anxiety was relieved. Hitler was entirely at my disposal, and would not Mrs Chamberlain come too![1]

Hitler was privately stunned that the British Prime Minister would make such an offer and, replying the next day, said would he would be 'very ready' to meet him on Thursday, suggesting his mountain home, the imposing Berghof in Berchtesgaden. By picking Berchtesgaden, Hitler ensured that Chamberlain would have to take the longest journey possible; his mountain retreat on the Obersalzberg lay in the very south of Germany, near the Austrian border. The meeting place was designed both to flatter and, more importantly, to intimidate.

At Heston aerodrome, supplies of sandwiches, whisky, cider, beer, sherry and tea were packed into the plane to fortify the Prime Minister for the trip. An attendant gave Chamberlain wads of cotton wool to stuff into his ears to help drown out the roar of the twin Pratt and Whitney engines. He was also handed a map for the journey, which traced the course of the plane across the Channel and down through France and the low countries before entering German airspace and heading south towards Munich.

Present on the tarmac to see him off were Lord Brocket, Lord Londonderry and Lord Halifax, together with two members of the German Embassy in London, Charge d'Affaires Theo Kordt and First Secretary Baron von Salzan.[2] Both Brocket and Londonderry were known Nazi sympathisers and prominent members of the Anglo-German Fellowship, a society set up in 1935 to broker good relations and mutual understanding between Britain and Nazi Germany. Brocket was such an ardent fan of Hitler that he had attended the Führer's fiftieth birthday, and was also a close confidant of the German Foreign Minister, Joachim von Ribbentrop.

On the flight, Chamberlain took with him Sir Horace Wilson, his Chief Industrial Advisor, and William Strang, the head of the Foreign Office Central European Department. Wilson, like Chamberlain, was a key architect of appeasement, but Strang was a tacit opponent of the policy. As the plane took off he experienced some 'slight sinkings when I found myself flying over London and looking down thousands of feet at the houses below, but that soon wore off and I enjoyed the marvellous spectacle of ranges of glittering white cumulus clouds stretching away to the horizon below me.' As they headed over the Channel, Chamberlain glanced at his map while also studying the cloud bank below. Halfway through the flight, to prevent any further queasiness, he ate a ham sandwich and downed a glass of whisky. Up to this point Chamberlain had coped with the flight quite well, but over Munich they hit storm clouds and the Lockheed 'for a time flew blind through the clouds while the aeroplane rocked and bumped like a ship in a sea.' Then the steward told Chamberlain they were descending and he had 'some more nervous moments while we circled down over the aerodrome,'[3] until a German plane guided them in to land. Chamberlain,

Wilson and Strang finally touched down at Munich airport at midday, where they were subjected to the full Nazi pomp reserved for visiting dignitaries.

The airport was festooned with Nazi and British flags and the party was met by a full detachment of SS Guards dressed in black. On the tarmac waiting for them was the German Foreign Minister, Joachim von Ribbentrop, and Hitler's interpreter, Dr Paul Schmidt. As he got out of the plane, Chamberlain said to Ribbentrop, 'I stood the passage very well, although we had bad weather part of the way and I have never been in aeroplane before.'[4] After exchanging greetings, Chamberlain then inspected the SS Guards. On entering the terminal it was discovered that, while the Prime Minister had a passport, he did not have a valid visa to enter Germany, such had been the haste with which his trip had been organised. Waving away protocol with a gesture of his hand, Ribbentrop ushered the PM's party through customs and into a waiting cavalcade of fourteen cars, all prominently flying the swastika flag.

The cars then set off, heading towards the station. To Ribbentrop's annoyance, and Chamberlain's delight, many Germans came out of their houses to cheer the Prime Minister, shouting 'Heil Chamberlain', some even waving British flags. In his letter to Ida dated 19 September, he said, 'I felt quite fresh and was delighted with the enthusiastic welcome of the crowds who were waiting in the rain and who gave me the Nazi salute and shouted "Heil" at the top of their voices all the way to the station.' Chamberlain, in return, turned, bowed and smiled broadly. According to Hitler's interpreter, Paul Schmidt, the people greeted Chamberlain very warmly, much more so than they had Mussolini the year before,[5] while the German press christened him 'Peace Envoy Chamberlain.'

Chamberlain lunched in Hitler's dining car on his armoured train at Munich station, the Führer having made elaborate preparations to ensure his visitor's comfort. As the countryside passed by, Chamberlain had turtle soup for starters, a delicacy greatly enjoyed by Hitler, followed by roast beef and Yorkshire pudding, and for dessert he had cheese, biscuits and fruit. These were washed down with white and red Rhine wines, followed by a port, coffee and a cigar. Writing to Hilda, Chamberlain stated, 'It was unfortunate that the weather was so bad as the scenery must be very beautiful but the mountains were covered in mist.' Commenting on this over lunch, he quipped to Ribbentrop, 'The weather was beautiful when we left London. Why is it that the clouds only began when we got over the continent?'[6] Chamberlain told his sisters, 'All the way up there were people at the crossings, the stations, and at the windows of the houses, all "heiling" and saluting and when we arrived there were crowds at the station and the hotel all busting with curiosity and excitement.'[7]

On arriving at the station at Berchtesgaden, which had been built specially for the Führer with a private entrance, another fleet of a dozen cars whisked them to the Grand Hotel. Upon leaving the car, Chamberlain was met by an honour guard from Hitler's personal bodyguard, the *Leibstandarte* SS Adolf Hitler, and the British flag was raised above the building. Next to Chamberlain's suite was Ribbentrop's room, his staff having taken up all the remaining forty rooms in the hotel. After a forty-five-minute rest, during which Chamberlain finally got a power nap, the convoy made their way up to the Berghof. During the three-hour journey from Munich to Berchtesgaden, military transports continually rattled past, crammed with heavily armed *Wehrmacht* (German Army) troops. When he saw them, Chamberlain stared out of the window in silence.

As the party reached the town of Berchtesgaden, it began to rain and dark clouds rolled down from the surrounding mountains. Hitler's mountain home, the Berghof, had undergone a massive transformation since he had originally purchased the property in 1933. Here, prior to Chamberlain's visit, Hitler had charmed and harangued a number of prominent guests, including Chamberlain's nemesis, the Liberal leader and former Prime Minister, David Lloyd George, in 1936, and the year afterwards the Duke and Duchess of Windsor. Earlier in 1938, it was also where he had met the Austrian Chancellor, Kurt Schuschnigg, and issued him with the ultimatum which resulted in the *Anschluss* (union) of Germany and Austria. Apart from foreign dignitaries, Hitler's inner circle also met there regularly and, unbeknown to any visiting guests, his mistress, Eva Braun, spent much of her time on the mountain, which was known as the Obersalzberg.

After winding its way up the steep mountain road and passing through three SS security check points, Chamberlain's car finally reached the imposing Berghof, 2,000ft up in the Bavarian Alps. Hitler received Chamberlain and his party at the foot of a flight of steps leading up to the house. Although they were very familiar with each other, it was the first time that the two had met face to face. The contrast in their respective attires spoke volumes about their attitude towards peace. Hitler was every inch the military dictator, dressed in his familiar black trousers and grey *Wehrmacht* jacket, complete with swastika armband and Iron Cross First Class. Chamberlain, in his tweed overcoat and wing-collared shirt, carrying his Homburg hat and trusty umbrella, looked more like a provincial accountant.

Writing to Hilda four days later, Chamberlain said, 'Half way down these steps stood the Fuehrer, bareheaded and dressed in a khaki-coloured coat of broadcloth with a red armlet and a swastika on it, and the military cross on his breast. He wore black trousers, such as we wear in the evening, and black patent-leather lace-up shoes. His hair is brown, not black, his eyes blue, his expression rather disagreeable, especially in repose, and altogether he looks entirely undistinguished. You would never notice him in a crowd and would take him for the house painter he once was.'[8] (Later on his return to London, addressing the Cabinet, Chamberlain was even more critical, describing Hitler as 'the commonest dog' he had ever seen, but that 'it was impossible not to be impressed with the power of the man').

Hitler then took Chamberlain up the steps to the entrance and introduced him to his staff. The only one Chamberlain could recall, when writing to Hilda four days later, was the 'distinguished General Keitel', head of the Armed Forces, whom he described as 'a youngish pleasant-faced smart-looking soldier'. 'We then entered the house and passed along a very bare passage through a smaller room to the celebrated chamber, or rather hall, one end of which is entirely composed of a vast window,' recounted Chamberlain, adding, 'The view towards Salzburg must be magnificent but this day there were only the valley and the bottoms of the mountains to be seen.' Once inside, Hitler told the party about the improvements he had made to the house, but Chamberlain cared little for the furnishings, commenting sniffily to Ida, 'On the walls were a number of pictures by old German and Italian masters. Just behind me was a large Italian nude!'

After his brief tour, Chamberlain sat down at the large tea table adjacent to the Berghof's centrepiece, a massive picture window measuring 32 square metres with ninety individual panes of glass, which could be lowered on a good day to give an unhindered view of the snow-covered Untersberg across the valley and, in the distance, Hitler's Austrian homeland. Ominously, as they surveyed the panorama, the spectacular view over the mountains disappeared completely beneath a veil of threatening clouds.

Chamberlain sat next to Hitler, with his interpreter on his other side, and attempted to break the ice. Following a strained twenty-minute discussion about the journey, Chamberlain raised the intriguing possibility of Hitler visiting England:

> We sat down, I next to Hitler, with the interpreter on his other side.
> He seemed very shy, and his features did not relax while I endeavoured to find small talk.
> I. "I have often heard of this room, but it's much larger than I expected."
> H. "It is you who have the big rooms in England."
> I. "You must come and see them sometime."
> H. "I should be received with demonstrations of disapproval."
> I. "Well, perhaps, it would be wise to choose the moment."
> At this H. permitted himself the shadow of a smile.

After taking tea, Hitler asked abruptly how Chamberlain wanted to proceed and if he 'would like to have two or three present at our talk.' Deciding to seize the initiative, Chamberlain asked instead if he could see Hitler on his own, 'Thereupon he rose, and he and I and the interpreter left the party and walked upstairs, and through a long room with more pictures (and more nudes), till we arrived at his own room. This was completely bare of ornament. There wasn't even a clock, only a stove, a small table with 2 bottles of mineral water (which he didn't offer me), 3 chairs, and a sofa. Here we sat and talked for 3 hours.'[9]

The Führer had been somewhat taken aback at Chamberlain's request, despite having frequently used exactly the same tactic on others to get his way. Momentarily thinking it over, he had agreed, but insisted that his interpreter Schmidt must be present. The request was a clear rebuke to Hitler's Foreign Minister, Ribbentrop, who Chamberlain neither rated nor liked. According to Schmidt, this had been settled beforehand as 'both sides felt that our Foreign Minister would prove a disturbing element in any endeavour to achieve a friendly settlement between England and Germany.'[10]

Ribbentrop remained downstairs, angrily kicking his feet, while Chamberlain, Hitler and Schmidt disappeared to the Führer's study on the first floor. During the next three hours, the charged atmosphere inside the bare room reflected the bad weather outside. The Führer began fairly quietly by repeating the long list of grievances that he always quoted when dealing with foreign dignitaries: these included the inequities of the Versailles Treaty, the ineffectiveness of the League of Nations and the need for disarmament. He also boasted how the National Socialist revolution had turned around Germany's economic fortunes and banished unemployment. Chamberlain was then scolded for Britain's continual interference in German affairs, the Führer singling out the British press in particular for its negative reporting of German news.

Putting on his best poker face, Chamberlain listened to Hitler's reproach attentively before dealing with each of his points individually, only breaking into a conciliatory smile when mentioning the freedom of the press. 'Nothing in his clear-cut, typically English features, with their bushy eyebrows, pointed nose and strong mouth, betrayed what went on behind his high forehead,' recalled Schmidt. In his letter to Ida on 19 September, Chamberlain said, 'For the most part H. spoke quietly and in low tones. I did not see any trace of insanity but occasionally he became very excited and poured out his indignation against the Czechs in a torrent of words so that several times I had to stop him and ask that I might have a chance to hear what he was talking about. I soon saw that the situation was much more critical than I had anticipated. I knew that his troops and tanks and guns and planes were ready to pounce and only awaiting his word and it was clear that rapid decisions must be taken if the situation was to be saved.'[11]

Moving on to the subject of the Sudeten Germans, Hitler said, in a long and rambling rant, that he was concerned with all Germans so felt the three million living in Czechoslovakia must come into the Reich. It was impossible, he said, 'that Czechoslovakia should remain like a spearhead in the side of Germany.'[12] Chamberlain replied that, in principle, he had nothing against the separation of the Sudeten Germans from the rest of Czechoslovakia, provided that the practical difficulties could be overcome. He went on, 'There is one point on which I want to be clear and I will explain why: you say that the three million Sudeten Germans must be included in the Reich; would you be satisfied with that and is there nothing more that you want? I ask because there are many people who think that is not all; that you wish to dismember Czechoslovakia.'

Then, looking Hitler straight in the eyes, Chamberlain said calmly that he was prepared to discuss any German grievance but that the use of force must be excluded in all circumstances. At the mention of force Hitler became enraged. '"Force" he exclaimed "Who speaks of force? Herr Benes [the Czechoslovak President] applies force against my countrymen in the Sudetenland, Herr Benes mobilised in May, not I".'[13] By this time it was pouring with rain outside, sheets of water running down the window and the wind was howling around the Berghof.

Hitler then launched into another long speech. He wanted to achieve racial unity so did not want a lot of Czechs, only the ethnic Germans. He continued, 'But all this seems to be academic; I want to get down to realities. Three hundred Sudetens have been killed and things of that kind cannot go on; the thing has got to be settled at once. I am determined to settle it. I do not care whether there is a world war or not. I am determined to settle it and to settle it soon, and I am prepared to risk a world war rather than allow this to drag on.'[14]

Translating the Führer's words, Schmidt emphasised that Hitler meant to settle the issue one way or another, making Chamberlain acutely aware that this meant war. 'I observed then and later (this) to be an extreme danger signal – its meaning now and on later occasions amounting to "Either the other side gives in, or a solution will be found by means of the application of force, invasion or war".'[15] Up to this point Chamberlain had kept his counsel, and his calm, but he now reacted, raising his voice and becoming visibly angry. 'At one point he seemed to be saying that he was going in at once, so I became indignant, saying that I did not see why he had allowed me to come all this way, and that I was wasting my time,' he told his sister, adding, 'He quietened down then.'

At this point Hitler, surprised at Chamberlain's tone and the sudden turn of events, hesitated. Schmidt recalled, 'If he really wants it to come to war,

I thought, now is the moment; and I looked at him in agonising suspense. At that moment the question of peace or war was really poised on a razor's edge. But the astonishing happened: Hitler recoiled.'[16] Thinking quickly, Hitler now changed his tone, switching in an instant from raging indignation to a considered response. 'If, in considering the Sudeten question, you are prepared to recognise the principle of the right of peoples to self-determination then we can continue the discussion in order to see how that principle can be applied in practice.'[17]

Recalling the moment to his sister, Chamberlain stated, 'If I could assure him that the British government accepted the principle of self-determination (which he had not invented), he was prepared to discuss ways and means.' The principle of self-determination was a controversial part of British policy under Chamberlain, but he was in no position to give this assurance without Cabinet approval:

> 'I said I could give no assurance without consultation. My personal opinion was that on principle I didn't care two hoots whether the Sudetens were in the Reich, or out of it, according to their own wishes.' Sensing that Hitler was now stepping back from the threat of war, Chamberlain raised a complication, 'But I saw immense practical difficulties in a plebiscite. I could, however, break off our talk now, go back and hold my consultations and meet him again. "That is a possible procedure", he said, "but I am very sorry that you should have to make two journeys. However, next time I shall come to meet you somewhere near Cologne." Then I asked him how the situation was to be held in the meantime, and he promised not to give the order to march unless some outrageous incident forced his hand.'[18]

At this point Hitler, seeing Chamberlain's face, had looked uncomfortable, but after Schmidt had translated that he would meet with him again, he visibly relaxed. The atmosphere had gone from one of intense hostility to resigned relief. 'On the way downstairs he was much more cordial than on going up. He asked what time I had to leave, with a view to my seeing his scenic beauties in the morning, and when I said I must go early, since lives were being lost, he said, "Oh well, when all this is over you must come back, and I will take you to my tea house at the top of the mountain".' Chamberlain had secured a promise that, in the intervening period, no aggressive action would be taken against Czechoslovakia, but little else. Even this had a caveat, Hitler as ever needing to have the final word by adding that it would not apply if the Czechs initiated any particularly 'outrageous incident' first. The discussion had ended with Schmidt concluding,

'After Hitler's change of direction, the prospects for the maintenance of peace seemed to me more hopeful. I drove with the English to the Berchtesgaden hotel where we dined and spent the night.'[19]

Exhausted after the encounter by Hitler's mood swings and histrionics, Chamberlain was also pleased that he had seemed to back down. Talking to reporters on the steps of the Grand Hotel in Berchtesgaden, he was circumspect, saying dishonestly that, 'It was a most friendly talk.' He told the media scrum that he would be flying back as soon as possible to consult with the Cabinet. At the hotel he began to compose a letter to Hitler, summarising his position. Referring to Hitler as 'His Excellency', the letter was designed to appeal to the vanity of the dictator and buy him time. It stated that he would consult his Cabinet colleagues as soon as he returned and also ask Lord Runciman for his view. Appealing for calm, he signed off, 'I should like to express my pleasure at having established personal contact with Your Excellency and to thank you for your courtesy during my brief stay at Berchtesgaden.'

The journalists who filled the lobby of the Grand Hotel, after being selectively briefed by von Ribbentrop, then had to find telephone lines to file their copy, but found that all the lines were choked with official coded telegrams. As a result, news of the meeting did not begin to filter out until nearly midnight. In the meantime, in his room, assisted by two secretaries, Schmidt tried to dictate his report of the meeting. As no other person had been present, Chamberlain was entirely reliant on Schmidt for a copy of the minutes to take back to the Cabinet when he flew back to Heston early the following morning. However, the report was not forthcoming so Chamberlain sent Henderson, the British ambassador, to see what the delay was. There he found von Ribbentrop standing over Schmidt, an angry look on his face. Unbeknown to Henderson, Ribbentrop had forbidden Schmidt from giving his report to the Premier. 'You think you're still in Geneva,' he said aggressively to Schmidt, 'where all the secret papers were freely handed about to everybody. We don't have that sort of thing in National Socialist Germany. This report is intended for the Führer alone. Please note.' As a result, Schmidt had to inform Henderson that the minutes of the meeting would not be made available to Chamberlain, 'He complained emphatically, stating that in these circumstances he must have his own interpreter at the next conversation, or at any rate bring someone with him who could make him a report.' Ribbentrop had got his revenge for being excluded from the meeting.

Schmidt finished the note at three o'clock in the morning. Five hours later Ribbentrop and Schmidt drove with Chamberlain and his party back to the airport at Munich. Exactly twenty-four hours after he had left, Chamberlain flew home. In the absence of the official minutes, Horace Wilson, Chamberlain's

Chief Industrial advisor, wrote some long notes on the flight home, commenting that 'Hewel (von Ribbentrop's personal secretary) who seems to spend a good deal of his time at Berchtesgaden and to have ready access to Hitler, spoke to me this morning of his impressions of a conversation he had with Hitler last night. He confirmed what the others had said, adding "Hitler told me that he felt he was speaking to a man".' He rather grandly signed off his note as being written 'somewhere over Germany.'[20]

Upon his return, King George VI also wrote personally to Chamberlain, saying how much he admired 'his wisdom in going to see Hitler in person,' adding, 'You must have been pleased by the universal approval with which your action was received.' Both notes transformed Chamberlain's mood and his analysis of the meeting. He was particularly impressed that Hitler thought he was dealing with 'a man'. Buoyed by the flattery, Chamberlain was pleased that Hitler had pulled back from the threat of war and he had his word that no military action would be taken until his return. He wrote to his sister, Ida, that he had come away from the encounter feeling he had 'established a certain confidence which was my own, and on my side, in spite of the hardness and ruthlessness I thought I saw in his face I got the impression that here was a man who could be relied upon when he had given his word.'[21] It was to prove a fatal error of judgement.

Chapter 13

A quarrel in a far-away country

'The integrity of the upright guides them, but the crookedness of the treacherous destroys them.' Proverbs 11:3

An emergency Cabinet meeting was held the day after Chamberlain's return from Munich, Saturday 17 September, at which ministers listened with 'breathless interest' to his account of his meeting with the Führer. 'I have been hard at it ever since,' he told Ida on 19 September. 'I saw Runciman on Friday on my return and had over an hour with the King who sent me a most charming note and was excited as a boy.' At the meetings, Chamberlain conveyed that he thought Hitler was genuine in his desire only to take back the Sudetenland, and that his objectives were 'strictly limited'. While there were dissenting voices who felt that Chamberlain had 'surrendered' to Hitler, the majority of the Cabinet reluctantly accepted that self-determination was a price worth paying if it avoided a wider war. The next day the French Prime Minister, Édouard Daladier, and his foreign minister, Georges Bonnet, were summoned to London to endorse Chamberlain's plan, which consisted of sending a blunt and uncompromising message to the Czech government that they must accept the transfer of German-speaking areas in return for an international guarantee of the new frontiers. After some haggling, the French agreed to the plan (thereby helping them save face in light of their obligation to stand by Czechoslovakia). The Cabinet endorsed the plan the next day, though, privately, many had grave misgivings.

While the negotiations with Hitler had clearly been stressful, Chamberlain was optimistic and secretly delighted that he had pulled off his dramatic coup, a move he thought that his father Joseph would have been proud of. 'I have still many anxious days before me but the most gnawing anxiety is gone for I feel that I have nothing to reproach myself with and that on the contrary up to now things are going the way I want. Luckily I feel fit and well and surprisingly untired. Annie is splendid but I fear when it is all over she will feel the terrific strain she has gone through. Thank you and Hilda ever so much for your letters. Hilda is quite right. It was an idea after Father's own heart.' He signed off his letter as he always did, 'Your affect brother Neville,' and added triumphantly, 'I hear from a German source that I am the most popular man in Germany! "He came to save us from a war".[1]

The problem with the British and French plan was that, unsurprisingly, the Czech government was extremely hostile to the dismemberment of their country. It was only after two days of unrelenting British and French diplomatic pressure that they finally gave in. A Cabinet meeting on 21 September also insisted that if Hitler made any similar demands in relation to German-speaking minorities in Poland or Hungary, or if he refused to allow an international boundary commission to report prior to the transfer of the Sudetenland, that Chamberlain had to get their approval before making any further concessions. In Germany, Hitler's propaganda minister, Joseph Goebbels, had ramped up reports of Czech aggression against Sudeten Germans to fever pitch. On 22 September, a solemn and much more subdued Chamberlain made his second flight to Germany.

Chamberlain again flew from Heston aerodrome to Cologne airport, this time without the fanfare that had accompanied his first flight. His destination was the Rhineland town of Bad Godesburg, where he was due to hold talks with Hitler. He again addressed the waiting reporters on the tarmac, 'A peaceful solution of the Czechoslovakia problem is an essential preliminary to a better understanding between the British and German peoples; and that, in turn, is the indispensable foundation of European peace. European peace is what I am aiming at, and I hope this journey may open the way to get it.'

In addition to taking with him Horace Wilson, his Chief Industrial Advisor, and William Strang, the head of the Foreign Office Central European Department, Chamberlain also took William Malkin, the head of the Foreign Office Legal Department, and two secretaries. He had good weather throughout the flight but this did little to lift his mood. Before his arrival, the Nazis had again made elaborate preparations for his visit, festooning the area with British and swastika flags. Godesburg itself was a popular tourist town on the river Rhine and home to 24,000 Germans. Hitler was a regular visitor there and had kept a reserved suite in the Hotel Dreesen for the last twelve years. But the town had never before been visited by both the German Chancellor and a British Prime Minister and it basked not only in the glorious autumnal sunshine but also in the opportunity to be at the centre of history in the making.

In the Hotel Dreesen Hitler stayed in the 'Führersuite', room number 106. It had been especially adapted for his convenience, with a large reception area, a sitting room that doubled as working office, and a large, comfortable bedroom with a bulletproof window. Chamberlain was staying opposite, in the luxurious Hotel Petersberg, so he and Hitler faced each other across the Rhine. Both hotels had been decorated with fresh pine and bunting, and hung throughout with the Union Jack and swastika flags.

Hitler's armoured train arrived at the spa town at 10am in beautiful sunshine and Chamberlain's plane touched down at Cologne airport just after 12.30pm. A scrum of reporters met the Prime Minister off the plane but he said nothing to the waiting press. So preoccupied was Chamberlain that he left his trusty umbrella onboard and an aide had to be sent back for it. Waiting on the tarmac was Ribbentrop, who was this time joined by Ernst von Weizsäcker, his secretary, and the German ambassador from London, Herbert von Dirksen. A full band played a variety of Nazi marching songs, including the German national anthem, *Deutschlandlied*, with the lines 'Deutschland, Deutschland über alles, über alles in der Welt' (Germany, Germany above all, Above all in the world), and, incongruously, *God Save the King*. Chamberlain inspected an SS guard composed of 'youthful giants, with black steel helmets, black uniforms, white collars and white gloves.' As Chamberlain's motorcade made its way to Bad Godesburg, he was again greeted by long lines of people saluting and 'Heiling'. At the Hotel Petersberg, after briefly admiring the view, he had lunch with the British ambassador, Nevile Henderson. Here he told him, 'I had a good flight. Weather was fine. We flew very low and I could enjoy the landscape.'

Just before 4pm, Chamberlain emerged from his hotel and, accompanied by Ribbentrop, went in one of the waiting Mercedes down to the quay where he travelled across the Rhine on a ferry, accompanied by two police boats, to the Hotel Dreesen. Thousands of onlookers lined the shore, reminding the British ambassador in Berlin, Nevile Henderson, of the 'Varsity boat-race day'. There, at the entrance, he was met by Hitler, who welcomed his guest warmly asking about his journey and accommodation. Afterwards, they sat down in the hotel conference room at either end of a long table, Hitler again with his interpreter, Schmidt. Due to the problems that Chamberlain had experienced in getting a report of the last meeting, he had bought with him Ivone Kirkpatrick, First Secretary at the British Embassy, who spoke excellent German.[2]

Chamberlain opened the meeting by telling Hitler that his Cabinet had agreed to the principle of self-determination for the Sudeten Germans, as had the French government. The Czech government, he said, had acquiesced and he then outlined his plan for the transferal of the disputed areas to Germany and the new frontiers. This involved a complicated system of checks and balances overseen by an international commission, with Germany also having to sign a non-aggression pact with Czechoslovakia. After this he visibly relaxed, content that he had covered all the points he and Hitler had discussed at the Berghof. Schmidt noted he had an expression of satisfaction, as much to say, 'Haven't

I worked splendidly during these five days.' Translating Chamberlain's points for the Führer, Schmidt too was impressed, 'That was what I felt too, for the agreement of the French, and still more the Czechoslovaks, to a definite cessation of territory seemed to me an extraordinary concession.' Hitler, however, was not impressed and said quietly, but with menace, 'I'm exceedingly sorry Mr Chamberlain, but I can no longer discuss these matters. This solution, after the developments of the last few days, is no longer practicable.'[3]

The developments that Hitler was referring to were the increasing number of 'attacks by Czechs on defenceless Sudeten Germans' as they claimed back some border areas, a development that had been reported extensively in the German press. Chamberlain, mistakenly thinking the Führer would instead thank him for his endeavours over the last few days, sat up with a start. After translating Hitler's diplomatic bombshell, Schmidt watched on in silence at Chamberlain's response, 'He flushed with anger at Hitler's attitude, at the ingratitude for his pains. I noticed that his kindly eyes could gleam very angrily under their bushy eyebrows.' Chamberlain was stunned and could not understand why the solution he had worked so hard to secure following their last meeting was now not acceptable to the German Führer.[4]

Recovering his composure, Chamberlain challenged Hitler directly over his change of mind. The Führer at first avoided replying, but then stated categorically that he could not sign any non-aggression pact with Czechoslovakia while there were outstanding border claims by Poland and Hungary which remained unresolved. Speaking calmly but indignantly, he then criticised each of the points in Chamberlain's plan, particularly the time taken for the transfer of Czechs out of the Sudetenland, stating, 'The occupation of the Sudeten territories to be given over must take place forthwith.' Hitler had not only moved the goalposts, he was now playing an entirely different game.

Chamberlain replied curtly that he was sure the Czech government would now have no option but to forcibly resist. Instead, he proposed an alternative that there be an 'agreement whereby law and order in certain agreed Sudeten German areas could be entrusted to Sudeten Germans themselves by creation of a suitable force'.[5] At this Hitler suddenly switched from being calm to angry, which considerably increased the tension in the small conference room. Demanding that the Sudetenland be evacuated immediately, he raged, 'The oppression of the Sudeten Germans and the terror exercised by Benes [the Czechoslovakian President] must end without delay,' before putting forward his own proposals, which would, in effect, have seen the unconditional surrender of Czechoslovakia. At this point Hitler brought the meeting to an abrupt end and stormed off to find Ribbentrop. An aggrieved Chamberlain returned to his hotel, a journey made worse by the fact that the ferry wasn't working, so he had to drive five miles along the Bonn road by the Rhine before he could find a bridge.

On arriving back at the Hotel Petersberg, he issued a terse statement to the waiting press pack, calling for calm. The only saving grace from Chamberlain's perspective was that another meeting had been agreed for the next day. The newspapers that evening reported extensively on the talks, but also noted that Sudeten Germans had already taken matters into their own hands by occupying the Eger district, one of the disputed border areas. 'Wonderful Discipline – Indescribable Joy' was the headline in a Cologne evening paper reporting on the occupation. By the time Chamberlain turned the lights out in his hotel room the Nazi flag flew over the city hall, church and all public buildings in Eger.[6]

The next day, Chamberlain sent a letter to Hitler rejecting his proposals in no uncertain terms. It read: 'I do not think you have realised the impossibility of my agreeing to put forward any plan unless I have reason to suppose that it will be considered by public opinion in my country, in France, and indeed in the world generally, as carrying out the principles already agreed in an orderly fashion, and free from the threat of force ... In the event of German troops moving into the areas as you propose, there is no doubt that the Czech government would have no option but to order their forces to resist.'[7]

Although the letter was written in a friendly style, with Chamberlain referring to Hitler as 'My dear Reich Chancellor', its impact was 'explosive' according to Schmidt. All morning Chamberlain paced up and down the balcony with the British ambassador, Nevile Henderson, wondering what Hitler's response would be. By early afternoon Hitler had still not replied and it looked as though the negotiations had reached an impasse. In the lobby, journalists talked openly about war. When Hitler finally did dictate a reply to Ribbentrop it was an angry repetition of what he had said the previous day. He continued in this vein for four or five pages and, as there was no time for a written translation, sent Schmidt directly to Chamberlain's hotel to translate it *ad verbatim*.

Schmidt left Hitler's hotel at 3pm with a large brown envelope under his arm to convey the Führer's response. Pushing through the scrum of waiting reporters in the Hotel Petersberg lobby, he remained stony faced as they clamoured round and shouted, 'Do you bring peace or war?' Schmidt noted, 'I did not even to venture to shrug my shoulders, as even the smallest gesture might have been misinterpreted. I was thankful when a member of the British delegation met me on the stairs and at once took me to Chamberlain.' Schmidt met Chamberlain in his room and translated Hitler's reply, with Sir Horace Wilson, Nevile Henderson, and Ivone Kirkpartick looking on. This took over an hour and was so rambling in parts that he had to 'add some elucidations verbally'. Downing a whisky for Dutch courage, he then fought his way back through the pack of reporters in the hotel lounge before heading back to Hitler's hotel.[8]

On his return, Hitler demanded to know how Chamberlain had responded, asking 'How did he take my letter?' Schmidt reported that Chamberlain had remained calm and showed little emotion, simply saying that he would reply in writing that afternoon. An hour later, at 6pm, Henderson and Wilson delivered the Prime Minister's reply. In it he again attempted to placate Hitler, referring to him as 'Your Excellency', and stated that he was ready to mediate with the Czech government about his proposals 'on which Your Excellency absolutely insists as you did yesterday'. He then asked Hitler to let him have the proposals in the form of a memorandum, with a map to illustrate the areas under dispute, which he could take back to London before passing it on to the Czech government. The reply had the desired effect of lowering the political temperature and, in the ensuing discussion with Ribbentrop, it was agreed that Chamberlain would return to the Hotel Dreesen later that evening to receive the memorandum in person and hear Hitler's commentary.

Back at Downing Street, Chamberlain's 'Inner Executive' had been meeting, concerned by messages sent by Horace Wilson that Chamberlain might be forced into a position of making concessions not agreed by the Cabinet. At 10pm Halifax sent a strongly worded message to Chamberlain citing that public opinion was 'mistrustful of our plan but perhaps prepared to accept it with reluctance as alternative to war, great mass of public opinion seems to be hardening in sense of feeling that we have gone to the limit of concession and that is up to the Chancellor to make some contribution.' The message continued, '[it] seems to your colleagues of vital importance that you should not leave without making it plain to the Chancellor if possible by special interview that, after great concessions made by Czechoslovak Government, for him to reject opportunity of peaceful solution in favour of one that must involve war would be an unpardonable crime against humanity.'[9] Chamberlain read the message with an increasing sense of foreboding.

The discussions, which started at 11pm on 23 September, were, according to Schmidt, 'one of the most dramatic in the whole of the Sudeten crisis'.[10] They took place in a small dining room in the hotel where Chamberlain, Horace Wilson, Nevile Henderson and William Malkin sat around in a semi-circle with Hitler, Schmidt, Ribbentrop and Ernst von Weizsäcker. On hearing that Ribbentrop had finally managed to get himself included in the meeting this time, one of the German officials quipped, 'All the best people are invited.'

The session opened with Schmidt translating Hitler's memorandum: 'The news of hourly increasing incidents in the Sudetenland proves that the condition of the Sudeten Germans is quite intolerable, and has therefore become a danger to European peace.' At this point he produced a large map on which all the disputed areas had been carefully marked by German officials: the areas to be ceded to Germany were marked in red while those where a plebiscite would be held were marked green. Spreading it out over the table, he continued, 'Evacuation of which will start on September 26th and which will be ceded to Germany on September 28th.' He added that the territory was to be handed over in its 'present condition', that the Czech government was to release 'all prisoners of German origin arrested for political offences', and that voting in the plebiscite was to take place 'under the supervision of an International Commission'.

Chamberlain and his colleagues listened in silence, and with increasing incredulity, to each point. At the end, Chamberlain threw up his hands in exasperation claiming, 'But that's an ultimatum', in the process throwing his copy on the table and getting up as if to leave. '*Ein Diktat*', added Henderson, knowing that it was one of Hitler's pet words that he regularly used when describing the 'hated Treaty of Versailles'. Returning to his seat, Chamberlain said sternly that it would be quite impossible for him to put the memorandum to the Czech government as it would create a violent reaction in other European countries. 'With the most profound regret and disappointment,' he stated forcefully, 'Chancellor, I have to state that you have made no effort to assist my attempt to secure peace.' Hitler, taken aback by Chamberlain's reproach, countered by saying that his proposals were a 'memorandum, not an ultimatum', but Chamberlain remained unmoved. Now indignant, Chamberlain stated that it would give the Czech government barely four days to issue the orders and evacuate the disputed areas, which would almost certainly result in violence and war.

With the negotiations at an impasse, the door suddenly opened and an adjutant came in with a note for Hitler. After studying it, he asked Schmidt to read it to Chamberlain. 'Benes [the Czech President] has just announced over the radio general mobilisation of the Czechoslovak forces.' The Czech government, responding to widespread demonstrations in support of keeping the integrity of the country's borders, had voted in a new Cabinet. Stalin had also come to the support of Czechoslovakia, stating that Russia stood beside them. There was a stunned silence in the room with everyone thinking that war was now inevitable.

During the negotiations, Hitler had always stated that he would not make a pre-emptive strike against Czechoslovakia unless some 'violent incident' on their part forced him to act. Now it looked as though the Czechs had played into his hands and given him the excuse he needed to invade. All eyes around the table rested on Hitler. Sensing the situation had come to a head, he then said in a quiet voice, 'Despite this unheard of provocation, I shall of course keep my promise not to proceed against Czechoslovakia during the course of negotiations,' then adding, 'At any rate, Mr Chamberlain, so long as you remain on German soil.'

The moment of high tension had passed. Schmidt commented, 'All seemed somehow to be relieved at the postponement of the catastrophe. Negotiations were continuing. That was the great thing.'[11] Hitler then moved on to the evacuation dates, in the process making a clumsy attempt to flatter Chamberlain. 'To please you, Mr Chamberlain, I will make a concession over the time-table. You are one of the few men for whom I have ever done such a thing. I will agree to October 1st as the date for evacuation.' Hitler then altered the memorandum, using his ink pen to note the change, and asked one of his adjutants to make another copy. Returning to the offensive, Hitler said that the areas ceded to the Reich were much smaller than if he had been forced to take matters into his own hands by taking military action. After looking around at his colleagues, and with a resigned look of indignation on his face, Chamberlain agreed to take the memorandum to the Czechs.

The meeting then finally broke up, but only after Hitler and Chamberlain had spoken alone for ten minutes. Schmidt recalled, 'In the course of their conversation, Hitler thanked Chamberlain, in words which seemed sincere, for his work on behalf of peace and that the Sudeten question was the last great problem which, as far as he was concerned, required solution.' In a letter to his sister, Chamberlain said, 'The Czech problem was the last territorial demand which he had to make in Europe.' Hitler also wanted closer cooperation with the British, stating, 'There need be no differences between us. We shall not get in the way of the exercise of your extra-European interests, while you can leave us a free hand in Central and South-Eastern Europe without harm.'

Summing up the talks, *The Diplomatic Correspondent*, the newsletter of the German Foreign Office, wrote, 'The Prime Minister, within a short week, has accomplished a valuable work in the service of peace. He realises that the German demands still keep within the limits of the principle of self-determination which have been recognised in all responsible quarters.' The German press, however, responding to the mobilisation of the Czech army, put the blame squarely on Prague. Whereas the previous day they had published the headline, 'With Hitler and Chamberlain for Peace', they now declared, 'With Benes and Stalin for War'. The front page headline of the *Nachtausgabe* newspaper said, 'Prague's mobilisation – the Road to War. Adolf Hitler's Plan – A Proposal for Peace.' *Der Angriff*, the mouthpiece of the Nazi party run by Hitler's Propaganda

Minister, Joseph Goebbels, screamed 'Prague's rulers sabotage Chamberlain. Germany, England and France want to save European Peace.' The *Börsen Zeitung* put it more succinctly, 'Chamberlain and Adolf Hitler for Peace. Only Prague wants War.'

Exhausted, Chamberlain and his team returned to their hotel, he insisting, 'You cannot call this a complete breakdown'. Yet the struggles of the last couple of days had taken their toll on him and, though he had held up surprisingly well considering his age, by the time he got back to the hotel that night he looked a beaten man. Despite this, Chamberlain was convinced by Hitler's assurance that the Sudetenland was his last territorial claim in Europe and came to the remarkable conclusion that a relationship of confidence had grown between himself and the Führer. He even went as far to say to his sister that, once the Czech crisis was over, he could overcome 'other problems still outstanding with the Führer in a similar spirit.' When he finally got back to his room at 2am Chamberlain slept soundly.

The *Irish Times* of 24 September 1938 summed up what Chamberlain's two flying visits to Berchtesgaden and Bad Godesburg had achieved with an editorial that said:

> Mr. Neville Chamberlain has the sympathy and admiration of the whole civilised world because he has done more than any other individual to save mankind from another war – Mr Chamberlain has done what no other statesman in Europe would have the courage to do. He has gone twice to Germany to plead with Herr Hitler in the service of peace, thereby placing his own political career on the hazard. If he has failed, it has been a glorious failure, and Neville Chamberlain's name will go down in history as that of a man who dared all to save mankind from calamity.[12]

On his return to Downing Street, Chamberlain made a radio broadcast to the people of Britain as the country mobilised for war. It included the lines, 'How horrible, fantastic, incredible it is that we should be digging trenches and trying on gas-masks here because of a quarrel in a far-away country between people of whom we know nothing.' The broadcast was well received by a British public as desperate as Chamberlain to avoid war. Few commentators at the time picked up on the phrase, yet the incredulity in Chamberlain's voice when he said the words 'horrible, fantastic, incredible' would later come back to haunt him.

Following his meeting in Bad Godesburg, Chamberlain privately admitted, in a letter to his sister Hilda, dated 2 October, that he was feeling the stress of dealing with Hitler, telling her, 'In these strenuous days I have lost all sense of time and recollection of days and I hardly know and certainly have no wish to recall where I was a week ago.' Of his ever-loyal wife, Annie, he said, 'I think her own religious faith and the conviction that the prayers of so many millions could not be in vain upheld her most.' Yet for Chamberlain, a man who had relinquished his faith long ago, the prayers of millions mattered little in the face of Hitler's intransigence, 'For me, I confess that it seemed only too possible that all the prayers of all the peoples of the world including Germany herself might break against the fanatical obstinacy of one man.'[13]

On 28 September, a subdued Chamberlain gave a long statement to an ill-tempered Commons on developments in the Czech crisis. In summing up he stated, 'Whatever views hon. Members may have had about Signor Mussolini in the past, I believe that everyone will welcome his gesture of being willing to work with us for peace in Europe.' As he was speaking, a dramatic intervention took place which transformed Chamberlain's demeanour and the mood of the House of Commons. A message was handed to Lord Halifax, which was then passed from hand to hand before it finally reached Chamberlain. Reading it, he announced immediately, 'That is not all. I have something further to say to the House yet. I have now been informed by Herr Hitler that he invites me to meet him at Munich tomorrow morning. He has also invited Signor Mussolini and Monsieur Daladier. Signor Mussolini has accepted and I have no doubt Monsieur Daladier will also accept. I need not say what my answer will be.'[14] Jubilant scenes, seldom seen in the Commons, ensued as Members leapt to their feet, cheered and waved their papers, with one MP shouting, 'Thank God for the Prime Minister!'

Chamberlain concluded his speech:

> We are all patriots, and there can be no honorable Member of this House who did not feel his heart leap that the crisis has been once more postponed to give us once more an opportunity to try what reason and good will and discussion will do to settle a problem which is already within sight of settlement. Mr. Speaker, I cannot say any more. I am sure that the House will be ready to release me now to go and see what I can make of this last effort. Perhaps they may think it will be well, in view of this new development, that this Debate shall stand adjourned for a few days, when perhaps we may meet in happier circumstances.[15]

Recalling the events afterwards in his letter to Hilda dated 2 October 1938, Chamberlain commented, 'That the news of the deliverance should come to me in the very act of closing my speech in the House was a peace of drama that no work of fiction ever surpassed.' He continued, 'The events of the next 48 hours entailed terrific physical and mental exertions. I was up the night before till after 2 a.m. preparing my speech. Then came the early rising, the scenes at the aerodrome and the long flight to Munich. The rest of that day till after 2 o'clock next morning was one of prolonged nightmare and I have only gradually been able since to sort out my impressions.'[16]

On his visit to Munich, Chamberlain told Hilda, 'Hitler's appearance and manner when I saw him appeared to show that the storm signals were up, though he gave me the double handshake that he reserves for specially friendly demonstrations. Yet these appearances were deceptive. His opening sentences when we gathered round for our conference were so moderate and reasonable that I felt instant relief.' An obsequious Chamberlain believed that Mussolini had played a key role in brokering the agreement, stating 'Mussolini's attitude all through was extremely quiet and reserved. He seemed to me cowed by Hitler but undoubtedly he was most anxious for a peaceful settlement and he played an indispensable part in attaining it.'[17] What didn't impress Chamberlain was Mussolini's appearance, 'It was of course the first time I had seen him. He is short, much shorter than I, so that I looked down on him. His head is closely shaven and to my eyes he would look much better if he let what hair he has grow. The centre part of the crown appeared to be bald, but the shaving of the rest of the head gives him a rather animal look, which is increased by his dark and sallow complexion.'

On the subject of the historic document proclaiming peace for our time – Chamberlain's so-called piece of paper – he told Hilda that Hitler had been extremely enthusiastic to sign it:

I asked Hitler about 1 in the morning while we were waiting for the draftsmen whether he would care to see me for another talk. He jumped at the idea and asked me to come to his private flat in a tenement house where the other floors are occupied by ordinary citizens [Hitlers private flat in Munich]. I had a very friendly and pleasant talk, on Spain, (where he too said he had never had any territorial ambitions) economic relations with S.E. Europe, and disarmament. I didn't mention colonies, nor did he. At the end I pulled out the declaration which I had prepared beforehand and asked if he would sign it. As the interpreter translated the words into German Hitler frequently ejaculated Ja! Ja! And at the end he said Yes I will certainly sign it. When shall we do it. I said "now", and we went at once to the writing table and put our signatures to the two copies which I had brought with me.[18]

Chamberlain then revealed that the whole ordeal had resulted in him coming close to a nervous breakdown, 'We came here (Chequers) yesterday immediately after lunch and walked up through Crow's Close to the Chequers Church way. I came nearer there to a nervous break down than I have ever been in my life. I have pulled myself together for there is fresh ordeal to go through in the House. After that I must make an effort to get away if only for a week. Sometime I suppose I shall see you two and we can let loose something of what we have felt – but that perhaps is better deferred till emotion is less intense.'[19]

The 'fresh ordeal' in the House began on 3 October, when Chamberlain made a statement to the Commons which was preceded by Duff Cooper, the First Lord of the Admiralty, dramatically resigning. In response Chamberlain did not seek to defend himself against Cooper's attacks but instead tried to explain his reasons for signing the four power agreement, 'The real triumph is that it has shown that representatives of four great Powers can find it possible to agree on a way of carrying out a difficult and delicate operation by discussion instead of by force of arms, and thereby they have averted a catastrophe which would have ended civilisation as we have known it. The relief that our escape from this great peril of war has, I think, everywhere been mingled in this country with a profound feeling of sympathy.'

At this point the House of Commons echoed to shouts of shame. Addressing his proclamation of 'peace for our time', he went on, 'I hope hon. Members will not be disposed to read into words used in a moment of some emotion, after a long and exhausting day, after I had driven through miles of excited, enthusiastic, cheering people – I hope they will not read into those words more than they were intended to convey. I do indeed believe that we may yet secure peace for our time, but I never meant to suggest that we do that by disarmament, until we can induce others to disarm, too.'

Following his speech, the Labour leader, Clement Attlee, taunted Chamberlain about Cooper's resignation and angrily said, 'This has not been a victory for reason and humanity. It has been a victory for brute force.'[20] The debate lasted eleven and a half hours and continued for another three days, and although the government easily won with a majority of 222, it was a painful and debilitating experience for Chamberlain. Twenty-two Conservatives, including Churchill, Anthony Eden and Duff Cooper, abstained from voting. The mood of the House was slowly but surely shifting away from his policy of appeasement to the defiant stance taken by Churchill.

Chapter 14

Poems, pipes and pianos

'There are different kinds of gifts, but the same Spirit distributes them.' 1 Corinthians 12:4

In contrast to the hostile atmosphere in the House of Commons in the days which followed the signing of the Munich agreement, letters, telegrams and gifts poured into Downing Street from all over the world eulogising Chamberlain and his role in delivering peace for our time. The City of Versailles, where the peace treaty, so hated by Hitler, had been signed in 1919, made him an honorary citizen, and the Belgians, not to be outdone, said every city that had suffered in the Great War should have a street named after him. The Maharajah of Nepal sent a personal commendation beginning 'Blessed be the peace maker', the Peruvians crowned him the 'Knight of Peace', and Portugal proposed a statute inscribed to 'Grateful Mothers'. Closer to home, ceremonies were held before all forty four Football League matches while the Chairman of Blackpool Football Club built a terrace of twelve houses for ex-servicemen in his honour. The Stock Exchange sent him a message of thanks before trading and in Birmingham, Sir Charles Hyde, a businessman and owner of the *Birmingham Post*, donated £10,000 to fund a Neville Chamberlain scholarship at the city's university.[1]

Sponsoring hospital beds in the name of peace proved to be particularly popular. On 3 October Bernard Docker, Chairman of Westminster Hospital, donated £1,000 for a 'Neville Chamberlain Bed' in the men's ward 'in perpetual remembrance of this victory of peace.' This was quickly followed on 5 October when Sir William Edgar Horne, a businessman and Chairman of the Prudential Assurance Company, donated another £1,000 to create 'The Mrs. Neville Chamberlain Bed' in the women's ward. On 28 October Mrs Meyer Sassoon donated £1,000 to create another 'Neville Chamberlain Bed', this time in the new St George's teaching hospital in Tooting. Chamberlain beds were even created abroad. On 8 April 1939 a 'Chamberlain Bed' in the Lisbon maternity hospital was 'inaugurated in the presence of the British Ambassador.' *The Times* reported that it was paid for from subscriptions raised by the Portuguese newspaper *Diario de Noticias* in recognition of Mr Chamberlain's unprecedented work for peace.[2]

In the three months following the signing of the Munich agreement, an estimated 40,000 gifts and letters flooded into Downing Street from an immensely grateful public.[3] In the first few days alone, over 20,000 letters and telegrams arrived, Chamberlain commenting in the House of Commons debate on Czechoslovakia on 5 October, 'Since I first went to Berchtesgaden, more than 20,000 letters and telegrams have come to No. 10, Downing Street. Of course, I have only been able to look at a tiny fraction of them, but I have seen enough to know that the people who wrote did not feel that they had such a cause for which to fight, if they were asked to go to war in order that the Sudeten Germans might not join the Reich. That is how they are feeling.'[4]

The congratulatory letters even included one from Spot, Chamberlain's favourite Chequers' dog. Whereas many of the letters received a standard reply (with the exception of Spot), the gifts proved much more of a headache for Chamberlain's private office as many required an individual acknowledgment. The number of presents was staggering and ranged from the humble (St Christopher crosses) to the expensive (gold watches), and also included the downright bizarre (kippers). The gifts reflected Chamberlain's hobbies and included ones for Mrs Chamberlain and their grandchildren. They included, in alphabetical order:

A – angling accessories, apples (two boxes of Canadian dessert apples from Nova Scotia Fruit Growers Association), Chamberlain coat of arms, art (numerous);

B – bags, bells (to ring out the peace), books (numerous, especially on fishing and birds), bootees, brochures, bulbs, bulldog (stuffed), burgundy (wine), bust (of Joseph), butterflies (specimens);

C – caddy clock, cakes, calendars, carnations, cat (black), champagne, charms, cheese, china, cigarette boxes, cigars, clotted cream, coats, Cornish cream, cots, crocodile dressing case (for Mrs Chamberlain from French newspaper *L'Oeuvre*), cross (St Christopher), cuff links;

D – delft ware, dictionary, dinner service, dolls, drawings

E – eggs, elephants (carved), engravings, etchings;

F – fishing rods (numerous including one with a personalised inscription), flies (fishing, numerous), flowers (box of wild), fruits;

G – gingerbread, gloves, gold (locket), grapes (box), grouse (box), gun butts;

H – handkerchiefs, hats, heather, honey, horlicks (to help Mrs Chamberlain sleep), horse shoes;

I – 'illuminated quotation', inscriptions, Irish Terrier (dog);

J – Jamaican paper knife, jelly (home made), Jersey milk can;

K – kippers, knives (paper);

L – lavender, laurels, lilies, lullabies, livre d'or (visitors book signed by 903 mothers, wives and sisters of war veterans and young French soldiers from La Baulle, Brittany)

M – Maltese model boat (silver), maps, marble (portrait), mats, meat (saddle of Welsh lamb), medals, mimosa (plant), miniatures, money ('peace donations'), moths (many specimens);

N – napkins, necklaces;

O – oil paintings, oranges (from the South African Co-operative Citrus Exchange), orchids, ormers;

P – pastries, peas (sweet), photographs, piano, pictures, pin cushions, pipes ('Hurricane'), plates (china), plaques (including a bronze), plumbs (stuffed), poems, port (Very Fine Old Tawny), portraits, posies, prayers, prints (including one of the Duke of Wellington), promise box, pullovers;

Q – quills, quilt;

R – records (gramophone), residences (fund for a house in France donated by *Le Soir* newspaper), roses, rugs;

S – scarves, scholarships, shamrocks, shawls, shortbread, shrimps, silhouettes, sketches, skis, silver ware (tea caddy, christening cups etc), socks (numerous), spinners, spoons, stitchwork, strawberries, streets (named after him);

T – table decorations, tapestries, tea sets, ties, tiles, toys, tributes, tweed;

U – umbrellas (numerous);

V – venison (hamper), verses, violets (parma), vinaigrette;

W – watches, watercolours, whisky, bottles of wine (numerous), woodcuts;

X – X-ray machine (for Wrexham hospital from Lord McAlpine);

Y – 'Yoshida' fishing tackle;

Z – Zeeland eighteenth century cabinet (from the people of Zeeland in Holland).[5]

Chamberlain's office was initially flattered to receive so many gifts from all over the world but soon found itself struggling to cope. On one day alone it took a secretary over seven hours just to open the telegrams. Despite taking on more staff to deal with the deluge, Downing Street at times ground to a halt, with some letters taking weeks to be answered by overloaded civil servants. Dealing with the flood of presents not only took up a lot of civil service time, it also proved a distraction at a time when everyone in Downing Street should have been focused on preventing another war.

One of the first of a plethora of poems eulogising Chamberlain was published on 29 September in the *Daily Express* by the poet Ernest Marston Rudland. In keeping with the times and Hitler's view of Chamberlain it was heroically called 'This is a Man' and in true biblical style cited God to thank for his deliverance. The final verse read:

Once more he cleft the air, but now,
With gladness on his tired brow.
And great lands' leaders met, and wrought,
Man's peace, alone the aim he sought.
We thank Thee, God! that in our span,
Hast given us in our need, a man.

Companies were also quick to cash in on the Prime Minister's new found fame, none more so than the makers of 'The Hurricane Pipe' – marketed as 'The

Cleverest Pipe Ever Made' – who were based in Oxford Street, London. On 30 September Mr Nutt, their appropriately named and resourceful manager, dispatched a 'Hurricane' to Chamberlain as a 'small token of great appreciation of one of millions, both in this country and round the world.' Mr Nutt also let it be known that King George VI was a fan of the Hurricane Pipe, which was designed to 'prevent spilling ash and burning tobacco' and 'wet tobacco sumps in the bottom of the bowl'. For this reason he proclaimed the pipe was 'Recommended by our most eminent doctors as the healthiest pipe to smoke.' Would the Prime Minister, Mr Nutt enquired, be willing to endorse the pipe?[6]

By 4 November, having heard nothing back, Mr Nutt phoned Downing Street offering a second pipe. He was informed in a follow-up letter the next day by a patient Miss Campbell, one of Chamberlain's private secretaries, that the Prime Minister was 'not a heavy smoker and the fact that he has lately been slightly indisposed has inclined him to smoke even less than usual.' She also added that Chamberlain had been laid low with gout. This resulted in a further letter of 14 November, with Mr Nutt hoping the Prime Minister was able to enjoy his pipe 'even in bed', and revealing that he suffered from sciatica so could 'fully sympathise with our Prime Minister.'[7] To improve Chamberlain's condition, he offered six other pipes and said he would be honoured if 'Mr Chamberlain will choose and accept any that he prefers.' Three days later Mr Nutt, who was nothing if not persistent, dispatched a third letter with a 'Nu-type' cigarette holder he had in production, asking if Mr Chamberlain would accept one and try it out.[8] A clearly exasperated Miss Campbell replied three days later with the curt note, 'Thank you for sending me a "Nu-type" cigarette holder.' Mr Nutt finally got the hint.

In response to the increasingly strained atmosphere in Downing Street regarding the escalating workload, Chamberlain's Principal Private Secretary, Osmund Somers Cleverly, wrote to his staff on 7 October seeking to clarify the situation: 'The Prime Minister has an extraordinary collection of presents from various people abroad and he thinks it would be ungracious to refuse them. He is therefore accepting them all; at any rate, all the portable ones. He proposes to get out of accepting the various houses, rivers, mountains and so on.' Cleverly's dry sense of humour was little consolation to a staff disappearing under a mountain of correspondence. Worse still, over the coming weeks Chamberlain's policy of accepting only the 'portable presents' was to cause his private office a lot of political headaches and lead to serious questions about his judgement.

As the gifts coming into Downing Street piled up, Chamberlain's private office became increasingly concerned, not only about the amount of work they were creating, but also in the blind adoration expressed about the Prime Minister by a public who had taken his declaration of peace for our time at face value. Yet some letters Chamberlain received must have moved even the jaded Downing Street staff to tears. On the 13 October an incredibly poignant letter and a 'small' pair of socks were sent to Chamberlain from a Mrs Janet Brown of 46 Burnhouse Street in Glasgow:

My dear Prime Minister

Will you please accept this small gift from a grateful mother as an appreciation of her gratitude to you for your great efforts for peace. I am seventy-three years old and have very vivid memories of the last war, as I had five sons on service, two of whom were killed and another died through illness contracted on service. My two surviving sons were ready to go if war had been declared again, but thanks to Almighty God and your heroic efforts, that has been averted.

My late husband was with Lord Robert's Army in the march from Kabul to Kandahar. Again I thank you with all my heart and I trust that God will grant both you and Mrs Chamberlain many years of peace and prosperity.

I am,
Yours in humble gratitude
(Mrs) Janet Brown

Chamberlain's office replied five days later, thanking Mrs Brown for sending the socks 'which he is very glad to accept', but in a clear sign that the workload was getting to them, didn't offer any sympathy for her loss. Another unrelated Mrs Brown also offered the Prime Minister some socks, but this time there was a much more enthusiastic response:

38 Huron Rd
S.W.17

Nov: 5-'38

To Mrs Chamberlain

Dear Madam
May we have the pleasure of sending our dear Prime Minister a Xmas present of socks? My friend & I are makers by machine, will you kindly

let me know his size of shoe, does he like 2 or 3 Ply or both, shades Grey, Navy, Black or mixture.

We have an unshrinkable wool, ½ Doz [Dozen] Prs[Pairs]: wear for two years, we reinforce the Toes & Heels.

Thanking you
Yrs: Faithfully

E.W. Brown[9]

P.S./ We are very pleased to note our dear Prime Minister is better, we always remember to ask God to bless & help him in his noble work.

Replying a week later Chamberlain's Private Secretary wrote:

Dear Madam

I am asked to write in answer to your very kind letter offering to give the Prime Minister a Christmas present of socks.

Your kind thought is very much appreciated and in answer to the questions which you ask may I say that the Prime Minister takes size nine in shoes and likes dark grey socks knitted in two ply wool.

Yours truly[10]

At a time when the country was in grave peril it seems extraordinary that the Prime Minister's office should spend time sorting out his sock requirements, but clearly delighted with his dark grey, two-ply wool socks, his office duly wrote back on 16 December, acknowledging them and passing on his festive good wishes.[11]

It was not just ordinary people who wrote to thank Chamberlain. The popular children's author Enid Blyton (1897-1968), who was just finishing her first full-length adventure novel, *The Secret Island*, took time out from it to pen a poem to rival Rudland's, eulogising Chamberlain and, again, crowning him a 'Man':

Here is a man who did not fear to lose
His reputation, high position, fame
A man with courage wise enough to choose
What might be deep humiliation, shame;

A man direct enough in mind and heart
To brush aside all precedent and fly
Straight to the problem's core to play his part;
Persistently, with dignity, to try
His lonely strength against relentless force;
No politician he – a statesman rare
Who champions all the lands at peace, a source
Of brilliant common sense beyond compare
To make the issues crystal-clear he fought
Reduced the angry turmoil to a plan
And ranged behind him hope prayer and thought
The moment came – and with it rose the Man.[12]

Chamberlain's office was clearly less than impressed with the best-selling author's efforts, referring to Enid Blyton as 'Madam' and curtly replying on 26 October that Mrs Chamberlain had 'safely received' the poem and conveying 'her warm appreciation' of it. Peace and questionable poetry seemed to be the order of the day.

On 14 October, in response to complaints from various embassies about the deluge of gifts, Chamberlain's private office tried to get a grip on the situation. Cleverly, in a letter to Harold Caccia (1905-1990), Assistant Private Secretary at the Foreign Office, tried to downplay the problem and distinguish between the role of Prime Minster and Chamberlain as an individual, saying:

> We have, I think, already accepted one or two quite small articles [a classic case of civil service understatement], but clearly if the flow of presents continues we shall have to call a halt. I think that in this matter we should wish to give a wide discretion to the Embassies and Legations, but our general line would be that, while the Prime Minister very much appreciates the kind thoughts and generosity which prompted the donors, he has received so many offers of the kind that he hopes he will not be misunderstood if he asks to be excused from accepting them. It might perhaps be suggested to the donors that, if they liked to give something to Mr. Chamberlain himself, he would be very pleased. Where to use such a suggestion is, I think again rather a matter for the Embassies' discretion.

The vexed subject of how to deal with gifts was again raised by the arrival, on 7 November, in Downing Street of an 18-carat gold presentation hunter watch from the people of Neuchatel in Switzerland, the result of a fundraiser in a local newspaper. It was delivered in the diplomatic pouch from Berne and engraved:

Neville Chamberlain
Hommage neuchatelois

Septembre 1938

Heureux Ceux Qui Procurent La Paix

The watch was a magnificent timepiece encompassing a 52mm diameter white enamel dial with arabic numerals and a 21-jewel movement. While clearly a highly desirable gift, it presented the Foreign Office and Chamberlain's private office with yet another difficult diplomatic dilemma. However, on seeing it, Chamberlain had no such qualms and was only too keen to accept it. He asked his staff to send off the following letter in his name:

This morning there arrived at my house the beautiful gold watch presented to me by the inhabitants of the canton of Neuchatel. Its actual presence here has made me feel that in this case I should relax the almost invariable rule which I have set myself of asking to be excused from accepting similar generous offers. I therefore accept with most sincere thanks this munificent gift of the Neuchatelois, which I shall value for its beauty, for its craftsmanship and for the spirit which inspired its donors.

The arrival of the watch and Chamberlain's letter caused consternation in Downing Street. As a result the following memorandum was sent to Chamberlain by Cleverly:

PRIME MINISTER

The arrival of the gold watch from Neuchatel has raised once more the question of your acceptance of gifts, about which My. Syers [Cecil, Private Secretary] minuted to you on 4th October ... The Neuchatel present is, however, sponsored by a newspaper, which will probably mean that your reply is likely to be published and might lead to a further number of presents being sent to you without previous consultation, these it is impossible to refuse. A draft reply as regards the Neuchatel gold watch is attached which attempts to show, without being at all ungracious that your general rule is to ask to be excused from accepting.

It was not just gifts from citizens, communities and countries that flooded into Downing Street. In response to Chamberlain's massive popularity around the world, manufacturers had been rushing out mementos of Munich encompassing everything from delft plates to tea pots, and from souvenir medals to handkerchiefs. On 14 October Chamberlain received a letter from the editor of the *Sunday Times*, William Hadley, informing him that the *Daily Sketch* had offered to its readers an 'Art Plate' of a photo of Annie and him at Downing Street. To receive the plate a coupon had to be filled in and forwarded with 3d in stamps. 'They had already had over 90,000 applications and they are still pouring in,' Chamberlain told Hilda on 15 October, adding, 'They had never known anything like it.' Reflecting on the deluge of gifts, he commented, 'Gifts indeed keep coming in embarrassing profusion. This week I have been notified of two cases from different senders of the finest German Rhine wine and flies and salmon rods, watches, lucky horseshoes, tweed for sporting suits and socks have all arrived this week.'

Some gifts, however, proved to be not just a problem for Chamberlain's overworked staff but also caused him political embarrassment. On 14 October Chamberlain received a letter from The House of Farnell, manufacturers of 'Alpha Soft Toys and Joyday Dolls', who had come up with a unique idea to cash in on Chamberlain's new found global fame:

The Rt. Hon. Neville Chamberlain M.P.
10 Downing Street,
London. S.W.1.

Sir

We thought that, after your successful efforts the week before last in maintaining the Peace of the World, many people both at home and abroad would like to have a replica of yourself as a souvenir of a great historical occasion.

We have, therefore, designed and placed on the market, a Doll representing you in ordinary daily dress and also pursuing your favourite pastime as a fisherman and we are glad to say the public response to these souvenirs is very gratifying.

Under separate cover we are taking the liberty of sending you one of each model and would ask you kindly to accept these with our compliments and trust you will like them.

Should you desire to present any models to your personal friends we shall be only too happy to supply them to you for that purpose, on the condition that you allow us to present them to you.

May we most respectfully add our congratulations on your wonderful efforts and achievement and sincerely hope that your recent success is only the forerunner of bigger successes to come in the International field.

I have the honour to be, Sir,

Your obedient servant
A.G. R. Rose
Director

Failing to see the political storm about to blow up, on 18 October Chamberlain's secretary Cleverly loyally wrote back on his behalf, thanking Mr Rose for 'the two replicas of himself which have duly been received under separate cover.' He went on in his own ingratiating style, 'The Prime Minister greatly appreciates your thought in sending him these figures, which he is interested to have.' Cleverly finished, 'The Prime Minister much appreciates the tribute which you pay to his work on behalf of your firm and the good wishes you send him for the future.'

A week later Patrick Gower, Head of Publicity at Conservative and Unionist Central Office, sent a letter to Cleverly giving him a good dressing down.

My dear Cleverly

My attention has been drawn to the advertisement on page 7 of this trade magazine. Although it is a small matter I cannot help thinking that something ought to be done about it. The manufacturers of the doll reproduced in the illustration have probably acted with the best intentions in the world but I could well imagine our political opponents making unfriendly use of it with a view to exposing the Prime Minister to ridicule.

I wonder whether you would care to get in touch with the Managing Director of the firm and explain to him that, while you fully appreciate their desire to publicise the Prime Minister, this particular form of publicity might be open to serious objection. If he were approached in a friendly way I should think that he would appreciate the point,

I see that the name and address of the firm are contained in the advertisement on page 54.

Yours sincerely
Patrick Gower

Whether or not Chamberlain's staff did get in contact with the company again is not recorded, but it went to show the degree of sensitivity now surrounding effigies of the Prime Minister. For Chamberlain's overworked staff, particularly the hard-pressed Cleverly, the scandal associated with the dolls was to prove child's play in comparison to one which would engulf Downing Street over a a piano. On 17 October the Downing Street office received a letter from Julius Blüthner, the famous German piano manufacturer, 'on behalf of the German people':

17 October 1938
To the Right Honble. Neville Chamberlain, P.C., M.P.
10 Downing Street
London S.W.1.

Sir,

Feeling strongly as I do that your strenuous efforts and exertions during recent weeks have saved both your own and my Country and the rest of Europe, from the disaster of a great War, I should like to show some token of my gratitude and appreciation. I hope, therefore, you will forgive me if I approach you with the following suggestion.

My desire is to make a present of one of my Boudoir Grand Pianofortes to your gracious lady, Mrs Chamberlain, whom I understand to be interested in Music.

If Mrs Chamberlain will accept this gift she will be conferring a very great honour upon me, and to avoid misunderstanding may I say at once that I would see to it that no publicity were involved.

I earnestly hope, therefore, that you will see your way to accept this token of my very great esteem and gratitude to you as one who has conferred untold benefit upon mankind.

In the event of your accepting this present my London Agents will make all the necessary arrangements for delivering the Piano so that you will be put to no trouble whatsoever in the matter.

I have the honour to be, Sir,

Your obedient Servant,
Julius Blüthner

After a delay of nearly ten days Chamberlain's Private Secretary wrote back, enthusiastically accepting the gift, 'Mr. Chamberlain feels that an offer, coming from a German, is a symbol of the good-will which he is so anxious to foster between the two countries and that, in such circumstances, he would very much like to accept it.' The letter went on to ask Blüthner's London Agents to get in touch to 'let Mrs. Chamberlain know the approximate dimensions of the pianoforte in order that Mrs. Chamberlain may decide upon a suitable place for it in the house.'

For years, Blüthner's business had been in decline under Hitler while his arch-rival, Carl Bechstein, a Nazi supporter from the early 1920s, had prospered. Blüthner's piano was, therefore, not just a way of honouring Chamberlain's efforts for peace, it was also a way of trying to steal a march on his rival and revive his company's fortunes. On 18 November Blüthner's London Agents, in the shape of the Managing Director, A.W. Whelpdale, duly got in touch, offering Mrs Chamberlain a piano by the end of the month and stating, 'The Boudoir Grand which he [Blüthner] originally offered is 6ft.1 in. in length but he would be quite willing to give you either a larger Piano or if you prefer it, a smaller instrument.' Annie, who by Chamberlain's own admission was a 'child of luxury', unsurprisingly decided to accept the larger Grand Pianoforte at 6ft. 9in. in length. Much to her delight the company also made the case in dark mahogany with 'egg-shell finish' so it would match the Chamberlain's table.

On 13 December, Chamberlain wrote back in person thanking Blüthner for his very generous gift, stating, 'I am writing to say how much both of us appreciate this magnificent addition to our household goods. Although she nor I is able to play the piano, our daughter is quite a good pianist and I hope that I shall have the pleasure of listening to her very often in the future as she plays your instrument.' Summing up, Chamberlain added, 'Perhaps I need hardly say that I value your gift not only for its intrinsic interest, but because of the spirit in which you have offered it – a spirit of friendliness which is, I believe, sincerely reciprocated in this country and which I hope nothing may ever occur to disturb.' He then added in his own hand, 'Believe me, Yours Sincerely, Neville Chamberlain.' In order to avoid any embarrassment to Mr Blüthner, the letter was sent via the diplomatic pouch in Leipzig to the British Embassy in Berlin.

While the Chamberlains were only too willing to accept gifts they thought would enhance their affluent lifestyle, the acceptance of the piano from a German manufacturer not favoured by the Nazis caused grave disquiet in the Foreign Office. For the British Embassy staff in Berlin, who were living under constant Nazi scrutiny and threat, the letter put them in a very dangerous position. On 23 December Adrian Holman, the First Secretary in the Berlin Office, wrote in diplomatic terms a highly critical letter to Oliver Harvey, the Private Secretary at the Foreign Office, stating:

> We feel sure that this practice of making presentations is by no means smiled upon by the German authorities, with the result that such gifts are brought to us for safe transmission ... To be quite frank, we feel sure that the best line of action would be the refusal of any further presents. For instance the acceptance of a piano might well be regarded by the donor as placing the Prime Minister under some form of obligation, if complications arose at a later date. Further if the letter signed by the Prime Minister himself were to fall into unauthorised hands and given publicity, it might do infinite harm both to Herr Blüthner and the Prime Minister.

It was a devastating critique of the Prime Minister's judgement. On 3 January 1940, Oliver Harvey took up Holman's case and wrote directly to the Prime Minister's Principal Private Secretary, Cleverly, on the subject, again asking for 'a firm rule against the acceptance of any further presents. It would, I suppose, be impossible to apply this rule to Germany alone and we should have to apply it to presents offered by persons in other countries as well.'

While the piano incident may not have been music to the ears of the Foreign Office, Chamberlain continued to be fêted by the public, despite the increasingly critical view of Munich being expressed in Parliament. 'Letters and presents still keep rolling in,' he told Ida on 24 October, 'I believe they include 5 fishing rods and innumerable flies, two gold watches, two clocks, an umbrella and quantities of rubbish.' The 'rubbish' was the many small, heartfelt items sent by an adoring public who were not used to the doublespeak practiced by politicians and who had taken Chamberlain at face value when he pronounced 'peace for our time.'

Despite the concerns of the Foreign Office and the embassies, gifts continued to arrive from all over the world. On 9 November, Chamberlain wrote to his sister Hilda, 'The tide of letters, flowers, testimonials and gifts continues to flow in without much abatement.' He reported that Annie was getting some seventy letters a day and that this was on top of a significant number in arrears. Even with four paid secretaries, she was struggling to cope. To help, she had recruited two friends, Pearl and Hester, 'Not only have they come with great enthusiasm but they have bought Mabel Catterson Smith as well, so I hope we shall now make some headway.'

While Chamberlain was happy to follow guidelines dictated by his civil servants when it came to everyday gifts, it seemed that protocol could be put aside when highly desirable ones arrived. On 17 November, a letter arrived from Domaines Cordier, a Bordeaux vineyard owner. Cordier owned six chateaux in France and offered Mr and Mrs Chamberlain twenty-four bottles of Lafaurie Peyraguey 1921 (White), twenty-four bottles of Lafaurie Peyraguey 1929 (White) and twenty-four bottles of Gruaud Larose 1925 (Claret). Mrs Chamberlain was only too happy to accept the bottles, despite Cordier's London agent writing, 'I had warned him that there was very little chance of his offer being accepted and he will feel himself, rightly, very highly honoured, that his "flowers of France" in bottles are going to Mr & Mrs Chamberlain.' No doubt the 'flowers of France' went down very well with the Prime Minister and his wife, both of whom were well-known wine connoisseurs.

Whether or not they wanted them, some other gifts had to be rejected simply because they were highly impractical. On 1 December, one of Chamberlain's private secretaries wrote:

> The Prime Minister desires me to thank you very much for your letter of 28th November and he would be glad if you would kindly convey to Mr. Fitzgerald his appreciation of his generous offer to present him with an Irish Terrier. The Prime Minister feels however that it would be neither very easy nor suitable to keep a dog in a house such as this and he would therefore prefer to be excused from accepting this offer. Mr. Chamberlain would like Mr. Fitzgerald to know however that he is happy to hear of his appreciation of the work he has been able to do in the cause of Peace.

Some gifts, however, had a much more serious purpose, and were used as a means of informing the Prime Minister about what was really going on in Hitler's Germany. One in particular was used to secretly send Chamberlain a message about the plight of the Jews. On 9 December a Mrs Lister, who was the niece of Lord Halifax, met with Edith Watson, one of Chamberlain's private secretaries, at Downing Street. Mrs Lister had just got back from Germany and she handed over a book from a Mr Alexander Oldenburg, a publisher in Munich. The book was a thank you for the Munich agreement and had been signed by all of his staff. Mrs Lister told Ms Watson that she had smuggled the book out but could not bring the accompanying letter for fear of them all being put in a concentration camp. Discussing the situation in Germany, Mrs Lister told Ms Watson, 'The feeling in Munich for the Prime Minister is as strong as ever, but no one is allowed to give expression to it, and no one can mention his name there.' She went on to explain that everyone who had sent flowers to Chamberlain's room during his visit and could be traced had received a threatening letter from the Nazi authorities making it clear that the credit for the Munich agreement was entirely down to Hitler.

Ms Watson discussed with Mrs Lister how Chamberlain could get an acknowledgement to Mr Oldenburg safely and decided that the best course of action was for it to go in the Foreign Office bag so 'it did not get into unauthorised hands.' The conversation then moved on to conditions in Germany, in particular the increasing acts of violence against German Jews. In a note of the meeting sent to Caccia, the Assistant Private Secretary at the Foreign Office, Ms Watson stated, 'She herself had seen an old Jewish woman whose face had all been slashed and cut, and a Doctor friend of hers had attended an old woman in Dusseldorf who had been trampled to death. She said the tragedy was that many of the people who were now suffering were Christian Jews, and had been for so long that they were not even aware until now that they were Jews. She also instanced the hardship of the old Jews whose children had got away on British passports [*Kindertransport*, an organised rescue effort whereby Jewish children were transported to Britain] and who were still left wholly unprovided for.'

The book and the accompanying conversation were duly conveyed to Chamberlain who, after hearing it, can have been under no illusions about what was really going in Germany. Yet, having risked everything on his high profile policy of appeasement, Chamberlain found himself in the unenviable position of not being able to publicly criticise the Nazi regime for fear of Hitler withdrawing from the Munich agreement. The gifts, while creating an immense amount of work for his private office and embassies around the world, had opened his eyes to what was happening in Hitler's Germany. They also pointed to another uncomfortable truth, that the British public had latched onto to the phrase 'peace for our time' and were now deaf to the political realities that were becoming increasingly apparent. After Christmas 1939, the number of gifts coming into Downing Street began to slow and, following Oliver Harvey's letter of 3 January 1940, Chamberlain accepted no more gifts from abroad. However, by accepting gifts from Germany and ignoring protocol when it suited him, those around Chamberlain, even his Principal Private Secretary Cleverly, began to question his judgement at a time when the world teetered precariously on the brink of war.

Chapter 15

Depression, Paris and a scaup

'He will renew your life and sustain you in your old age.' Ruth 4:15

On 1 October 1938 a new weekly photojournalism magazine was launched called *Picture Post*. It was published by Edward George Hulton, whose stable included *Farmers Weekly* and *Lilliput*, a men's art and soft porn monthly magazine launched the year before.[1] The *Picture Post* broke new ground with full-page photo features on all aspects of British life, from corsets to conductors, together with more in-depth special features, articles and stories. Edited by Stefan Lorant (1901-1997), a pioneering Hungarian-American photojournalist, its use of stunning photography and colour in its eighty A3-sized pages made it stand out from its competitors. At a cost of just three pence, it was an instant hit, selling over one and a half million copies in two months.

The second issue, published on 8 October, featured on its cover a head and shoulders shot of Chamberlain with the caption 'I have done all one man can do to save peace.'[2] Inside was an image of Chamberlain addressing the crowds from a first floor window at Downing Street with the caption 'My good friends … I believe it is peace for our time', accompanied by a four-page illustrated spread on his life story, from his birth to his meeting at Berchtesgaden with Hitler. After the article, the *Post* ran a double-page spread with pictures from the First World War of dead bodies and men blinded by tear gas with the headline, in one-inch capitals, 'Hitler! How can you forget this?'

Sadly, Chamberlain was in no state to enjoy his new-found fame following the gruelling debate in Parliament over the Munich agreement. The subsequent euphoria that had gripped the nation had left him mentally exhausted. Concerned about Chamberlain's health following his near breakdown at Chequers on 1 and 2 October, his friend and Parliamentary Private Secretary, Alec Douglas-Home, offered his home, 'The Hirsel', as a place to convalesce. It was a stately pile near Coldstream in the Scottish Borders and had been a seat of the Earls of Home since 1611. Looking back over the last few days, Chamberlain admitted to Ida that it had been a 'pretty trying ordeal, especially as I had to fight all the time against the defection of weaker brethren and Winston was carrying on a regular conspiracy against me with the aid of Masaryk, the

Czech Minister [Jan Masaryk, Czechoslovak Foreign Minister, 1886-1948].'
He also sensationally revealed that, using his powers as Prime Minister, he had
authorised the Special Branch to spy on both Churchill and Masaryk, bug their
phones and send the transcripts to him: 'They, of course, are totally unaware of
my knowledge of their proceedings. I had continual information of their doings
and sayings which for the nth time demonstrated how completely Winston can
deceive himself when he wants to and how utterly credulous a foreigner can
be when he is told the thing he wants to hear. In this case the thing was that
"Chamberlain's fall was imminent".'[3]

Chamberlain continued, 'These inside troubles which formed a background
to the ceaseless stream of vituperation being poured out upon me had a somewhat
depressing effect on my spirits. I tried occasionally to take an antidote to the poison
gas by reading a few of the countless letters and telegrams which continued to pour
in expressing in most moving accents the writers' heartfelt relief and gratitude.
All the world seemed to be full of my praises except the House of Commons,
but of course that was where I happened to be myself so naturally its voice spoke
loudest in my ear.' After complaining further about the Commons, in particular
Winston's duplicitous and bullying behaviour, he signed off by stating, 'Presents
still pour in, of every kind sort and description. It's most embarrassing!'[4]

On Saturday 15 October, Chamberlain sent off another letter from The
Hirsel, this time to his sister Hilda. In it he reflected ruefully on his situation
stating, 'In two days I must go back to work at the numerous problems which lie
before me.' Chamberlain had two Cabinet places to fill following the resignation
of Duff Cooper and the death of Dominion Secretary Edward Stanley (1894-
1938). As a result, Chamberlain's confidant and fellow appeaser, Lord Halifax,
had urged him to bring Labour members and his former Foreign Secretary,
Anthony Eden, back into the Cabinet to create 'national unity on foreign policy.'
But Chamberlain thought his differences with Eden were too great, 'If we had
Labour men in I see them forming a group with him which would keep up a
constant running fight over every move in the international game. That would
soon make my position intolerable.'[5]

On the weekend of 24-25 October, Chamberlain mused over his Cabinet at
Chequers. The problem, he told Ida, was, 'A lot of people seem to me to be losing
their heads and talking and thinking as though Munich had made war more
instead of less imminent. The papers are largely responsible for it and I want to
try and get them back to the view that though there are gaps to fill up we need
not believe that we have got to make huge additions to the programme now being
put into operation.' One addition he did think was necessary was a Ministry of
Civil Defence, 'under a new Minister, to take over ARP [Air Raid Precautions]

and to organise the various civilian corps required for Air Raid Wardens, extra police and fire brigade, trench digging, ambulance driving, Red Cross etc. might be a good thing and might tend to create greater confidence. But it wants rather careful working out.'[6]

On 27 October, a by-election was held in Oxford following the death of the sitting Conservative MP Robert Croft Bourne (1888-1938) in August.[7] The by-election was the first to be held since Chamberlain had signed the Munich agreement and it was seen as a barometer of his popularity. The contest saw two Oxford graduates take on each other: Quintin Hogg, a supporter of Chamberlain and his foreign policy, and Sandie Lindsay, who had been selected following the Labour and Liberal parties standing down their candidates in favour of an independent anti-appeasement one. The *Picture Post* covered the campaign in its 5 November issue, describing the by-election as of 'world importance'. Its editorial stated:

> In the past few weeks the whole politics of Britain have been shifted by events which seemed at first remote, the business only of a small, unspellable and distant state. For years the ordinary person has been most concerned with home, family, neighbours, street. In the past month foreign affairs have forcibly taken a front-page place for weeks on end. Via the gas mask it has been brought home (literally) to every elector that foreign policy may be as important as street lighting, new housing, or the price of milk. Within the next few weeks a long list of by-elections is being fought, on the one main issue of foreign policy. Briefly, was Chamberlain right? And is the present Government to be relied upon?'[8]

The campaign was a predictably dirty one, with Hogg being supported by his 'attractive wife' who, according to a *Daily Express* reporter, 'Smiled so merrily with Cupid's lips and bright blue eyes that at once she put 400 votes in his bag.' By contrast, Lindsay's supporters tried to paint Hogg as a friend of Hitler, using the slogan 'Hitler wants Hogg for Christmas' (The campaign was also notable for featuring two future politicians, then students at Oxford University: Edward Heath and Roy Jenkins, who both supported Lindsay). Hogg summed up what was at stake: 'Mr Chamberlain came back admist the applause of the entire British Public. And the people of this country will vote for him. It is not enough that we should win. We must win by a vast, an overwhelming majority.' On polling day the campaign resulted in an increased turnout and Hogg winning, but with a reduced majority of 3,434. The people of Oxford, like the country as a whole, were split on the signing of the Munich agreement.

On 27 October, Chamberlain had some ornithological relief from politics when one of his Treasury staff, N.E. Young, reported that he had seen a flock of long-tailed tits *Aegithalos caudatus* in the plane tree outside Number 10. By now Chamberlain's birdwatching obsession had become well known within his own private office and the surrounding government departments. Cleverly and his other private secretaries rightly deduced that watching or 'twitching' birds, even if it was just in the environs around Number 10 and in nearby St James's Park, played an important role in managing the stress level of their boss. Not believing the sighting, Chamberlain queried it. Young replied that he was quite certain about his observation and provided a detailed description, which he sent to the Prime Minister in a long memo.

Long-tailed tits are readily recognisable by their distinctive black and silver colouring, their undulating flight and their tail, which, as their name suggests, is longer than their body. Gregarious and noisy birds, they most often occur in small, excitable flocks composed of family groups of up to twenty birds. Their distinctive 'see-see-see' call was probably what first brought them to Young's attention, and seeing a flock flit from one tree to the next, pause, grab an insect and then move rapidly on would have been a real delight. Although common, long-tailed tits would have been infrequent visitors to the garden at Number 10 and, as a result, one of Chamberlain's secretaries was asked to dispatch a letter to his ornithological mentor, Gilbert Collett.

10 Downing Street
Whitehall

29 October, 1938

Dear Sir

Mr. Chamberlain thinks that you would be interested to know that Mr. N.E. Young of the Treasury informed him two days ago that he had seen from his window in the Treasury several long tailed tits in the plane tree just outside the garden wall of this house. Mr. Chamberlain enquired whether Mr. Young was quite certain of his observation and received a note in reply to say that Mr. Young was absolutely positive that they were long tailed tits. From his detailed description it seems quite unlikely that he can be making a mistake.

Yours truly

C.M Campbell
Private Secretary.[9]

The joy of birds apart, Chamberlain was having a bruising time. On 1 November, in a House of Commons debate on the international situation, the Labour leader, Clement Attlee, made a fierce attack on the Munich agreement and the state of the British economy in comparison to Germany's, in particular reports in the press that social services were being cut to pay for armaments. 'To cut down, whether it be pensions, education, schools or unemployment benefit – any of these things – will do precisely the wrong thing from the point of view of the strength of this nation,' he told the House. 'It is to give priority to Ascot and the Ritz. At the present moment we have widespread malnutrition in this country. We claim that the first thing for the defence of this country is a healthy, sound population. You will not get the kind of service you want in this country unless you base it on that.'[10] This incensed Chamberlain and he retorted that the story, which had been in the *Daily Herald*, was 'entirely an invention'. It was another heavyweight political encounter that left Chamberlain reeling.

By the beginning of November, the heavy burden of Munich and its toxic aftermath were beginning to take a serious toll on Chamberlain's health to such an extent that his personal staff were urging him to take time off. Chamberlain ignored them, citing the Chief Whip, David Margesson, who had commended him on the 'best speech [he] had ever delivered' on the Munich agreement. The strength of it had also seen off the Labour Party and their planned machinations, in which, he fancied 'Winston was to play a part'. In the ensuing debate, he wrote to Hilda, 'No argument of any weight could be brought against the agreement and after the usual round of repetition we got a spanking vote to finish up on.'

In his letter he also revealed that he and Halifax were going to Paris with their wives and then on to Rome to see Musso, the man he had been courting for so long, 'I feel that Rome at the moment is the end of the axis on which it is easiest to make an impression.'[11] In Germany, however, there were increasing signs that Hitler no longer cared about international opinion. On 10 November 1938, Jewish homes, shops and synagogues were set on fire or destroyed in what became known as *Kristallnacht*, or 'The night of the broken glass'. The attacks were nominally in revenge for the shooting of Ernst vom Rath, a secretary at the German Embassy in Paris, by a Polish Jew. Chamberlain stated that he was 'horrified by the German behaviour to the Jews.' He then added, fatefully, 'There does seem to be some fatality about Anglo-German relations which invariably blocks every effort to improve them.' Resigned to raising the issue, he concluded, 'I suppose I shall have to say something on the subject tomorrow as there will certainly be a private notice question and it will be problem [sic] how to avoid condonation on the one side or on the other such criticism as may bring even worse things on the heads of these unhappy victims. It is clear that Nazi hatred will stick at nothing to find a pretext for their barbarities.'[12]

At the end of November, Chamberlain, Halifax and their spouses flew to Paris to shore up Daladier in the face of British government efforts to schmooze Italy and appease Germany. Chamberlain was impressed with the reception he received from the French people who were clearly as enamoured with him as their British counterparts: 'I drove in the first car with Daladier and the whole route from the station to the embassy was lined with cheering crowds … [I had] to tell the chauffeur to aller doucement (go slowly) so that the people might have some chance of looking at me.'

In Paris, Chamberlain's conversations with French ministers proved 'most satisfactory'. On the way back, at the behest of the King, he visited the Duke and Duchess of Windsor. Upon meeting the Duke in his 'modest apartment', Chamberlain was struck by how well he now looked, 'He had lost his harassed look and now the pouches under his eyes and the lines about the mouth and eyes had disappeared.' Before he left, the Duke said the Duchess would like to see him, 'Opening a door into the next room he called for "Darling". So Darling appeared very smartly groomed and got up and I guessed very nervous and anxious to please. I only stayed five minutes but came to the conclusion she was not my style!'[13]

The 4 December found Chamberlain working at Chevening House, the government's grace and favour country house in Kent. Referring to his critics as 'persistent and bitter', he told Ida, 'At my age and in my position there can be nothing more for me to want. Personal ambition therefore does not count. The only thing I care about is to be able to carry out the policy I believe, indeed *know*, to be right and the only distress that criticism or obstruction can cause me is it prevents my purpose.' He also told her that he was becoming exasperated with the dictators. On 30 November, Italy made public its long-held demands for the annexation of Nice, Corsica and Tunis in the belief, as Mussolini put it, that 'Sudeten methods' would bully the French into surrender. 'What fools the dictators are,' Chamberlain protested, 'After the Jews in Germany the Italians go and work up this ridiculous demonstration against France.' However, Chamberlain's forthcoming visit to Italy would, he believed, reign in Musso, 'But the fact that Mussolini sent word to us on Saturday that he would like to publish the date of the Rome visit today shows I think that it may be possible to keep him quiet between then and now.'[14]

On 1 December, John Anderson, who as Lord Privy Seal was in charge of air raid preparations, announced government plans for National Service in the House of Commons. These excluded plans for a compulsory national register but instead promoted voluntary registration pending a national recruitment plan to start in the New Year. 'But insufficient preparation has been done,' Chamberlain told Ida and, to get their message across, he proposed instead the radical course of following 'the Dictators in starting a Ministry of propaganda, though I would hope on far more better lines than theirs.' It was a familiar gripe. Chamberlain complaining about the limitations of being in charge of a democracy while trying to negotiate with dictators who did not have to balance competing political interests or deal with a critical press. Anderson also announced plans for an evacuation scheme, which was meant to show that the government had learnt the many hard lessons from the chaotic mobilisation it had tried in September 1938. 'Of course the crisis caught us unprepared,' Chamberlain told her, 'and in the rush of the sudden emergency many things went very wrong.'[15]

On 9 December, to escape from the pressure cooker environment of Number 10, Chamberlain slipped out and went in search of a very rare bird which had turned up on the lake in St James's Park in the depths of winter. Chamberlain's daily walks around the park with his wife Annie had become a habitual part of his routine and they were a vital way of dealing with the stress he was under. Chamberlain had been tipped off by his fellow ornithologist Gilbert Collett that a scaup *Aythya marila* had been seen there the previous day. The scaup was a rare sea duck that resembled, superficially, the black and white tufted ducks that were very common on the lake. However, Collett, with his expert eye, spotted that the bird's grey back and greeny black head, together with its lack of a distinctive tuft, marked it out from the 'tufties' as a scaup. It was a significant sighting in central London, especially as the wintering population of around 5,000 birds were almost wholly confined to coasts, with a few turning up each year on large, deep, inland waters, usually near the sea. St James's Park was neither deep nor near the coast and, to crown it all, was in the middle of one of the largest urban conurbations in the world (the scaup, then as now, was also the rarest breeding duck in Britain).

Despite his heavy workload on hearing of the scaup's presence, Chamberlain was determined to see it. Together with Annie, his Principal Private Secretary Cleverly and his exasperated personal bodyguard – for whom the Prime Minister's daily walks were a constant source of anxiety – he scoured the lake until he found it. A delighted Chamberlain, on getting back to Number 10, asked Cleverly to send a letter to Collett on his behalf:

Dear Mr Collett

The Prime Minister was greatly obliged to you for reporting the presence of the Scaup on St. James's Park lake. He looked particularly for it when he went for his walk this morning and I am glad to say that it was still on the water.

Yours very truly
O.S. Cleverly[16]

The sighting was so significant that *The Times* dedicated a piece on it the following week entitled 'From the Sea':

Last Friday morning the Prime Minister came to the breakfast table showing definite signs of excitement. "I have received information," he said (he did not add "from a reliable source"), "that a Scaup has arrived in St. James's Park. Don't you think we ought to go out and try to find it?" I must hasten to inform readers – if they do not already know – that the Scaup is a very rare bird that comes from the sea. It is, I believe, a white bird with black feathers and strange peregrinating habits.

The Prime Minister and Mrs. Chamberlain started from Number 10 on their joyful quest. No doubt he thought a bird from the sea would be likely to seek a body of water, and the deduction was correct. After a careful search the Scaup was discovered on the pond in St. James's Park. Later in the day when we saw Mr. Chamberlain in the House his face had assumed its normal seriousness. The flapping of wings over Tunisia could be heard, and he was back to the endless, thankless business of trying to maintain a measure of sanity in a mad world.[17]

After the excitement of seeing the scaup, the endless, thankless business of being Prime Minister in a mad world continued on 11 December, when Chamberlain found himself back at Chequers facing a barrage of hostility in the media over comments that his former minister, Duff Cooper, had made in Paris. Claiming the Munich agreement was a defeat for both England and France, Cooper also criticised Chamberlain's proposed visit to Rome. It was not just the dictators and the media who were depressing Chamberlain, 'What makes my position so unhappy however is not only the vagaries of dictators but the instability of my own party who seem to be all over the place.' As a result of his troubles at home and abroad Chamberlain was slowly but surely beginning to wonder how long he could survive.

To get away from it all, the following month Chamberlain went to Farnham Royal in Buckinghamshire, a royal hunting estate where he was meant to be shooting pheasants, but because he was so tired he couldn't hit any. 'This has not been a nice day, bitterly cold,' he wrote to Ida on 17 December, 'and the keeper was disappointed because the birds did not show well.' Complaining that it had been a 'pretty awful week', he said, 'Sometimes I feel that I wish democracy at the devil and I often wonder what P.M. ever had to go through such an ordeal as I.'[18] That Monday he had received thirty questions on foreign affairs, in addition to the ones addressed to him as Prime Minister. It was a clear sign that not only had appeasement come to define his foreign policy, it had also come to define his Premiership.

The Foreign Office questions were followed by 'two or three supplementaries', all in the hope of 'trapping me into some imprudent declaration and always with the object of injuring my foreign policy.' While Chamberlain felt that the opposition didn't gain much from these tactics, he believed their attacks were a gift to Dr Goebbels, Hitler's propaganda minister, 'To stir up more ill feeling on the other side.' Feeling particularly unsupported, he ruefully wrote, 'While S.B. [Stanley Baldwin] was Prime Minister he had me to help him, but I have no one who stands to me in the same relation and consequently I have to bear my troubles alone.' As a result, he had decided to use his precious holiday to make some changes to the junior ranks, but, he added, 'The material available is meagre in the extreme and I don't remember any time when there was so little promise among the younger men in the Government and on the back benches.'[19]

On the 13 December, Chamberlain had given the traditional annual speech to the Foreign Press Association, an experience, he told Ida, that had given him 'no end of worry'. Foreign affairs had now become the bane of his life, a situation made worse by knowing 'that every word you say will be analysed and dissected and that there are any number of people in various countries on the watch to make mischief.' Looking ahead, he had to make two more foreign affairs speeches in the House of Commons and was the guest of the lobby correspondents at a lunch where, 'I am expected to make a witty reply to the toast of my health. It is my one consolation that Thursday will close the House of Commons for a whole blessed month.' Annie was also counting down the hours as 'every day she is opening a bazaar or attending a reception or some social function.' If that wasn't bad enough, the correspondence flowing into Downing Street showed no signs of abating, 'Christmas cards and Christmas presents are pouring in often accompanied by such touching letters that one doesn't like to leave them unanswered.'[20]

Isolated, unsupported and increasingly besieged on all sides, Chamberlain retreated for his Christmas break to Hever Castle in Kent, the guest of the American millionaire William Waldorf Astor. His Christmas card for that year featured a full-page picture of the gleaming, silver Lockheed 14 aircraft that he had used on his famous trip to visit Hitler in Munich.[21] It was meant to signify his greatest triumph, but just three short months later the image and all it stood for had come to haunt him.

Chapter 16

A 'savage mistrust of the P.M.'s motives'

'A time to love and a time to hate, a time for war and a time for peace.'
Ecclesiastes 3:8

The year 1939 started with Chamberlain busy planning his trip to Rome to meet 'Musso' for his long-planned attempt to forge a partnership with the Italian dictator and drive a wedge once and for all between him and Hitler. 'I shall be very glad when this Rome visit is over,' he told Ida on 8 January, writing from Hever Castle, 'for it is evidently going to be not merely strenuous but very possibly anxious and difficult.' Despite his break at the castle, his mood had not improved, 'Everything seems to go against me (as usual, I feel inclined to say).' However, he refused to be downbeat, stating, 'Musso is most anxious for Anglo-Italian friendship to develop.' Some close to Chamberlain had been urging him to cancel the visit and instead make a grand alliance against Germany, 'In other words better abandon my policy and adopt Winston's!' he railed, 'Fortunately my nature is as Ll.G. [Lloyd George] says extremely "obstinate" and I refuse to change, but if anything happened to me I can plainly see that my successor would soon be off the rails and we should once more be charged with that vacillation which in the past has made other diplomats despair.'[1]

From 11-14 January, Chamberlain and Lord Halifax visited Rome, and despite staying three days, his conversation with Mussolini lasted less than three hours. To many observers this was a clear sign of where relations were heading, but Chamberlain again ignored the warning signals and instead took great solace from his reception by the Italian people. 'I hardly know where to begin my account of a truly wonderful visit,' he breathlessly told Hilda in a letter dated 15 January from Downing Street, 'At all the receptions the society men and women were extraordinarily cordial and all wanted to express their gratitude and appreciation many of them saying "You don't know how we *love* you".' While in Rome, Chamberlain and Halifax also met with King Victor Emmanuel III (1869-1947) and Pope Pius XI (1857-1939). 'We had a most interesting talk with the Pope who was much stronger and more vigorous than I expected',[2] he told his sister. The Pope was clearly suffering in silence for his faith as he subsequently died a month later, on 10 February.

On his return, Chamberlain gave a major speech in Birmingham, on 28 January, reiterating Britain's desire for peace, while declaring that rearmament was 'purely defensive'. Hitler responded two days later in a speech to the Reichstag, marking six years since he had taken power. In a long and rambling monologue he thanked Chamberlain for his willingness to reach an agreement over the Sudetenland, but, more ominously, stated that Nazi Germany would be prepared to fight a world war if the 'Jewish question' was not resolved. Reflecting on his Birmingham speech while staying at Chequers on 5 February, Chamberlain wrote to Hilda, 'What a power broadcasting is. I realise it because I have had letters from all over the country about my Birmingham speech saying "We listened sitting by our fireside" and then adding how much comfort or relief or inspiration it had given.'[3] Chamberlain was relying more and more on support from the public while turning a blind eye to the warning signs about Hitler.

The 19 February found Chamberlain at Chequers contemplating the impact on Britain of Franco's victory in Spain. Again he found himself at odds with the Foreign Office over the Spanish, as well as the Germans and Italians. 'The dislike they have of the totalitarian states is so strong that it will keep bursting out,' he told Hilda. Prophetically, he pointed out, 'There is no doubt that we are getting near to a critical point where the whole future direction of European politics will be decided.' To get away from politics, Chamberlain went to Chequers the following week to look for the first signs of spring. 'Your letter sounds spring like and here with a thrush singing in the garden the sun shining and the rooks beginning to discuss among themselves the prospects of the coming nesting season I feel as though spring were getting near,' he told Hilda. '[I'm] going about with a lighter heart than I have had for many a long day. All the information I get seems to point in the direction of peace and I repeat once more that I believe we have at last got on top of the dictators.'[4]

At the end of February, Chamberlain was still in high spring spirits and staying as the guest of the Astors (William Waldorf Astor 1879-1952 and Nancy Astor 1879-1964, the first female Member of Parliament) at their magnificent Cliveden home in Buckinghamshire. Here, on 26 February, he wrote to Ida, telling her about a speech he had given in Blackburn to record crowds. Over 600 had packed into the hall and another 3,000 gathered in the rain outside to hear him say that peace was within his grasp and that many Socialists were 'openly saying that the P.M. was right and that they wish him success.' Looking ahead, Chamberlain told Hilda he was accompanying the King and Queen on a visit to Birmingham, 'I have got to attend the annual meeting of the B.U.A. [Birmingham Unionist Association] there on the 17th and they have found out, confound them, that I shall be seventy next day.'[5]

On the 5 March 1939, Chamberlain wrote his weekly letter to his sister Hilda. He had given a speech the previous week recognising the new Franco government and had been attacked by the Labour leader, Clement Attlee, who, according to Chamberlain, described him as 'not only a Fascist in theory but a Dictator in practice'. However, Attlee had been criticised for his language and the government had acquitted itself well in the subsequent debates on air raid protection and national defence. More encouragingly, Chamberlain had accompanied the King and Queen on their visit to Birmingham, 'It was fortunately a fine day and the streets were lined everywhere by enthusiastic crowds.'

Following Attlee's onslaught, Chamberlain suffered a further savage attack, this time by the Chairman of the League of Nations, Gilbert Murray (1866–1957), in *The Times* newspaper. Murray was an outstanding scholar and a serial haranguer who had written or co-signed almost 300 letters to the editor of *The Times*. His eclectic topics ranged from Liberal politics and the League of Nations to improving the national diet and banning smoking in cinemas. In a letter dated 1 March, Murray said millions of young people had a 'savage mistrust of the P.M.'s motives', that Chamberlain's kind words are 'all for the oppressors; his unkind words for the sufferers,' and that he wanted to 'make money out of the agonies of others'. Chamberlain in turn made plain his disdain for Murray, telling Hilda, 'On the contrary I believe most of the young people today are grateful to me for saving them from war.'[6]

On 12 March, Chamberlain wrote to Ida that he was looking ahead 'to a big milestone, 'On Saturday is that portentous event, my seventieth birthday … Barring accidents therefore I ought to be good for at least one more Parliament after this, to exasperate and infuriate the Gilbert Murrays of this world.' But to deliver 'peace for our time' he needed his party and the British people to grant him a few more years at the top. He went on, 'One man told me that he had been doing a lot of speaking in different parts of the country … he had known five Prime Ministers but he had never known anything like the personal regard that was felt for me. Then he went on to say that at one meeting when he had been speaking of me and of father someone called out "Hurrah for the two Chamberlains". Whereat another voice cried "And don't forget the third". I liked that incident very much.'[7] The Chamberlain dynasty, culminating in Neville aged seventy, now held sway over British politics but events over the next few days would show only too clearly how tenuous that hold was.

On 14 March, in breach of the Munich agreement, Hitler sent German troops into Moravia and then Prague. In a Commons debate on Czechoslovakia on 15 March, Chamberlain was again attacked from all sides of the House, but there was a noticeable change in his tone, from one of insisting appeasement was right to one of disappointment and regret. However, he continued to defend the Munich agreement and declared he would never be deflected by others from his efforts to 'substitute the method of discussion for the method of force in the settlement of differences.' The next day Hitler occupied the remainder of Czechoslovakia by force and declared it the 'German Protectorate of Bohemia, Moravia and Slovakia'.

Increasingly isolated, Chamberlain wrote to Hilda on 19 March from Downing Street, thanking his sisters for their steadfast support and their 'sympathy and understanding in this black week.' Labour had tabled a debate about the Czechoslovakian crisis on 15 March. In response Chamberlain had hatched a plan for a four-power declaration signed by Britain, France, Russia and Poland to support each other in the case of further aggression, but it had been vetoed by the Poles, leaving him even more out on a limb. Despite his unpopularity in the Commons, he still had the support of the monarchy, stating, 'I had a long talk with the King tonight. He and the Queen had listened in on Friday and were thrilled. They approve enthusiastically.'[8]

The end of March saw Chamberlain at Chequers lamenting the ever-worsening political situation in Europe. 'From your letter I think you have realised that this has been a grim week though how grim even you couldn't know,' he wrote to Ida on 26 March, 'I think perhaps the climax came on Tuesday night when we attended the State Banquet at Buckingham Palace. No sooner did I arrive than Hore-Belisha came up and whispered "We have just got word that the Germans have mobilised twenty Divisions on the Western frontier".' On 21 March, German troops had occupied the Lithuanian port of Memel, claiming it back for Germany (who had occupied it up until 1919). Chamberlain wrote, 'You can imagine that with these things on my mind it was more than usually difficult to keep a smiling face. Nevertheless one of the Frenchmen did remark to me upon my bonne mine and appeared comforted by the fact that I was always "calme et soriant" (calm and smiling).'

Despite outward appearances, behind the calm smile Chamberlain was struggling to cope. He had taken a sleeping pill one night but assured Ida that it was a one off and that he had done without them ever since, 'And that is remarkable because I was much worried over the possibility of a surprise attack. It didn't seem to me in the least probable but with this fanatic you can't exclude entirely the conception.' Chamberlain then summed up Hitler's mindset perfectly, 'He might well say "This is life or death to my people: I am justified in breaking all unwritten or written rules if I can deliver a knock-out blow before the other fellow has had time to prepare".'[9]

Chamberlain now hoped for the best but increasingly feared the worst. He spoke with his army chiefs and had covertly posted soldiers with anti-aircraft guns and searchlights around London to watch the skies night and day. 'It all sounds fantastic and melodramatic,' he told Ida, 'but I cannot feel safe with Hitler. We are not strong enough ourselves and we cannot command sufficient strength elsewhere to present Germany with an overwhelming force. Our ultimatum would therefore mean war and I would never be responsible for presenting it.' It was pragmatic talk born out of realism, but it was also dangerously defeatist.

As dark, threatening clouds gathered over Europe, Hitler gave a major speech on Saturday, 1 April in the German port of Wilhelmshaven where he was launching the battleship *Tirpitz*. Defending German rearmament, he said his forces were not there to attack other countries, as long as they left Germany alone and it was not surrounded. The same day, Chamberlain wrote to his sister, Hilda, 'Well it has been another week of nightmares and momentous decisions. Halifax says all this is child's play compared to last September and of course he is right but all the same it is bad enough to destroy all one's peace of mind.'

In the Commons and in the press there were now increasing calls for conscription to counter the threat from Nazism, but Chamberlain's focus was elsewhere. Referring instead to Hitler's speech, he said, 'I thought it very significant that in that rambling ineffective speech, hastily thrust together at the last moment in great disorder of mind, he never even formulated a demand for Colonies, nor did he say a word to egg on Mussolini. After all I begin to wonder whether I shan't get away for my Easter fishing which had nearly faded out.' Referring to his Chequers retreat, he added 'It is wet foggy and gloomy here but oh so peaceful. I have had more trees planted, tulip trees walnuts and black walnuts and am planning for next year.'[10]

Parliament broke up for its Easter recess on Wednesday, 6 April and Chamberlain managed to get away for his fishing to Castle Forbes, a nineteenth-century country house near Alford in Aberdeenshire and the ancestral home of the Forbes family. However, the troubles of the world followed him and the holiday had to be curtailed. Writing to Ida on 9 April 1939, he told her, 'Your letter arrived at Castle Forbes just as we were leaving, so we read it in the train. In these days events come so quick that any letter becomes out of date before it can reach its destination.' Illustrating his point, two days earlier, on 7 April, Mussolini had invaded Albania, a country formerly part of the Roman Empire and which he had long coveted for its strategic importance in giving control of the Adriatic Sea. Always too forgiving of Mussolini, Chamberlain hoped it was a coup he could make 'look like an agreed arrangement' to 'raise as little as possible questions of European significance.' Unfortunately for him, Mussolini put together a huge force consisting of 100,000 men supported by 600 airplanes, so it looked to all the world exactly what is was; an invasion. Albania was rapidly overrun, its ruler, King Zog I, was forced into exile in Greece and the country was made part of the Italian Empire.

What didn't help matters abroad was the continual badgering he received at home in the House of Commons, 'By the two Oppositions and Winston who is the worst of the lot, telephoning almost every hour of the day. I suppose he has prepared a terrific oration which he wants to let off. I know there are a lot of reckless people who would plunge us into war at once but one must resist them until it becomes really inevitable.' In addition, Chamberlain had received 'several abusive telegrams from Communists yesterday and I see Mr Barnes of the Coops [1887-1974, Alfred Barnes, former Labour MP and Chairman of the Co-operative Party] is calling for my resignation.' Chamberlain's defence was again to contrast his popularity in the country with his standing in the House of Commons. 'On the other hand whenever I go the people collect in crowds to give me their good wishes and I don't believe that Hitler and Mussolini have shaken my position.'[11]

Despite the pressures of his role, Chamberlain continued to make time to study nature, 'This afternoon we went down to Kew to see the Magnolias, which were magnificent and the new Alpine house full of lovely tulips, fritillaries, saxifrages and irises. The Director took us round in such a way as to avoid being mobbed, but when we went to tea with him a card was brought in to ask if 5 newspaper photographers could take a picture! I suppose someone must have telephoned to them to tell them we were there. Downing St was packed from end to end as we drove off – all shouting Good Luck and Well Done.'

With Germany becoming ever more threatening towards Poland, Chamberlain was visited on 4 April by Józef Beck (1894-1944), the Polish Foreign Minister. Commenting on Chamberlain's ill-fated four power declaration, Beck said Poland did not want to be in any agreement with Russia in case it provoked Hitler 'to make an attack which otherwise he hoped it might still be possible to avoid'. On Russia, Chamberlain said he viewed her as a 'very unreliable friend with very little capacity for active resistance but with an enormous irritative power on others.' However, this was not the view of the opposition. 'Unhappily we have to strive against the almost hysterical passion of the Opposition egged on by Ll.G [David Lloyd George] who have a pathetic belief that Russia is the key to our salvation.'[12]

On Thursday 13 April, Parliament was recalled from its Easter recess to hear Chamberlain's account of the Italian invasion of Corfu and British guarantees towards both Greece and Romania. However, his critics in the House of Commons, including the opposition and Churchill, all demanded an alliance with Russia as a bulwark against German aggression. The debate left Chamberlain 'profoundly depressed and unhappy.' 'In fact,' he told Hilda two days later, 'I have been at the nadir all this week. The interruption of my holiday made it much worse than if I had never gone away and it cannot be denied that Musso has behaved to me like a sneak and a cad. He has not made the least effort to preserve my friendly feelings – on the contrary he has carried through his smash and grab raid with complete cynicism and lack of consideration.'

Chamberlain was finally coming to terms with the fact that he had been led on by Mussolini and that his policy of friendship towards Italy as a way of isolating Hitler had failed. It was a bitter blow. He concluded, 'Any chance of further rapprochement with Italy has been blocked by Musso as Hitler has blocked any German rapprochement.' However, stubborn as ever, Chamberlain refused to admit he had been mistaken. 'That does not show that I have been wrong as my partisan critics declare. The fruits can be seen in the consolidation of world opinion and in the improvement of the military position of ourselves and France.'[13]

By now, opposition attacks led by Clement Attlee, with Churchill often joining in, were beginning to wear down Chamberlain, despite his best efforts to win them over by sharing briefings on the European situation. 'I have done with confidences to the Labour Party,' he told Hilda, 'They have shown themselves implacably partisan and this game in which they have all the advantages of a truce and none of the disadvantages is too one-sided for me to go with it.' He went on to say that he had hoped for better from Winston but there was an 'acid undertone which brought many cheers from Labour benches and again I felt depressed when he sat down.' Chamberlain's explanation was that Churchill was still smarting from not being offered a key role in the government. He considered it a 'rotten debate unworthy of the House ... marked by frequent personal attacks on me to which I perhaps paid too much importance in my rather "edgy" condition. But it is hard when one is fighting against such odds abroad to continually be having to ward off attacks at home.'[14]

The media did not help. The *News Chronicle* had run a scare story about Chamberlain starting a new Mediterranean pact with Mussolini and then followed it with, 'A violent attack upon me for my obstinate faith in a man who could not be trusted.' So furious was Chamberlain that he sent for the editor and gave him a dressing down, after which the paper issued an apology the next day. Churchill had again let it be known that he would like a major role in government, either the Admiralty or as Lord President. But Chamberlain did not trust him and was unsure whether he would help or hinder the Cabinet. As a result, the following day he summoned Halifax to Chequers and, while walking through the woods, they discussed Churchill, conscription and a new Ministry of Supply for the Army. Resuming their talk in the afternoon, they were told that Roosevelt had made an appeal to Hitler and Mussolini to give guarantees to thirty countries that they would not invade them. In his letter to Hitler dated 14 April, Roosevelt wrote: 'Are you willing to give assurance that your armed forces will not attack or invade the territory or possessions of the following independent nations: Finland, Estonia, Latvia, Lithuania, Sweden, Norway, Denmark, The Netherlands, Belgium, Great Britain and Ireland, France, Portugal, Spain, Switzerland, Liechtenstein, Luxembourg, Poland, Hungary, Rumania, Yugoslavia, Russia, Bulgaria, Greece, Turkey, Iraq, the Arabias', Syria, Palestine, Egypt and Iran.'[15]

Chamberlain knew nothing beforehand of the letter but it was a gift to Hitler who would go on to parody it to roars of laughter in the Reichstag (Hitler's speech was, in fact, a masterclass in using mockery to mask ambition as he would go on to invade or attack over half of the listed countries). On Sunday 23 April, Chamberlain wrote to Ida from 10 Downing Street, asking, 'How are we to interpret all this? Perhaps Hitler has realised that he has now touched the limit and has decided to put the best face on it. But we won't take any chances.' He then told her, 'Look out for news on Wednesday afternoon.' This was his announcement three days later of a Military Training Bill, which, for the first time, introduced a six-month period of conscription for men aged 20 to 21.

Following his woodland walk with Halifax, he again mulled over bringing Churchill back into government. 'The fact is the nearer we get to war the more his chances improve and vice versa. If there is any possibility of easing the tension and getting back to normal relations with the Dictators I wouldn't risk it by what would certainly be regarded by them as a challenge.' The *Evening Standard* and other newspapers had been urging Chamberlain to bring Churchill back, a campaign Chamberlain resented. Summarising his power over them, he told Hilda, 'So I believe I can snap my fingers at Winston and Attlee and Sinclair [Archibald, leader of the Liberal party].'[16] It was a rash remark made out of frustration, and it said more about Chamberlain than his tormentors.

The end of April 1939 saw Chamberlain back at his beloved Chequers, writing to Hilda, 'As you supposed we did not find anything in Hitler's speech to prevent our coming down here last night … The trouble is that he finds it so easy to tear up treaties and throw overboard assurances that no one can feel any confidence in new ones from him and he has so managed his affairs as to create an atmosphere in which further discussion with him would command no support in this country.'[17] Hitler, an inveterate poker player, was running out of cards, but Chamberlain, in continuing to gamble on his policy of appeasement, had played a busted flush.

Chapter 17

An innate sympathy with Fascism

'I am for peace, but when I speak, They are for war.' Psalm 120:7

Chamberlain's answer to Hitler's intransigence was again to approach Mussolini, a relationship in which he had already invested so much but had yielded so little: 'From certain information which comes to me it would appear that Musso has been getting more and more irritated with Hitler ... I have a feeling that if he is now handled judiciously it might be possible to give the axis another twist and that this might be the best way of keeping Master Hitler quiet.' Pleased that his announcement about conscription had come out before Hitler's speech, he told Hilda that it was 'impossible to represent it as a reply or a refusal to respond to a peaceful gesture.'[1] On 27 April 1939 in Parliament a vote had taken place on his Military Training Bill, which had been approved by the Lords without a division and in the Commons by 376 votes to 145. It was a small but important victory.

Chamberlain also took heart from the the that fact negotiations were progressing to create an anti-German alliance, though not with Russia. 'I must confess to being deeply suspicious of her. I cannot believe that she has the same aims and objects that we have or any sympathy with democracy as such. She is afraid of Germany and Japan and would be delighted to see other people fight them. But she is probably very conscious of her own military weakness and does not want to get into a conflict if she can help it,' he told his sister. Russia was, according to Chamberlain, 'Thoroughly distrusted by everyone except our fatuous opposition.'

On 1 May, after reading the Sunday papers, which were full of stories of impending war, Chamberlain told Hilda in his weekly letter, 'I don't take such a gloomy view myself. I believe every month that passes without war makes war more unlikely and although I expect to have more periods of acute anxiety yet in cold blood I can't see Hitler starting a world war for Danzig [the Polish port with a German-speaking majority long claimed by Germany].' Once again, in the midst of great political challenges, it was to nature that Chamberlain turned to forget about politics, 'Sometime I must show you the enlarged photos I have had made of our best trees; they are most successful. I have got 6 boxes occupied by tits: one is sitting. I was going to see what else I could find but not in this weather!' Chamberlain also consoled himself that, for a man of his age, he was in remarkably good condition given the international situation, 'It is really astonishing to me that I keep so well, as everyone remarks ... [I] spent two hours in sawing cutting and carrying away various trees ... It was quite hard work but I felt none the worse for it and awoke this morning quite fresh and free from any stiffness.' The same was not true of Annie who, following a trip to Hull to open a bazaar, spent 'most of yesterday lying down in her parlour or in bed.'[2]

At the beginning of May, Chamberlain saw the King and Queen before their tour of Canada. He reassured the King that he thought nothing would happen in Europe while he was away, but in a letter on Sunday 7 May, confided to Ida, 'One can never exclude any possibility with the dictators.' The same day Italy said it would sign a military alliance with Germany which became known as the Pact of Steel. Despite this, Chamberlain still clung on to his belief that he could win 'Musso' over, telling Ida, 'The Italians evidently don't want Hitler to get them into a war. But I see that they have been forced to sign a military alliance and no doubt the Germans are doing all they can to nail them down.'[3]

A week later Chamberlain was entertaining at Chequers. On the Sunday morning he took his guests, who included the US ambassador, on a walk around the grounds. It was a chance for him to impress his visitors with his botanical knowledge, 'What a wonderful moment of the year it is,' he told Hilda on 14 May, 'The beeches and limes are nearly out but not quite full out. In Crows Close the ground is covered with forget-me-not which makes a shimmering blue carpet a little lighter in shade than the bluebells which are in other parts of the woods ... Tulips, daffodils and cowslips are all unusually good this year and I find a good crop of *Cephalanthera eurfolia* coming along [narrow-leaved or sword-leaved helleborine, a rare orchid whose Latin name is now *Cephalanthera longifolia*].' Chamberlain also told Hilda he was delighted to be handing over responsibility for the woodlands on the estate to the Forestry Commission, 'I have no doubt I shall get it through now and that we shall get rid of the rabbits and see the woods regenerated. It is quite a load off my mind but I *must* remain P.M. a little longer to see the scheme well under way. Besides I have a number of further planting schemes that I want to get done before someone else comes who will take no interest at all in the place.'[4]

On Sunday 21 May, Chamberlain wrote to Ida, updating her on negotiations with Russia and opposition attacks at home. It was a letter shorter than his usual ones as it was already well after midnight when he started it. Two days previously he had been mauled in the Commons on a debate over Russia, with Churchill warning that the government needed to get 'some brutal truths into their heads' in regards to the position with Germany, and Lloyd George criticising him for 'staring this powerful gift horse in the mouth.' On any alliance, he told her, 'It is all very well for Ll.G who was as vicious as ever to praise the dictators for their superior efficiency, but they have no press and no opposition to contend with or they would do no better than we.' He consoled himself by quoting the minutes from a leaked Labour Party Executive meeting, which stated, 'There had never been known such support for the Government as had been manifested in recent weeks and if there were a general election now it would spell disaster.' He finished by wishing her many happy returns for her birthday, commenting, 'We are all going so strong that we bid fair to rival Aunt Alice and G.H.K.[5] [Uncle George or George Hamilton Kenrick, who was then 89 years old but gravely ill].'

On 28 May, Chamberlain wrote to Hilda from Weir House in Alresford, Hampshire (the home of Sir Francis Oswald Lindley, a retired attaché at the Foreign Office), where he was spending the bank holiday fishing. Although he had forgotten, it was the second anniversary of him becoming PM:

> You say, I don't quite know why, that it is an "amazing fact". Well that's how I feel about it and I often think to myself that it's not I but someone else who is P.M. and is the recipient of these continuous marks of respect and affection from the general public who collect in Downing Street or at the station to take off their hats and cheer. And then I go back to the H. of C. and listen to the unending stream of abuse of the P.M. his faithlessness his weakness his wickedness his innate sympathy with Fascism and his obstinate hatred of the working classes and I say to myself This is the real thing, this is truly myself that I hear being misrepresented or misunderstood. In the end I believe I am neither unduly exalted by the one nor unduly depressed by the other, though like every one else I have my better and my worse moments.[6]

It was a brutal, if honest, character assessment, which pitched the love of the people against the vitriol of the House of Commons, with Chamberlain as ever caught in the middle.

Despite the slings and arrows of office, Chamberlain was in a 'happier mood'. Working with the ever-faithful Horace Wilson, he had managed to find a way of getting the Russians onside without signing a formal alliance. His answer was a declaration of intent to fulfil the British government's obligations under article XVI of the Covenant of the League of Nations. 'It really is a most ingenious idea,' he told Hilda, 'for it is calculated to catch all the mugwumps and at the same time by tying the thing up to Art XVI we give it a temporary character.' However, in reality it was a legal compromise that kept no one happy.

When it came to Hitler's fate, Chamberlain couldn't understand why the Jews hadn't assassinated him. It was a sentiment shared by much of Europe, as he was now threatening to invade the Polish port of Danzig, 'We are therefore still in the danger zone but I myself still believe that Hitler missed the bus last September and that his generals won't let him risk a major war now. But I can't yet see how the detente is to come about as long as the Jews obstinately go on refusing to shoot Hitler!' He signed off, 'I came here in time for lunch yesterday and before tea had landed eight fat trout. I must go out again now, I only wish my host would not insist on accompanying me together with a fellow guest!'[7]

Later that day, Sunday 28 May, Chamberlain received the sad news of the death of his Uncle George, the entomologist and natural historian who had taught him so much. A glowing obituary to George Kenrick was published in the *'Entomologists Record and Journal of Variation'* which mentioned his close relationship with Chamberlain[8]. George had been ill since the beginning of the year but his passing devastated Chamberlain who had lost his mentor and a great friend. It was the end of another great Chamberlain and an uncomfortable reminder of his own mortality.

Chamberlain's grief was cut short by more problems abroad, this time in the Far East. On 14 June, Japanese troops blockaded the British and French settlement at Tientsin in northern China after four Chinese men suspected of murdering the Japanese Federal Bank manager had fled there, claiming diplomatic immunity. The blockade, and the treatment of British settlers, caused a major diplomatic incident. 'Once more I ask myself whether any Prime Minister ever had to contend with such a series of critical events,' he told Hilda on 17 June, 'The behaviour of the Japs has been increasingly insolent and aggressive for a long time and the Tientsin incident is only the culmination of successive acts of provocation.' On the blockade, he commented, 'If the Americans would come in with us of course it would be all over directly. But I am sure they won't.' To add to his woes he was making no progress with the Russians, who were 'the most impossible people to deal with', and the French were quarrelling with 'every one with whom they ought to make friends, Italy, Spain, Turkey.' The Poles caused him great anxiety and the Germans had gone strangely quiet, 'Perhaps that is the most ominous of all. I can tell you I am glad to get away from it all for a few hours.'[9]

On Sunday 25 June, writing from his desk in Downing Street, Chamberlain was buoyed by how well a visit and major speech to Cardiff had gone, 'I have always regarded South Wales as an enemy stronghold but evidently I must revise that opinion for the welcome I get everywhere was quite sensational.' He had also met the King and Queen on their return from Canada, 'When I went to the Palace in the evening they both received me and gossiped away in great spirits about their journey for a long time before the Queen left us to do some business.' He finished on a note of personal triumph, '[P.S.] The Chequers Trustees have passed the Forestry Scheme. Hurrah.'[10]

The beginning of July marked another 'worrying and miserable week' for Chamberlain, telling Hilda, 'What with Japan and Russia and Danzig, I feel relieved that we have come through it without any development of an acute crisis.' In a letter dated 2 July he told her that foreign affairs had driven him to distraction but, 'Fortunately I continue to sleep and Horder [his doctor] and Miss Hultman [his physiotherapist] unite in certifying the satisfactory condition of my health in their respective spheres.' Progress was being made with Tokyo following the Tientsin incident, but Russia was proving to be unyielding, 'But things are not made easier by these constant assertions in the British and French press that we are on the point of concluding an agreement when in fact we have never been in sight of it.'[11] As for Danzig, he believed it was very difficult to see a way out but not impossible, provided that Hitler didn't really want war.

The following week was a quieter one, ruined only by further political machinations to get Churchill back into government and the prospect of his holiday being curtailed by Hitler. 'It is evident that Australia and South Africa are rather alarmed at the bellicose tone in the country,' he told Ida on Saturday 8 July, 'and they think as I do, that if Winston got into the Government it would not be long before we were at war. My impression is that August will be the difficult month and that once again Hitler will spoil my holiday. In the meantime I have sent a personal message of warning to Mussolini and it will be interesting to see how he reacts.'[12]

By mid-July, Chamberlain was back at Chequers, complaining this time about the state of the weather and the garden. Summer gales and rain storms were the order of the day and the garden was 'betwixt and between time when the poppies campanulas and delphiniums are over and the later summer flowers aren't yet out … I am sorry to see one or two more of my trees dead, but that will give something to do in the autumn if I am not more grimly employed.' Writing to Hilda on 15 July, he stated that he had refused to take Churchill into the Cabinet 'to please those who say it would frighten Hitler'. He continued, 'I have told Musso plainly that if Hitler tries to get it [Danzig] by force it will mean starting the European War to which he replies "Let the Poles agree Danzig goes to the Reich and I will do my best to get a peaceful agreed solution". But that is not good enough. That is just what we tried at Munich, but Hitler broke it up when it suited him. I doubt if any solution, short of war, is practicable at present but if the dictators would have a modicum of patience I can imagine that a way could be found of meeting German claims while safeguarding Poland's independence and economic security.'

It was an incredible turnaround. Despite a tacit admission that Munich had failed and that war was now likely, Chamberlain still clung on to the vain hope that a way could be found to appease Hitler. 'As always I regard Rome as the weak end of the axis and we should always be trying to bend it.' But increasingly, rather than bending the Italian dictator to his will, he was clutching at straws. His efforts elsewhere gave little cause for hope. An agreement with Russia continued to elude him, Chamberlain commenting wryly, 'I put as little value on Russia's military capacity as I believe the Germans do.' The situation with the Japanese also remained on 'tenterhooks' thanks to the 'ineptitude of our Foreign Office.'[13]

A week later, Chamberlain was close to despair again and 'sick of the perpetual attacks on me at home.' One thing was certain, he told Hilda, 'When I cease to be P.M. I shall have finished with politics. I would like to have long enough to see my policy through and I believe that if I am allowed I can steer this country through the next few years out of the war zone into peace and reconstruction. But an interruption would be fatal and I should have then to leave it to someone else to try some quite different line.' What kept him going was the thought of his holiday, but he and Annie had yet to agree where it would be. She was not relishing the long journey to northern Scotland, 'But I should get a more complete change of thought and mental rest there than anywhere else.'[14]

On Sunday 23 July, Chamberlain wrote to Ida, looking ahead to the summer break. He now expected to go to Loch More for his holiday, but was resigned to coming back to London early, 'if only to keep the press quiet'. But before then he still had two weeks left and Parliament was awash with conspiracy theories. He had heard that 'Winston and his group are plotting a conspiracy to set up a Council of State which should have the responsibility for summoning Parliament.' Chamberlain now believed that, despite Churchill's denials, he was plotting behind the scenes to remove him. Writing from Chequers, he signed off, 'We arrived here in soaking rain on Friday and I was much disappointed to find that Spot [Chamberlain's favourite Chequers dog] had had to go back to the vet as his foot had got bad again. I miss him dreadfully and keep looking for him and then remembering he is not here. Luckily Valerie [another Chequers dog] is here and she is nearly as good and helps me in my forestry operations.'[15]

The final weekend in July found Chamberlain at Chequers again, where he received Hilda's usual fortnightly letter. In it she had included an enclosure from M[ax?][16] Sichel, a German Jew who had written about Nazi persecution.

She had also flagged up stories that Hitler's health was not good. In response Chamberlain wrote:

> Your enclosure from M. Sichel is very interesting. I had no idea that Jews were still allowed to work or join such organisations as the Hitler Youth in Germany [Chamberlain was mistaken as Jews could not join the Hitler Youth, and by 1939 most had been driven out of professions though about a quarter still worked in more menial roles]. It shows, doesn't it, how much sincerity there is in the talk of racial purity. I believe the persecution arose out of two motives, a desire to rob the Jews of their money and a jealousy of their superior cleverness. No doubt Jews aren't a loveable people; I don't care about them myself – but that is not sufficient to explain the pogrom.[17] [Although Chamberlain's attitude towards the Jews would today be anti-semitic, at the time his view would have been more commonly voiced in British culture]. The stories about Hitler's health are no doubt current in Germany, and I daresay there is truth in the accounts of his moods of depression or exaltation. That would be characteristic of a paranoid. But it would be foolish to conclude from these symptoms that he has any organic disease. Still I did say when I returned from Munich that I could not imagine Hitler living to be an old man and I have often heard since that he himself does not expect to live long. So I cherish hopes that I may see what happens "after Hitler"! [Hitler would in fact live four and a half years longer than Chamberlain].

Chamberlain was now in the final week before the summer break. A vote of censure brought by the Labour Party on his refusal to increase the state pension had been defeated, the opposition accusing him of being the 'Artful Dodger' after he promised instead to set up an inquiry. However, the last week was going to be 'extra strenuous', with a debate on foreign affairs again dominating proceedings. On 11 July, as part of Britain's attempts to intimidate Hitler, over 100 RAF bombers had flown across France. Two weeks later over 250 did the same. Commenting on the show of strength, Chamberlain wrote to Hilda on Sunday 30 July, that he would not be surprised to hear about a big German military build-up near the Polish border, 'That is part of the war of nerves and no doubt will send Winston into hysterics. But to summon Parliament to ask questions and demand counter measures is to play straight into Hitler's hands and would give the impression that we are in a panic. But I warn you so that you may not be unduly agitated if you hear of fresh excursions and alarums [sic].'[18]

The fact that Chamberlain fully expected a massive German military build-up on the Polish border but considered it merely a game of nerves spoke volumes. Against all the odds he was still holding out for an agreement with Hitler: 'My critics of course think it would be a frightful thing to come to any agreement with Germany without first having given her a thorough thrashing to larn her to be a toad. But I don't share that view. Let us convince her that the chances of winning a war without getting thoroughly exhausted in the process are too remote to make it worthwhile. But the corollary to that must be that she has a chance of getting fair and reasonable consideration and treatment from us and others if she will give up the idea that she can force it from us and convince us that she has given it up.' But it was force, not fair and reasonable consideration, that drove Hitler.

Signing off as he often did when at Chequers, he told Hilda about his plans for the grounds and his love of nature:

> I get an extraordinary amount of pleasure and satisfaction out of my outdoor amusements here, especially in connection with trees. I have now completed my album of tree photographs which I will show you next time you are here; it looks fine. The spotted flycatchers brood is almost ready to fly and it is comic to see them standing up in their box. I got an interesting bird record in St. James's Park last Friday when I saw a heron flying up the lake with the gulls [this is one of the few instances where Chamberlain did not share the record of what he had seen in St James's Park with his fellow birder, Gilbert Collett; he was probably too busy]. I can't remember ever seeing one before. I miss my dog who is still staying with the vet awaiting a last operation on his foot.[19]

On 5 August 1939, Chamberlain was at Chequers bemoaning the weather as it was bucketing down with rain. As part of Britain's preparations for war, the first militia camps had been formed, leading him to conclude, 'The conditions are, I am told, too awful and things are not improved when a large number of the cooks who had volunteered for service calmly walk out saying this was more than they had bargained for.' As an army marches on its stomach this was a not a good sign. The last week in Parliament had been, as Chamberlain predicted, extremely strenuous. He had to speak to the House of Commons four times, 'I call that pretty rough on the P.M. in the last week of a very exacting session.' The press had been kinder to him though and he had easily defeated a Labour motion, supported by Churchill, that Parliament should reconvene on 21 August because of the crisis, by making the amendment a vote of confidence in himself.

To placate Churchill, Chamberlain had exchanged words with him before the vote and commented, 'He is so sensitive to criticism that he couldn't stand even my joking remark about a *tu quoque* [Latin: you also] when he said he couldn't trust my judgement … That is Winston all over. His are summer storms, violent but of short duration and often followed by sunshine. But they make him uncommonly difficult to deal with.'[20] To enable him to visit Loch More, a secure telephone line had been installed and an aeroplane was on standby. He boarded the 7.30am train north. War or no war, Chamberlain was not going to miss out on his fishing.

A week later, at the Duke of Westminster's shooting estate at Loch More, near Lairg, Chamberlain was relieved not to have been called back, but doubted he would get a second week of holiday. Writing to Hilda on 13 August he said, 'Things are working according to the plan which I told you of before you left England [Hilda and Ida had departed for Royat, in Auvergne, central France, on their holiday] and that, as you will remember, contemplated a period of strain about this time. I expect that the next two days will show whether or not a real crisis is coming.' The only disappointment had been the weather which 'could hardly have been worse from the fishing point of view,' but the storm clouds had finally lifted. He signed off, 'Today is a perfect day with blue sky and light clouds. The river should be in excellent order this sabbath – but by tomorrow it will be too low.'[21]

On 19 August, Chamberlain had a call from Downing Street saying that, due to the worsening crisis, he would have to cut short his precious holiday. It was a day earlier than he had intended but 'I have never enjoyed a carefree mind the whole time I have been here and have had a good deal of work sent up to me.' He had put off his return pending what was awaiting him in London but told Hilda and Ida there was no reason they should curtail their holiday 'but if at any time I think you ought to come back at once I will wire you the words "I agree".'[22]

On 23 August, Hitler stunned the world by signing the Nazi-Soviet Non-aggression Pact with his nemesis, Stalin. The secret part of the pact was the division of Poland, leaving the way clear for his planned invasion. On 27 August, writing to Hilda from Downing Street, Chamberlain said, 'Phew! What a week. One or two more like this one would take years off my life.' (the statement was grimly prophetic as Chamberlain would die just fourteen months later). 'Whether this be a war of nerves only or just the preliminary stages of a real war it takes very strong nerves to stand it and retain one's sanity and courage.'

On his return, the atmosphere in Downing Street was extremely tense and the place buzzed with rumours. The British Secret Service were continually sending reports 'of the most alarming character' from the Polish border. 'I don't know how many times we have been given the exact date and even hour when the Germans would march into Poland and the machinery started which must inevitably drag us into its cogs. Yet they haven't marched yet and, as always, I count every hour that passes without catastrophe as adding its mite to the slowly accumulating anti-war forces.'

Hitler's attitude to peace left him incredulous. 'The mentality of that extraordinary man would be incredible to anyone who had not seen and talked with him. I believe that in his excitement over the prospect of this Anglo-German alliance, the possibility of which has come upon him with a new force after the ease with which he brought off his Russian agreement, he has almost forgotten Poland! But we can't forget it and so for the moment we are no further advanced.' He signed off, 'We are not through the jungle; on the contrary the issue is still doubtful but on Friday the motto on my calendar was "Remember that the tide turns at the low as well as at the high level"!'[23]

At dawn on 1 September the tide of war didn't turn but swept all before it as German troops invaded Poland. An Anglo-French ultimatum demanding the immediate withdrawal of German troops was ignored. As a result, at 11.15 am on Sunday 3 September 1939, Chamberlain broadcast to the nation that a state of war existed between Britain and Germany. He said, 'You can imagine what a bitter blow it is to me that all my long struggle to win peace has failed. Yet I cannot believe that there is anything more or anything different that I could have done and that would have been more successful.'

Chapter 18

Speak for England

'Fear not, for I am with you' Isaiah 41:10

On the night of 3-4 September, ten Whitley bombers from Numbers 51 and 58 squadrons dropped a personal leaflet from Chamberlain to the German people over Bremen, Hamburg and the Ruhr.[1] Written in German it was entitled 'Warning! A message from Great Britain':

> German Men and Women: The Government of the Reich have, with cold deliberation, forced war upon Great Britain. They have done so knowing that it must involve mankind in a calamity worse than that of 1914. The assurances of peaceful intentions the Führer gave to you and to the world in April have proved as worthless as his words at the Sportpalast last September, when he said: "We have no more territorial claims to make in Europe" … You, the German people, can, if you will, insist on peace at any time. We also desire peace, and are prepared to conclude it with any peace loving Government in Germany.[2]

The leaflet was Chamberlain's attempt to explain to the German people why he had been forced by events to declare war on Germany and that he was willing to negotiate with any 'peace loving Government' or one not led by Hitler. In September alone, twenty million leaflets with five different messages would be dropped over Germany as Chamberlain sought to justify his actions and win over the German people.

Writing a week after he had declared war on Germany, Chamberlain said to his sister Ida, 'It is only a fortnight since I wrote to you last but it seems like seven years. In such days of stress and strain one loses all sense of time. One day is like another and Sundays are only more trying than other days – and life is just one long nightmare.'[3] During the incendiary debate in the House of Commons on 2 September, as the acting Labour leader Arthur Greenwood, rose to give the opposition's response, Leo Amery – who Chamberlain had passed over for a job in government – shouted out to Greenwood 'speak for England', implying that Chamberlain did not. Worse still, some of his colleagues in government used the opportunity to mount a challenge to his leadership, which petered out but hurt Chamberlain.

Despite the declaration of war, peace negotiations had been going on behind the scenes through an intermediary. Chamberlain still believed that Hitler wanted a peaceful solution, claiming that, at the last moment, 'Some brainstorm took possession of him – maybe Ribbentrop stirred it up – and once he had set his machine in motion he couldn't stop it. That, as I have always recognised, is the frightful danger of such terrific weapons being in the hands of a paranoiac.' Mussolini had also intervened, proposing a revision of the Treaty of Versailles, while France had vacillated and demanded another forty-eight hours before declaring war, 'So we postponed our ultimatum and they advanced theirs.' Then he wrote to Ida, matter-of-factly, 'And so the war began,' adding, 'after a short and troubled night, and only the fact that one's mind works at three times its ordinary pace on such occasions enabled me to get through my broadcast, the formation of the War Cabinet, the meeting of the House of Commons and the preliminary orders on that awful Sunday which the calendar tells me was this day a week ago.'[4]

The nine-man War Cabinet that had been formed that fateful Sunday evening had included Churchill, who had gone back to his old haunt, the Admiralty. Now that war had been declared, and despite all Chamberlain's reservations, the party would have accepted nothing less for the man who had come to symbolise standing up to Hitler. Appeasement had been replaced by defiance. Also in the War Cabinet was the indispensable Halifax as Foreign Secretary, Simon at the Exchequer, Hoare as Privy Seal, Chatfield as Coordination of Defence, Wood in charge of Air, Hore-Belisha at the War Department and Hankey as Minister without Portfolio. 'Since then,' he told Ida, 'although I have had some dreadful anxieties, especially during one sleepless night, the tension has actually decreased and I have occasionally times, perhaps an hour or even more, when there has been nothing for me to do.' There had been false air raids while Poland was 'being rolled up much faster than our people had anticipated but on the West the war cannot have said to have begun.' Chamberlain was now preparing for 'a three years war' and was next going to see the French Premier, Daladier, 'Once again I think the moment for a mildly spectacular move on my part has come.' He went on, ruefully, 'While war was still averted, I felt indispensable for no one else could carry out *my* policy. Today the position has changed. Half a dozen people could take my place while war is in progress and I do not see that I have any particular part to play until it comes to discussing peace terms – and that may be a long way off.'

What kept him going was again the support of the public. 'We are getting a great number of very wonderful letters and many of them express the writer's sympathy with us even though they often report that their sons or husbands have been called up.' Ida had written that she hoped he didn't think that all his efforts to secure peace had been in vain. He replied, 'Indeed I don't think so and have said so. It was of course a grievous disappointment that peace could not be saved but I know that my persistent efforts have convinced the world that no part of the blame can lie here. That consciousness of moral right, which it is impossible for the German to feel, must be a tremendous force on our side.'[5] For security reasons the Cabinet had agreed a rotating policy under which only three of the nine would remain in London each Sunday. Chamberlain commented, 'By this arrangement I shall have twenty-four hours away two Sundays out of three and I expect I shall mostly spend them here [Chequers].'

Sunday 17 September, exactly two weeks after war had been declared, found Chamberlain at Chequers admiring the garden. 'The rose garden outside my window is full of colour and one cannot believe in this marvellous silence and stillness that we are at war,' he told Hilda. 'It certainly is an immense boon to have this place to come to occasionally.' They had entertained guests, including his daughter, Dorothy, and her husband, Stephen, his son, Frank, and the Halifaxes. Frank had turned up looking very smart in his Royal Warwickshire Regiment uniform and told Chamberlain that his field artillery battery was being sent to France, thus causing 'fresh anxieties for his parents'. In the Commons Chamberlain claimed Britain had destroyed six or seven German submarines. German propaganda had hit back, claiming that Churchill had sunk the liner *Athenia*, with the loss of 112 lives, including 28 Americans, in order to bring pressure on the US to enter the war. Goebbels had also released a cartoon of Chamberlain standing over a dead German woman with the caption, 'As a result of England's blatant support for Poland this German woman was tortured and murdered by inhuman Polish beasts in Bromberg. How do you feel, Herr Chamberlain?' Seeing the cartoon, Chamberlain told his sister that it 'revolted common sense and decency.'[6]

Chamberlain also updated Hilda on his flying visit to Daladier, the French Prime Minister. He had left his house at 8.30am on a rather 'dirty morning', arriving an hour later at a secret location outside Paris. 'The plane swayed and bumped a good deal but it got smoother as we approached the other side and the only member of the party who was actually sick was the steward!' The meeting had been very cordial and there had been complete agreement on the need to resist any planned German attack in the west. 'Moreover I think it did a lot of good throughout Europe to know that the Supreme Council had met and my flight (at my advanced age!) was highly approved here. Dorothy says the comment made to her was "What a sport!".'

In Cabinet he was getting on better with Churchill, but found that he talked a lot and generally did not stay on theme. He was also writing long letters to Chamberlain: 'As we meet every single day at the War Cabinet this would seem unnecessary, but of course I realise that these letters are for the purpose of quotation in the Book that he will write hereafter. Hitherto I haven't answered them, but the one I got yesterday was so obviously recording his foresight and embodied warnings so plainly for the purposes of future allusion that I thought I must get something on the record too which would have to be quoted in the Book.'[7]

In Britain, the evacuation of children from the towns and cities to the countryside had begun, a huge logistical exercise that separated families and produced some shocking stories. 'Dorothy heard of a child who wrote home "There are no bugs in this house and we have got rid of all our fleas", another who had never before seen a bed made up with sheets and didn't know how to enter it, others who had never sat up to a table to have tea.' These reports, and what he saw for himself as he travelled around the country, moved Chamberlain greatly. 'For the rest of my life I mean to try to make amends by helping such people to live cleaner and healthier lives,' he told Hilda, 'It certainly is a disappointment that all the care and money spent in the schools has not produced a better result but however bad conditions are I am still convinced that they are infinitely better than they were 20 years ago.'[8]

The 23 September found Chamberlain dealing with a 'tiresome catarrhal attack' and a 'quarrelsome' Commons. He, like everyone else in the country, had been busy speculating what Hitler would do next when, suddenly, the war became real with the large loss of life following a German submarine U-29 torpedoing the elderly aircraft carrier HMS *Courageous* on Sunday 17 September 1939. 'The loss of all these men in the Courageous weighs on my mind,' he told his sister, 'but I shall do as I always have done, go for what I believe to be the right course and risk the consequences.'

To try to relax, he and Annie had headed to Kew Gardens where they were escorted by their old friend, the director Arthur Hill. 'I enjoyed it very much, and not least the greenhouses. The number of extraordinary plants at Kew always amazes me and I never go there without learning something new. This afternoon we are going to the Zoo. I have received some magnificent dahlias named after me. The blooms are over nine inches across, the colour a mixture of yellow mauve and pink which is really very beautiful. Shall I ever grow flowers again?'[9] It was a melancholy line but it hinted that Chamberlain already knew that his time was limited.

On the morning of Sunday 1 October, Chamberlain attended the National Day of Prayer service at Ellesborough Church, near Chequers, then spent the afternoon trimming elders and planting trees in Crows Close. An Emergency War Budget had been announced on 27 September, resulting in a sharp rise in income tax, from 5s. 6d. (27.5p) in the pound to 7s. 6d. (37.5p) in the pound, an Excess Profits Tax designed to curtail wartime profiteering from armaments contracts, and increased taxation on beer, spirits, tobacco and sugar. Describing it to Hilda, he said it was, 'terribly stiff ... but we should begin now while the going is good.' Two days later the German-Soviet Boundary and Friendship Treaty was signed, carving up Poland. Commenting on the conduct of the war, he told his sister, 'The Germans are lying hard about the U-boat campaign.' As evidence he cited their false claim to have sunk the aircraft carrier *Ark Royal* when instead the British had destroyed six or seven of their submarines. 'One commander who we captured is such a nervous wreck that we are sending him back to Germany "pour encourager les autres",' he quipped.[10]

On Friday 6 October, Hitler addressed the Reichstag and proposed an Anglo-German conference, a move Chamberlain rejected as the Germans were 'not yet (being) sufficiently convinced they can't win'. His postbag had been dominated by people wanting to stop the war, the result of a letter-writing campaign organised by the Peace Pledge Union, run by Anglican clergyman 'Dick' Sheppard, and the Peace Council, run by the Bishop of Chelmsford. The letters were, according to Chamberlain, along the lines of 'You stopped war before, surely you can find a way out now, before we are pushed over the precipice'. The difficulty was that with the declaration of war there was now no turning back.

Chamberlain's answer was to replace appeasement with his new policy of containment, 'Hold on tight. Keep up the economic pressure, push on with munitions production and military preparations with utmost energy, take no offensive unless Hitler begins it.' He then added the rather amazing statement, 'I reckon that if we are allowed to carry on this policy we shall have won the war by the Spring.' What frustrated Churchill so much about Chamberlain was he required the unanimous consent of the Cabinet before taking military action. By contrast, Chamberlain believed Churchill was 'enjoying every moment of the war,' but he was 'prudent enough against risking our air force on operations which would not be decisive.' Instead, he told Hilda, 'We should keep it in reserve and go on adding to it till the decisive moment arrives.'

The press had not been helpful in keeping his Cabinet united behind him. Some of the more left-wing papers were calling for Churchill to become Prime Minister following a well-received broadcast on the state of the war he made on 1 October. Chamberlain had continued to receive long letters from Churchill, 'The latest of these went so far and looked so like a document for the Book that I resolved to put an end to it. I sent for him and had a very frank talk.' As a result, Churchill, who 'neither knows his own motives or sees where his actions are carrying him,' had acquiesced and had been 'extra friendly ever since.'[11]

Sunday 15 October, found Chamberlain at Downing Street having grave doubts about whether to carry on following the torpedoing of the elderly battleship *Royal Oak* by the German submarine U–47. On the night of 13–14 October, the U–47 skilfully sneaked into the Royal Naval base at Scapa Flow and avoiding the elaborate underwater defences, sunk the *Royal Oak* with the loss of 834 crew, many from drowning. It was a huge propaganda victory for the Nazis. On its return the U-boat was met by ecstatic crowds and Hitler personally gave its commander, Günther Prien, the Knights Cross of the Iron Cross, Germany's highest award for bravery. What made it worse was that Scapa Flow, Britain's main naval base, was deemed to be impregnable. Referring to the sinking a couple of days later in Parliament, Churchill said, 'It is still a matter of conjecture how the U-boat penetrated the defences of the harbour. When we consider that during the whole course of the last war this anchorage was found to be immune from such attacks, on account of the obstacles imposed by the currents and the net barrages, this entry by a U-boat must be considered as a remarkable exploit of professional skill and daring.'[12]

Rather than admiring the skill and daring of the U-boat commander, Chamberlain told Hilda, 'I do hate and loathe this war.' He bemoaned, 'I was never meant to be a War Minister and the thought of all those homes wrecked with the Royal Oak makes me want to hand over my responsibilities to someone else.' He damned Hitler, saying, 'We have to kill one another just to satisfy that accursed madman. I wish he could burn in Hell for as many years as he is costing lives.' His sole consolation was the view of the Downing Street garden out of his window, which looked beautiful after some rain the previous night. 'I see the drops of water still hanging from the twigs of the lime tree outside my window. It has lost nearly all its leaves now but it has been a constant joy all this week. I don't think I have ever seen anything in that way more beautiful than those red gold leaves on which we looked down from A's bedroom window.'[13]

One advantage of the bad weather, Chamberlain predicted, was that it made an attack in the west more difficult. 'I still retain my skepticism about any major attack [but] ... the soldiers are all against me. They think an attack is imminent.' Chamberlain had rejected Hitler's offer of an Anglo–German conference in a speech on 12 October, Hitler cleverly replying the British had been offered peace but chosen war. Despite this, Chamberlain was pleased with his speech, 'I must say Winston was most helpful not only in suggestions of phrases etc but also in his ready agreement with suggestions from others particularly myself that I did not think he would like.' To try to improve their relationship Chamberlain had dined with him the previous Friday and afterwards Churchill had shown him around the Admiralty room. 'There we saw plotted out the hourly movements of convoys, submarines, anti-submarines and the hunt that is going on for the raider in the S.Atlantic [referring to the *Graf Spee* which had sunk nine ships in two months in the South Atlantic, to the chagrin of the Royal Navy].'

To escape the war, Chamberlain visited Richmond Park on 14 October where, to his delight, he saw 'a green woodpecker as we strolled about.' He had also been 'methodically reading through all Shakespeare's comedies – one must have something to take one's mind off these perpetual war problems and the unending nagging of the Press and House of Commons.' A 'splendid' letter from his son, Frank, had also arrived to add to his reading list. 'He is in charge of two 4.5's [Field Guns] the only officer there. He sleeps in a dug out and is thoroughly enjoying himself besides being in the best of health. He finds life much more interesting than when he spent it in the service of the I.C.I.' At least one Chamberlain was having a good war.[14]

On 22 October, Chamberlain wrote to Ida, predicting 'a fresh peace offensive'. Hitler, he surmised, wanted a way of keeping his conquests without a major war, 'I cannot see how he can get a smashing victory and the attempt whether successful or unsuccessful would entail such frightful losses as to endanger the whole Nazi system.' Instead, he thought the Germans would wear down the British by 'boredom and impatience of controls and restrictions that irritate the more because they are not accompanied by the fear of death.' Whatever Hitler had in mind, boring the British into submission probably wasn't on his agenda.

In trying to second guess Hitler's next move, Chamberlain continued to dismiss an attack in the west, despite receiving daily updates to the contrary from his Chiefs of Staff and a steady stream of reports from the British Secret Service. His dismissive thinking was more reminiscent of the man in the street rather that the man in charge of the country. Comparisons with the First World War were also specious, but it didn't stop him making them, 'It must be admitted that in these first seven weeks our own losses of men have been insignificant compared with 1914 when our expeditionary force was decimated and I believe fourteen big warships lost. But the disasters to Royal Oak and Courageous are pretty heart breaking when you come down to the individual family or home and neither of them ought to have happened.' This had been powerfully brought home to him by the death of a close relative of one of his staff, 'Card lost a nephew in the Royal Oak, a fine boy and an only son. If we can achieve our purpose without a holocaust, what a relief!'[15]

The House of Commons continued to be the bane of his life, getting 'more and more ill-tempered and unreasonable.' In response, he had approached the

Chief Whip about limiting sittings in wartime, 'D. Margesson [Henry David Margesson, 1st Viscount Margesson, 1890-1965], will not give me any hope of getting rid of it before the middle of December but he does hope to cut it down to two days a week.' Chamberlain would not miss it, writing, 'You have no idea what a relief it is to think the House is not sitting for although I have taken no part in the tiresome debates that have been going on I have to be on the bench every day at question time and to be thinking in between whiles of how to ward off opposition attacks on the Govt for doing necessary but unpopular things.'

One compensation for having to put up with the troublesome Commons was personal access to the King and Queen. 'Annie and I went and had lunch with the King and Queen last Thursday. There were only the four of us and luncheon was served in what is really a sort of boudoir. It was all very simple and pleasant and we both enjoyed it. I see the King twice a week regularly now unless he is away, but I don't get so many opportunities of seeing the Queen who preserves all her charm and intelligence.' Chamberlain signed off by saying that another new book about him had appeared entitled *Neville Chamberlain: Man of Peace* by Derek Walker Smith, 'Annie reports that it is a very poor affair of scissors and paste without perspective or proportion but there is a good review in the Sunday Times by Hadley, the Editor.'[16]

On Tuesday 24 October, Hilda received a letter, unusually not from Chamberlain but from Annie, eulogising her husband, 'Neville is simply marvellous the way he keeps going,' she wrote, 'Much as one hates for him that this War should have come while he is Prime Minister, I rejoice all the time that he is there with his wise, never-tiring mind.' Like her husband, she had clearly developed a low opinion of the House of Commons, 'I simply do not know how he keeps his patience and balance when I go down as I sometimes do and listen to the Questions and the Labour Party's opposition afterwards. It is incredible that they don't seem to realise that a war is going on ... The majority of the Back Benchers behave just like schoolboys and you can see them grinning at each other whenever they think that one of their leaders has scored a point.'[17] Annie was not only his rock, she had now become his cheerleader.

On Saturday 28 October, Chamberlain wrote to Hilda from Chequers, again suffering from gout but sympathising with his sisters, who had been 'bothered by billeting'. It was, he supposed, 'in connection with the militia who are being called up for training and for whom camps cannot be built fast enough.' The war had now come home to the village of Odiham, with Chamberlain commenting scornfully, 'More marks against Hitler.'

Sunday 5 November, was Chamberlain's turn to stay in the capital so he had written to his sister from 10 Downing Street. The day before, he had again headed off to Richmond Park for a spot of birdwatching. 'It is extraordinary how people recognise one even where they couldn't be expecting you ... I was plagued to death with cars stopping for their occupants to stare, pedestrians and motorists waving their hands and even calling out their good wishes, and of course the ubiquitous autograph hunter,' he told Ida. 'There are still a lot of tales going round about the invasion of Britain,' he confided to his sister, adding sarcastically, 'Followed by the flight and suicide of the Prime Minister.' To Chamberlain's ears, it was all 'very fantastic', and could only become a reality if the Germans occupied Belgium and Holland, the chances of which he thought 'remote'.[18]

By the 19 November, Hitler still had not invaded Holland. Chamberlain noted in his letter to Ida, '[He] can't keep his armies "mounted" indefinitely and each day that goes by, renders his chance of success more uncertain.' Two days previously the Supreme War Council had met, with the French premier, Daladier, and his Chief of Staff, Gamelin (Maurice, French Army General, 1872-1958), visiting Chamberlain to agree a plan of defence against any unexpected attack against Belgium. 'I am told that Army officers are disgusted by his [Hitler's] intolerable brutality,' he told his sister. 'He is said to have shocked them by the way he gloated over the destruction and sack of Warsaw – and I guess it takes a lot to shock a German Army officer.'[19]

A week later, Chamberlain had at last recovered from his gout and, though still in pain, was able to resume his beloved daily walks around St James's Park. The war had not been going well, with the loss of several ships, notably the SS *Rawalpindi* in a fire fight with the German battleships the *Scharnhorst* and *Gneisenau*. By contrast, a meeting the previous week with the 1922 Committee had, he told Hilda, gone very well with nearly 200 MPs attending who gave him a wonderful reception. On 3 December 1939, Chamberlain wrote to Ida that 'well-informed sources' had told him that an attack on Holland was imminent today, but added, 'We have been given definite dates for offensives on so many previous occasions ... I have ceased to pay any serious attention to them.' Sticking to his belief that Hitler would not attack because any serious fighting would entail 'heavy losses whether among soldiers or civilians', Chamberlain instead thought Hitler would continue with minelaying and torpedoing British shipping.[20]

On 30 November, the international outlook became even bleaker when Stalin invaded Finland. Commenting to his sister, Chamberlain said it seemed 'to have provoked far more indignation than Hitler's attack on Poland,' and it had 'added a great deal to the general feeling that the ways of dictators make things impossible for the rest of the world.' On the home front, the Germans had laid so many magnetic mines that the Thames estuary and much of the east coast had been closed to shipping following the loss of twenty-seven ships. 'We are busy experimenting with his magnetic mine,' Chamberlain told Ida, adding, 'All the same this convoy business together with the diversion of cargoes to new ports does slowdown the passage of ships to an alarming extent.'[21]

Following the mounting loss of ships, the government had added sugar and meat to the rationing list, along with bacon and butter, which were already restricted. Chamberlain's rather novel answer to the food shortages was that people should keep communal pigs. 'But it certainly would want some enthusiastic and capable body to organise it. Why not the W.I.?' he mused, noting that he and Annie were getting tired, 'I hope we get a bit of a recess soon; it will be good for both of us.'

On 10 December, Chamberlain was joined at Chequers by his wife, and daughter Dorothy. Bemoaning a 'terrible week' in front of him, including a secret session in the House, he told Hilda that he would fly to France on Friday and 'spend a long and strenuous weekend with British and French troops, probably finishing up with a Supreme War Council in Paris.' After this, 'barring unforeseen developments in the war situation,' he was looking forward to an easier time. With the consent of the opposition, he had finally secured a month's Parliamentary recess, 'which is a heaven sent relief.'[22]

Inviting both sisters to spend Christmas Day with him at Chequers, Chamberlain looked forward to a well-earned break, but first had to visit France and sign off his Christmas card. His previous one was made of high quality paper and prominently featured the sleek Lockheed Super Electra 14 in which he had made his historic trips to Germany. One year on and the country was at war so, in keeping with the mood of austerity, his card was cheaper and had no picture. On the front it simply featured the words 'Christmas 1939' accompanied by a red ribbon. Inside was a quote from Shakespeare's *Henry VI, Part 2, Act 4, Scene 2:* 'Now show yourselves men; 'tis for liberty.' On the face of it the quote was simply about rallying the nation, but the underlying message would not have been lost on anyone who had bothered to look up the whole passage:

And you that love the commons, follow me.
Now show yourselves men; 'tis for liberty.
We will not leave one lord, one gentleman:
Spare none but such as go in clouted shoon;
For they are thrifty honest men, and such
As would, but that they dare not, take our parts.

On 15 December, he flew to France on a four-day visit to review the troops and Allied war plans. It was an exhausting trip and he missed the creature comforts he had come to take for granted as Prime Minister, particularly his bath. He had ended up sleeping on a railway siding and the cold had got to him. It was all a far cry from Chequers. After reviewing the Maginot Line (named after the French Minister of War, André Maginot, it was a line of connected concrete fortifications, obstacles and defensive positions), he had eventually flown home. Reflecting on the visit, he told Ida, 'It sickened me to see the barbed wire and pill boxes and guns and tank obstacles, remembering what they meant in the last war. I was glad when it was over.'[23]

On 22 December, Annie recorded an eight-and-a-half-minute appeal at the BBC, dedicated to the women of France. It was broadcast on New Year's Eve. She finished, 'My Friends, it is the certainty of the justness of our cause, which gives to every one of us, whether we be French or English, that spiritual faith which sustains us. Our faith is in God, who has given us those words, so full of comfort: "Fear not, for I am with thee".'[24] It was a skilful piece of propaganda, designed to rally the women of France in the face of an anticipated German attack, prop up her husband the Prime Minister and pave the way for the British Expeditionary Force. The problem was that her husband had not put his faith in God but in his own ability to second guess Hitler's next move.

The year ended with great disappointment when the family break that Chamberlain had so much been looking forward to had to be abandoned following another flare up of his gout. It was a painful end to a very challenging year, which had been characterised by too many days of 'stress and strain'.

Chapter 19

A fine patriotic spirit in wartime

'And you will hear of wars and rumors of wars. See that you are not
alarmed, for this must take place, but the end is not yet'. Matthew 24:6

The first weekend of 1940 found Chamberlain back at his beloved Chequers,
telling Ida that the gout was 'the least of my troubles this week' as he was
grappling with changes at the War Ministry. He had been looking for an
opportunity for some time to move the War Minister, Leslie Hore-Belisha,
because of a personality clash with Viscount Gort, the Commander-in-Chief
of the British Expeditionary Force. 'In wartime nothing could be worse than
perpetual friction and want of confidence between the Secretary of State and
the C.in C. in the field,' he wrote to Ida on 7 January.

Hore-Belisha, as well as being a controversial War Minister, was also the only
Jew in the Cabinet and as a result had come under fire from the British Union
of Fascists, with Oswald Mosley calling him a 'Jewish warmonger'.[1] He had also
been remorselessly targeted by the Nazi press who disparagingly referred to him
as '*Ein Jude Kriegsminister*'. Chamberlain's plan was instead to offer Hore-Belisha
a new role as Minister of Information. He consulted Lord Halifax, who thought
he was not right for the post but 'said nothing about his being a Jew, this point not
having occurred to him.' Churchill, on the other hand, thought he would do well,
but following a Cabinet meeting, Chamberlain reported, 'To my consternation
Edward [Lord Halifax] now declared that he was unhappy about the appointment
and he thought it would have a bad effect on the neutrals both because H.B. was
a Jew and because his methods would let down British prestige.'[2]

So at the last moment Chamberlain changed his mind and instead offered
Hore-Belisha the Board of Trade. 'It was a most painful interview. It came as a
complete surprise to H.B. and it was evidently a shattering blow.' In response
Hore-Belisha resigned from the government, later blaming the move on
prejudice and anti-semitism. Chamberlain, however, was more concerned about
the fuel it would provide to his many critics, 'Of course the enemies of the
Govt will do their best to exploit the incident … The friction is due to personal
incompatibility and not policy or administration.' He signed off, saying he had
to 'get back to this vile speech that I must deliver on Tuesday.'[3]

The next Saturday at Chequers, Chamberlain was enjoying spending time with his children and playing with his grandchildren. He noted with some satisfaction that the 'H.B. sensation had died down as quickly as it began.' His 'vile speech' had been delivered on 9 January at the Mansion House, where he had reviewed the military position and extolled ever greater sacrifices on behalf of the population to fight the Nazis. Reflecting on his speech, he told Hilda that it had 'a wonderfully good reception both at home and abroad'. Only in Germany was the speech deemed 'so poor as to need no reply.'[4]

The following day, Sunday 14 January, he continued the correspondence, ruefully reflecting, 'There is no peace for the wicked.' Belgium had been on a state of high alert following reports of a Nazi invasion and Churchill had rung him up four times the previous day so he had reluctantly decided to go back to Downing Street. He remained 'very skeptical about this German invasion,' rumours of which had been fuelled by the discovery of some papers on two downed German airmen, a story Chamberlain considered very 'fishy'. He signed off, 'One wonders what the purpose of a fake was but I could suggest at least three plausible motives. Well, we shall see.'[5]

On 17 January, Hore-Belisha gave his resignation speech in the House of Commons. Chamberlain had replaced him at the War Ministry with Oliver Stanley (1896-1950), a lawyer and Bristol West MP, whose father had held the same post during the First World War. Sir Andrew Duncan (1884-1952), a business man and City of London MP, took over at the Board of Trade while Chamberlain asked Lord Reith (1889-1971), the former Director General of the BBC, to head up the Ministry of Information. Hore-Belisha's resignation speech had, according to Chamberlain, been 'a flop, much to the disappointment of M.P.'s who had crowded the House in the hopes of a sensation and still more to the disgust of the "popular press".' However, Attlee, the Labour leader, had attacked him remorselessly over the resignation, leading Chamberlain to sarcastically conclude, 'A fine patriotic spirit in wartime!'[6]

Chamberlain's escape from the pernicious atmosphere of the House of Commons was to go birdwatching in St James's Park, which was now frozen over. Writing to his sister Ida on 20 January from Downing Street, he noted, 'There were 8° [degrees] of frost in the Park when we walked round this morning and last week the therm. registered 22° and 23° degrees F. in two successive days at 10.15 a.m. There is hardly any open water left and what there is crowded with ducks, among which is or was, so an ornithological correspondent [Gilbert Collett] informs me, a smew. But though I take my glasses every day I haven't been able to discover it. But the blue tits now come regularly to the bird table outside the window of this room.'[7]

The smew *Mergellus albellus* is an iconic winter bird, the male's striking black-and-white markings making it a revered species for birdwatchers. Visiting Britain in small numbers from Russia and Scandinavia each year, the species, with its 'cracked ice and panda' appearance, can turn up on even small bodies of water, particularly in hard weather. Despite this, a sighting on an ornamental lake like St James's in the middle of London would have been like hitting the birding jackpot. As a consequence, Chamberlain had searched hard for the bird, not only on his daily walks but on other occasions when he had slipped out without informing his bodyguard. However, the smew is a shy bird and easily takes flight when disturbed, so, much to his annoyance, Chamberlain had not been able to spot it.

The next day, Chamberlain had better luck when, on his daily walk around St James's Park, he saw a wading bird feeding at the muddy margins of the lake. Waders were extremely rare on the lake in winter and he raised his binoculars excitedly to look at it more closely. The bird flew off but its identification was betrayed by its three-note call, which Chamberlain recognised straight away. It was a common sandpiper *Actitis hypoleucos*. The common sandpiper, like the scaup he had seen the previous December, was, despite its name, anything but common in winter, most migrating to Africa. Finding one in the depths of winter was an achievement that any ornithologist would be proud of and on returning to Number 10 Chamberlain asked one of his private staff to send off a letter to his birding counterpart, Gilbert Collett.

10 Downing Street
Whitehall

Dear Sir,
The Prime Minister has asked me to write to tell you he saw yesterday (the 21st January) a common sandpiper at the west end of St. James's Park lake. He has no doubt that you will agree with him that it is remarkable that this bird should be seen at this time of year. He has also seen recently a pair of carrion crows in the Park, though this, of course, is much less unusual.

Yours truly,
A. Neil Rucker[8]

The common sandpiper is best known as a species that habitually bobs up and down, a behaviour known as 'teetering'. It also has a distinctive flight, with stiff, bowed wings. Following his flight to Munich, Chamberlain had teetered on the brink for too long, unable to decide whether to appease or stand up to Hitler. Now at war, Chamberlain's only release from the pressures of the job was to surreptitiously slip out of Number 10 to visit St James's Park lake.

By now, Chamberlain's sudden disappearances from Downing Street had become the subject of much gossip among those working there. He would often take a member of his private staff out with him to help in the search, including junior ones, who would then be tasked with writing the letter afterwards to his birding mentor, Gilbert Collett. A birdwatching guide was provided by Chamberlain to help his staff increase their ornithological knowledge. For many, these clandestine trips were a visit they looked forward to, leaving behind the colossal workload and highly charged atmosphere in Number 10 and allowing them to spend quality time with their Prime Minister. However, sometimes Chamberlain would ask them to go out on his behalf to recce the park on their own while, on occasions, despite the security risks, he sneaked out alone with his binoculars hidden under his coat or tucked into his pocket. He had learned from his experience of being mobbed in Richmond Park and would leave behind his trademark homburg hat and umbrella, instead disguising himself or simply hoping people wouldn't recognise him.[9] While some in Number 10 saw his passion for twitching, or ticking off birds, as a highly eccentric but essentially harmless pastime, others felt that it was distracting him at a time when the country had never been in graver peril. In particular it caused great consternation for the special protection officers assigned by the Metropolitan Police to guard him. However, whenever the subject came up in conversation, his Principal Private Secretary, Osmund Somers Cleverly, would always stoutly defend the Prime Minister, knowing that he was dealing with almost unbearable pressure. For Chamberlain, the freedom to escape the suffocating confines of Number 10 and go birdwatching had become a coping strategy for dealing with Hitler.

The end of January found Chamberlain back at Chequers reflecting on the reluctance of many of the neutral nations to join the Allies in the face of Nazi intimidation and threats. Annoyed at this, on 20 January Churchill had taken matters into his own hands and made a radio broadcast in which he urged them to take sides before it was too late, memorably stating, 'Each one hopes that if he feeds the crocodile enough, the crocodile will eat him last.' This analogy had gone down badly in the Scandinavian and Low Countries, who felt it made their already precarious position even more vulnerable and, as it had not been cleared by the Cabinet, Churchill had been forced to apologise to the Foreign Secretary, Lord Halifax. Reflecting on the situation, Chamberlain commented to Ida on 27 January 1940, 'Edward [Lord Halifax] tells me that "with as much signs of contrition as Winston ever shows" he has been mediating on the possibility of saying something to undo the incalculable harm done by his recent broadcast … It is a heavy price that we have to pay for our Winston.'

Elsewhere, the international situation was equally depressing. Chamberlain despaired at the US position, declaring, 'Heaven knows I don't want the Americans to fight for us – we should have to pay too dearly for that if they had a right to be in on the peace terms – but if they are so sympathetic they might at least refrain from hampering our efforts and comforting our foes.' The Japanese, meanwhile, continued to be a threat to British interests in the Far East. At home the partisan and personal attacks by the Labour Party had reached new heights and were only matched by the vitriol shown in the press. The result was that Chamberlain had, once again, thought of stepping down, 'Only I don't see that other to whom I could hand over with any confidence that he would do better than I.'[10] Despite it all, Chamberlain still thought himself indispensable.

On getting back to Downing Street on 30 January, he found a small consolation in the form of a tawny owl *Strix aluco* which had set up home in the grounds of Number 10. On hearing the owl's haunting call in the garden at night, Chamberlain got one of his private secretaries to send off a letter the next day to Gilbert Collett.

> 10 Downing Street
> Whitehall
> 1st February 1940
>
> Dear Sir,
> The Prime Minister thought you might like to know that last Sunday, the 30th January, before and after midnight, a brown owl was hooting either in the garden here or just across the road in the Park. This is not the first time Chamberlain has heard an owl in the garden, but he had not heard one for some time.
>   Mr Chamberlain has not yet succeeded in picking out the smew.
>
> Yours truly
> C.M. Campbell
> Private Secretary[11]

The tawny, or brown owl, is the commonest owl in Britain and is found in woodlands across Europe, from the Iberian peninsula in the south to Siberia in the east. It is nocturnal and mainly hunts rodents but in urban areas like Downing

Street its diet would have included a higher proportion of the song birds which Chamberlain was so keen to encourage. Ironically, the increased number of birds in the garden, as a result of Chamberlain putting up nesting boxes when he first arrived at Downing Street, would have attracted it. Nevertheless, the owl was a great source of inspiration to Chamberlain who would have been well versed with the folklore associated with it, from Wordsworth, who described the technique for calling an owl in his poem 'There was a Boy', to his literary hero, Shakespeare, who wrote in *Julius Caesar*, Act 1 Scene 3:

> And yesterday the bird of night did sit
> Even at noon-day upon the market-place
> Hooting and shrieking.[12]

As Chamberlain knew well, Westminster supported a good population of tawny owls which were present in St James's Park and other London parks, as well as Kensington Gardens and Buckingham Palace. From the beginning of the year to the end of March, the usually secretive owl comes into its peak territorial calling time and its characteristic night-time cry must have echoed eerily from the shrouded boughs and darkened parks of wartime London. Appropriately, the collective noun for a group of owls is a 'parliament'. Yet Chamberlain would also have been only too aware that the silent, night-time assassin had a long superstitious association as a harbinger of bad luck and death.

On Saturday 3 February, Chamberlain wrote to Ida that 'having got through my two speeches successfully I feel much less depressed.' The two speeches in question were: on 31 January to the City about their contribution to the war effort; and on 1 February in the House of Commons against a Labour motion to create a Ministry of War Economy, which he had compared to being a 'dictator over all … Departments'. In a poorly attended debate, the motion was defeated by 185 votes to 90. Writing as he was leaving for France, to attend the next Supreme War Council, he told Ida that his office had been bombarded with letters, not about the war but an IRA bomb attack in Coventry in which five people died, 'Asking that the Coventry murderers should be let off, many of them on the grounds that they are "innocent"!' Incredulous, he ordered the two men executed on 7 February, commenting, 'The Irish mind is incomprehensible to the English mentality.'[13]

A week later, Chamberlain wrote to Hilda from his desk at Downing Street, saying that his trip to France had been a great success as, in the face of a Nazi attack, there had been 'not only unity of purpose but unity of thought'. He had found it tiring speaking French constantly but Winston, who was in 'seventh heaven' over being asked to attend, did not contribute due to his poor French, Chamberlain quipping, 'Old Sir Dudley Pound, the 1st Sea Lord, who has a sly sense of humour, is said to have remarked "Well I've seen a miracle today. The first Lord sat all through the Conference and he was never allowed to open his mouth!".' On the boat journey across the Channel they had seen several floating mines, which had been dispatched with a Lewis gun, and they had been treated to an exhibition using depth charges:

> It was most impressive. We saw the charge describe its parabola as it was flung out of a mortar and then a minute after there was a tremendous shock which fairly shook us up though we were several hundred yards away. A second after, a huge mass of water rose into the air as high as the destroyer wireless mast, looking for an instant like an iceberg, and then it dropped again and there was only a thin cloud of smoke and a great expanse of foam. It gave one a vivid idea of what it must be to be shut up in a submarine with those things going off all around.[14]

On Saturday 17 February, Chamberlain was back at Chequers, looking in vain for the first signs of spring and in a more optimistic mood following some encouraging war news. 'I had promised to find the first aconites,' he told Ida, 'but there had been a fresh fall of snow and the ground was white everywhere with considerable drifts in the hollow places.'[15] At 7.45am he had been rung by Churchill with some good news about the *Altmark*, the supply ship for the German pocket battleship, the *Admiral Graf Spee*, which had been scuttled on 17 December 1939 at Montevideo following the Battle of the River Plate. On 16 February the *Altmark* had been located in a Norwegian fjord and boarded by HMS *Cossack* who rescued all the 299 prisoners on board, a considerable propaganda coup for the British.

The following Saturday, Chamberlain gave a speech at Birmingham Town Hall, the culmination of a series of speeches the Cabinet had been giving on the prosecution of the war. While speaking, he was heckled by peace protestors who shouted, 'We want Moselely [a suburb of Birmingham] for Peace', before they were escorted from the premises to boos from the audience. At the end, responding to the vote of thanks, he said that, paradoxically, he did not feel the same degree of strain now as he had felt after Munich when he still thought that war could be averted. He concluded, 'I am still young. Time is before me and I hope that even yet I may have some chance of putting my energies into the work of peace.'[16] It was a hopelessly optimistic statement coming from a man who knew he was neither young nor had time before him.

The next day, in his letter to Hilda from Downing Street, he reflected on the responsibilities associated with office, saying, 'How much more easily I carry it than Father did when he was several years younger than I.' Recalling the terrible headaches that had plagued Joseph's final years, he was thankful that he hadn't got to that stage yet and instead looked forward to a visit to Kew Gardens, one of his favourite haunts, that afternoon. His Birmingham speech had been broadcast, causing him to marvel 'at the power of the wireless'. The ticket collector on his way back had heard it, Chamberlain mimicking him when he said that it came across as 'something butiful' and the stationmaster at Euston had also tuned in, while his police chauffeur had heard it from a portable set on the top of a bus. On his return to Downing Street he had been met by a 'wildly enthusiastic telegram' about his 'noble words' from the Canadian Prime Minister, Mackenzie King (1874–1950). He did not know if Hitler had heard the broadcast but felt he was 'certainly getting madder' and that it could 'only be a question of time before he goes off his head altogether.'[17]

The war, meanwhile, continued to go badly. In Finland, they were heroically holding out against far superior Russian forces but it looked like only a matter of time before they would be overwhelmed. Chamberlain told Hilda that the Russians had, 'in their usual treacherous and cowardly way been trying to get us to convey their peace terms … This of course is copied from the Hitler technique in Poland and Czecho-Slovakia … the terms were so outrageous that we declined … and told the Russians to do their own dirty work.' He signed off while looking out of the window of his office into the garden, 'As I sit writing, a blue tit continually visits my bird table just outside the window and hustles off the sparrows. There was a hen blackbird there this morning though she seldom comes.'[18]

To bolster the British blockade of Norway, Churchill had been lobbying Chamberlain hard to use the Royal Navy to lay mines in their waters, but following a Cabinet meeting on 29 February, Chamberlain rejected the idea. Taking Churchill aside beforehand, he explained why he had decided against the operation. 'So in Cabinet he didn't fight at all but accepted my verdict and I paid him warm compliments. The relief of the rest of the brethren was comic. Simon whispered to me Splendid! You are a *real* Prime Minister.' It was again a case of keeping your friends close and your enemies even closer.

The deteriorating situation in Finland necessitated two emergency Cabinet meetings on 1 March. The Finns had made a demand for 100 bombers and 50,000 troops to be transported via Sweden or they would negotiate a surrender with Russia. Chamberlain was annoyed that the French had passed the buck, promising Finland unlimited support but claiming that the British 'can't or won't transport them … So he [Daladier] coolly passes the buck to the Nation

Amie and Alliée [the friendly and allied nation]. This is what the French always do and it is an unpleasing trait.'

In the Middle East, the future of Palestine also made demands on his time, with the Arabs threatening to withdraw from the peace process, 'I expect it will be like the I.R.A. a lot of threats beforehand, followed by a rather feeble row and then it's all over.' Closer to home, Chamberlain met with the Chairmen of the County War Agricultural Committees with a view to 'stirring up the ploughing campaign' (a Ministry of Agriculture campaign to grow more food).[19] To show his support, he had allowed the tenant farmer at Chequers to plough up some rough grass in front of the house.

On Friday, 1 March Britain ordered a naval blockade of Italian coal imports from Germany, a move designed to isolate Italy and put pressure on her industrial base. The blockade followed a visit from President Roosevelt's Under Secretary of State, Sumner Welles (1892-1961), who had come to Italy with peace proposals. Hitler, fearing the visit was designed to drive a wedge between the two countries, sent Ribbentrop to shore up the Italians and meet the Pope who was also trying to prevent Italy from joining the Germans. The British naval blockade, which had resulted in thirteen Italian ships being detained, was designed to coincide with Ribbentrop's visit on 10-11 March 1940. Commenting on it in a letter to Hilda on 10 March, Chamberlain wrote, 'How we are all chuckling this morning. What a delightful surprise Ribbentrop had when they bought him the news with his early tea this morning. What a nice temper he will be in when he goes to pay his visit to the Pope tomorrow.'

In family news, Chamberlain revealed that Annie had been in a nasty accident when her chauffeur-driven car had to stop suddenly to avoid a collision with a bus. She had suffered whiplash and would be taking no more engagements until she recovered. He had accompanied his son Frank to Wisley Gardens, where they had a pleasant walk in the sunshine admiring the spring flowers. In the evening Frank had taken his wife, Valerie, to see a play and then they went out dancing until the early hours. Ever the worrying parent, Chamberlain told Ida, 'With this blackout and the daily toll of accidents I do get nervous when the young people are out late, but of course they had gone to dance at some supper place.'[20] He had also visited London Zoo, one of his favourite haunts, with Valerie, but had found it a very different place to the one that had existed before the war.

At the outbreak of war, London Zoo, together with all other public attractions where people gathered in large numbers, had been closed by order of his government.[21] All the venomous reptiles and amphibians, including snakes, lizards and frogs, had been destroyed. The rather bizarre reasoning for the cull was that the last thing bombed-out Londoners needed was to be bitten by an escaped poisonous snake. However, the Chinese alligators, Komodo dragon and two pythons – one 25ft foot long and the other 28ft long – were deemed worthy of saving as they were not venomous. Together with two giant pandas, two orangutans, four chimpanzees, three Asian elephants and an ostrich, they were shipped off to Whipsnade Zoo for safety.

On the 15 September 1939, London Zoo had reopened, minus all the reptiles and most of the big animals. The aquarium had also been closed due to the danger of it being bombed and the excessive cost of running it. Most of the fish, including the trout, perch, dace and the salmon so beloved of Chamberlain, were destroyed, apart from the carp which were released into the flamingoes' pond. All the glass in the zoo, like the windows in people's homes, was criss-crossed with black masking tape to prevent it shattering. The cost of entry was one shilling for adults and sixpence for children. With no big animals, venomous reptiles or an aquarium, and with black masking tape covering all the glass cages, it can't have been either a great visitor experience or very good value for money.

After his visit to the remains of London Zoo on 16 March 1940, Chamberlain was again at Chequers contemplating the eradication of invaders who threatened the country; this time not Germans but rabbits. To help him in the task he had brought in Roy Robinson, a forestry expert, whose crack team was busy shooting them. 'They have destroyed about 200 rabbits so far,' he told Ida in his letter of the same date, 'but think it will take two years to eradicate them all.' When it came to Chamberlain's precious trees, a war on rabbits was something he was determined to prosecute with vigour.

In the real war, the Finns, as Chamberlain suspected, had sued for peace on 13 March 1940, the terms being 'much more severe than I had expected but their spirit was broken.' Following his visit to Berlin, Rome and Paris, Sumner Wells had arrived in London, dining with Chamberlain who initially found him 'distinctly stiff', a term usually deployed by the Americans to describe their reserved British cousins. However, after dinner, Chamberlain concluded 'He was the best type of American I have met for a long time.' The reason for his change of mind was that Wells had told him that the President 'had a deep admiration for me and would like nothing better than an opportunity of meeting though he realised this was not possible at present.'

The next day, Sunday 17 March, Chamberlain updated Ida on his all-important Easter holiday plans. He had provisionally decided to fish the river Test in Hampshire, staying as the guest of Viscount Wyndham Portal (1885-1949) at Laverstoke Mill, before returning to London on Easter Monday. His security services had informed him that 15 March had been earmarked by Hitler as a possible date to invade the west. It had again passed without incident, leading

Chamberlain to conclude, 'Frankly I remain sceptical of the Spring offensive and told Wells so, but I don't think he shared that view.'[22] The next day, 18 March, Hitler met with Mussolini at the Brenner Pass, on the German–Italian border, to persuade the Italian dictator to enter the war on the side of the Axis powers. Mussolini secretly said he needed longer to prepare, but Chamberlain again mistakenly interpreted this as showing a reluctance on the part of the Italians to join forces with Nazi Germany.

The final weekend of March 1940 found Chamberlain again at Chequers, writing to Ida that during a lull in the rain he had decided to go out for a walk to get some air and do some birdwatching:

> The result was that Spot and I got very wet on Beacon Hill as by the time we got there the rain came on hard again, but I was amply rewarded because as I passed by the Wellingtonia I perceived a tree creeper snugly ensconced in its little hole in the bark. I had so often looked for it before but never been lucky enough to find it at home though I knew by the droppings that it must roost there. This habit doesn't seem widely known – there is nothing about it in any book of mine. I also counted the rooks' nests and noted how steady the numbers remain – thirty-three now, thirty-four last year, thirty-one the year before. I wonder what keeps them down.[23]

The observations marked Chamberlain out as a first-class birdwatcher. In fact, unbeknown to him, an article had been published on 1 June 1936 in the magazine *British Birds* entitled 'Roosting Habitats of the Tree-Creeper', by the ornithologist P.G. Kennedy. He described how the birds bored holes into the soft bark of Wellingtonia trees *Sequoia gigantea* and slept in them at night. The article also stated that the treecreeper *Certhia familiaris* will use other trees, including oaks and Scots pines, Kennedy concluding, 'I should say that Tree-Creepers prefer dead trees … the birds use cavities or dents in growing trees as alternative roosts.'[24] However, as this behaviour was still new to ornithology it hadn't made its way into any of the bird books.

The answer to the mystery of the rook numbers was more mundane - they were shot. Rooks *Corvus frugilegus* are considered pests by some farmers, who believe they damage crops, but to ornithologists like Chamberlain they are admired, their cawing call and communal nesting sites or rookeries epitomising the quintessentially English countryside. Rooks are also steeped in folklore. Many people believe they bring good luck, but if they abandon the rookery, a death is imminent. To keep numbers down at Chequers, the young birds, after fledging, were probably shot before they were strong enough to fly and the meat used to make traditional rook pie, a supposed delicacy enjoyed by the shooting fraternity.[25] The reason that nobody told Chamberlain was because of his well-known love of ornithology and the fact that, had he known about the cull, he would have probably put a stop to it.

In contrast to the culling of rooks, when it came to the war it was Chamberlain who tried to call the shots at the next Supreme War Council. He reported to Ida that the meeting had been very successful, apart from the fact that he didn't entirely trust the new French Prime Minister, Paul Reynaud (1878-1966), who had replaced the injured Daladier (he had been injured in a riding accident). 'His face has a foxy expression which causes me to wonder if his real name is not Renard instead of Reynaud. But it is a comfort that he speaks English fluently and perhaps he is more courageous than Daladier of whom it is said that he is "a bull with snail horns".'

On his way to the meeting, the French news agency, Havas, had run with a story that the Allies were no longer going to respect neutral territorial waters because of violations by Germany. Chamberlain suspected that the cunning Reynaud had deliberately leaked the story so that the meeting would reach the conclusion he desired. He was furious, believing it might give away the Allies' plan to mine Norwegian territorial waters, but the French Prime Minister denied he had leaked it and blamed it on one of his new ministers. 'I hope he was telling the truth,' Chamberlain commented to Ida, 'but the French are a "rum lot".'[26] It also didn't go unnoticed in Germany, where they took it as a warning of imminent military action.

In Cabinet, Chamberlain had again to tackle the intransigent Churchill, this time over the government's Ministry of Information. He had spoken with Lord Reith and found that 'his ideas and mine about propaganda are pretty close,' but when the plans were put to the services, the Admiralty under Churchill refused to participate, despite the War Office and the Air Ministry agreeing. 'I am not unhopeful about getting my way,' he told his sister, 'Winston in spite of his violence and impulsiveness, is very responsive to a sympathetic handling. To me personally he is absolutely loyal and I am continually hearing from others of the admiration he expresses for the P.M.'[27]

Yet it had now become clear that it was Churchill, not Chamberlain, who was calling the shots. His praise for the increasingly beleaguered Prime Minister was a double-edged sword, designed to enhance Chamberlain's reputation in his own eyes while further weakening his position with the party. Chamberlain even felt obliged to consult Churchill about Cabinet changes he was planning. He dismissed out of hand the notion of offering roles to the opposition, and when the changes were finally announced to the War Cabinet they merely involved two ministers swapping portfolios; Hoare, who held the office of Privy Seal, exchanging with Kingsley Wood at the Air Ministry. Despite months of damning criticism of his leadership, Chamberlain was now too weak to remove his critics, chief among them Churchill. Instead making the position of Minister for Coordination of Defence – held by the former Sea Lord, Baron Chatfield (1873-1967) – redundant, he made Churchill chair of the Military Coordination Committee, which consisted of the three service chiefs and their ministers. Churchill was now effectively running the war.

On 6 April, writing from Downing Street, Chamberlain told his sister Hilda that, despite widespread criticism of his non-Cabinet changes in the press, he felt 'still in a strong enough position to treat them with the contempt they deserve.' Rejecting accusations of 'clumsy handling' by his enemies, he believed that he and Churchill could now work together to prosecute the war. He was pleased to have brought in Lord Woolton (1883-1964), the ex-Chair of Lewis's department store, as the new Minister of Food, telling Hilda he had 'great hopes that he will do well.' Turning to the war, he said there was a 'curious and some would say ominous lull in war activities.' Wondering what the 'Boche' were up to, he remained ever sceptical of an attack, 'I can't think any offensive on a large scale would pay the Boche as well as keeping quiet and developing relations with Russia.' At a speech to the Conservative Central Council that week, he reiterated his theory that any attack on the west would have happened last year and that 'Hitler [had] missed the bus'.[28] Those words would come back to haunt him as two days later German forces overran Denmark and invaded Norway.

Chapter 20

In the name of God, go.

'Now is my soul troubled; and what shall I say? Father, save me from this hour: but for this cause came I unto this hour.' John 12:27

On Saturday 13 April, Chamberlain wrote to Ida that Churchill was to blame for the Norwegian debacle. Churchill's plans for a naval attack to recapture Bergen and Trondheim and then occupy Narvik to cut off the German advance were abandoned because of the strength of the German Navy and indecision within the Admiralty. 'I judge from your letter that you, like many others, were disappointed that Winston was not able to give a more complete and satisfactory account of the operations of the Navy ... The blame has of course been put on to the Ministry of Information who were I believe blameless ... I suspect the real reason for the Admiralty's hesitations is that Winston has got everyone so terrified there that none of them dare take any responsibility.'

Chamberlain was now beginning to seriously feel the strain. 'I have had a pretty harassing week,' he told his sister, 'Twice I have been got out of bed early in order to hold a Cabinet at 8.30am and I find that sort of thing very tiresome and disturbing.' Again he highlighted Churchill's working methods as being at fault. 'But I confess that although Winston only means to be helpful he does give me more trouble than all the rest of my colleagues put together ... He goes to bed after lunch for a couple of hours or so and holds conferences up to 1 in the morning at which he goes into every detail, so I am informed, that could quite well be settled by subordinates.' Yet Chamberlain knew that, despite his shortcomings, Churchill had become indispensable. 'I say to myself that this is just the price we have to pay for the asset we have in his personality and popularity but I do wish we could have the latter without the former.'[1]

Chamberlain was told that an attack on the Low Countries was now 'imminent' but he still refused to believe it. 'My guess, and I can't pretend that it is more than that, is that Hitler is worried to death about iron ore and oil and that he has laid plans to secure both,' he told Ida before adding, 'I don't believe any of these tales ... the attack must I think come this week. If it does not materialise during the next seven or eight days I shall conclude that my theory is correct.'

The war continued to take its toll on his mental health, and he confided to Ida, 'This is a trying time and everyone's nerves are apt to get frayed.' Once more he turned to nature to find peace of mind, 'It has not been a very nice day but there has been enough sun to make me wish for the country and the garden blackbird has been singing constantly. I have had to confine myself to St. James's Park, but was rewarded for as we walked round this morning a number of pigeons rose from the grass and among them I spotted a Kestrel with a sparrow in its talons. It flew into a plane tree to eat it and I was able to walk across the grass near enough to see it very plainly before it took fright and flew off.'[2] Buoyed by the sighting, Chamberlain still found the time to dictate a letter about his observation to his birding mentor, Gilbert Collett, despite the huge pressure he was under:

10 Downing Street
Whitehall
13 April, 1940

Dear Sir,
The Prime Minister asks me to let you know that when walking round St. James's Park this morning, he saw a kestrel leave the ground with a bird in its talons which he thinks was a sparrow. The kestrel, a cock bird, flew into a plane tree and began devouring the bird on a branch about twenty feet from the ground.

Mr. Chamberlain walked across the grass till he was within about fifteen yards, when the kestrel, after watching him for a while, flew off.

Yours truly
C.M. Campbell
Private Secretary[3]

On Sunday 20 April, Chamberlain went to Chequers for the first time in three weeks. He told Hilda he was keen to go because, 'At this time of year there is so much going on in the garden that one doesn't want to be away too long. It is dull and inclined to drizzle every now and then but it is fairly mild and the daffodils, especially those that came from Holland are a wonderful sight.' Commenting that everything was late this year, he noted there were still 'quantities of violets' in Crows Close, and that the orchard was looking 'really interesting and in another fortnight there will be a lot out there.' He was busy planning the herbaceous borders, having obtained £50 worth of plants from the Parks Department, 'I have always thought the garden too monstrous with its red roses and red bricks and this is going to bring in a fine contrast.' Suddenly remembering there was a war on, he added, 'I could go on rambling about the garden but I must turn to more important matters.'

Weighed down by work, Chamberlain told Hilda, 'Your letter came down yesterday at midday when I only had three telephone calls and two bags by special dispatch rider!' He had again taken over chairing the Military Coordination Committee, describing it as a 'sad mess, quarrelling and sulking, with everyone feeling irritable and strained.' The reason for the unhappiness was that the old chair, Churchill, had 'superseded' the committee because, 'He believes so earnestly in all his own ideas … The result is apt to be that they are bullied into a sulky silence – a most dangerous position in war.' As a result, Churchill had, according to Chamberlain, 'recognised that he was getting into an impossible position and himself asked me to take the chair, remarking "They'll take from you what they won't take from me".'[4] The remark was a clever way of damning the committee and Chamberlain with faint praise. Yet, in another sign of his increasing dependence on Churchill, Chamberlain told Hilda that he was taking him to Paris for the next meeting of the Supreme War Council.

Reflecting on the war, Chamberlain crowed to his sister, 'Well you see the great offensive hasn't come off and though we are still told it is going to I remain more firmly convinced than ever that in its broad outline my guess is correct.' Chamberlain had asked Churchill for his opinion on the large build-up of German troops on the Baltic coast and he had replied at once 'An attack on Sweden.' Chamberlain thought he was mistaken. 'Well he is the professional strategist, but I believe he is wrong,' Chamberlain categorically told his sister. Like his prediction that Hitler would not attack in the west, he also held firm to his belief that 'Musso' would not risk war. 'I see no reason to change the view I expressed to the Cabinet last Monday, namely Musso will go as far as he dares to help Hitler without actually getting himself involved in the war.'[5] It was classic Chamberlain, but by being so overly optimistic he was also now dangerously in denial.

Chamberlain's new-found confidence, however, was short lived, and the end of April found him again close to despair. Writing to Hilda on Saturday 27 April, he said, 'The good public little realises the anxieties which continually weigh on Cabinet Ministers and of course the P.M in particular. Although you are better informed than most I daresay you will be surprised to hear that this has been one of the worst, if not *the* worst, weeks of the war and for once I feel really tired.' On 22 April he and Churchill had flown to Paris for the Supreme War Council, a meeting Chamberlain expected to be 'very sticky' but where the French, realising the precariousness of their position, had agreed to all the British joint war aims.

On his return he had chaired the Military Coordination Committee, where he received further 'disquietening telegrams', and where, 'Winston's attitude was most difficult, challenging everything the Chfs of Staff suggested and generally behaving like a spoiled and sulky child.' The next day Churchill was in an equally foul mood, 'complaining bitterly of being "thwarted" and not having sufficient powers.' Chamberlain talked through the issues with him and was told he wanted to become Minster of Defence. However, Chamberlain knew that if he granted Churchill's wish it would 'make him sole director of military policy without safeguards', a position that would fatally undermine his own already weakened authority.[6]

Reports getting through to him from Norway told of an increasingly desperate situation with complete German air superiority causing havoc with British and French supply lines. The Germans were bombing 'houses, piers, stores and ammunition at their leisure till there was nothing left to destroy.' As a result of the deteriorating military position in Norway, the Supreme War Council had met again, this time in London, and after some initial disagreements they had agreed to withdraw British and French troops from Norway. It was a humiliating retreat which piled more pressure on Chamberlain's and Churchill's strained relationship. Following further discussions, he agreed to Churchill again chairing the Military Coordination Committee in his absence and giving guidance and direction to the Chiefs of Staff, including the ability to summon them at will. Churchill was now effectively Minister of Defence in all but name.

Saturday 4 May, found Chamberlain relaxing at Chequers following a 'lull' in the war for a 'well needed rest'. Writing to Hilda, he said, 'You can imagine that I have had little peace during these last days, but though we have had some losses, I don't yet know how much. I am thankful that at least we got our men out of Norway.' Looking back, he did not see what else he could have done. The blame he felt was squarely on the shoulders of the Norwegians, who had not blown up any bridges to stop the German advance because, 'They couldn't bear the idea of spoiling their nice railway and except in a few cases they seemed to have no fighting spirit.'

The response from the international community was a rapid condemnation of German aggression, with the US in particular asking why, yet again, the Allies had been caught on the hop. Chamberlain's answer was that the Allies had manpower and equipment but no time to train and deploy it, in contrast to the Nazis who had 'spent years in preparing'. However, there was a shortage of air power and, for the first time, Chamberlain began to realise that an attack in the west was now a distinct possibility, something he had been in denial about for months.

Churchill continued to be a thorn in his side. His proposal that he give guidance and advice to the Chiefs of Staff had been met by resistance from two service ministers who threatened to resign over it. Chamberlain had called their bluff by offering to resign himself, '[Letting] W.C. be Prime Minister as well as Defence Minister, they said that would be too great a disaster and they would do what I asked them.' He concluded, 'It's a vile world, but I don't think my enemies will get me down this time. I should be sorry if they did because I should then have to leave this lovely place [Chequers]. You couldn't imagine anything more perfect than it is today.' As a PS, he added, 'Reith tells me that my prestige with the chfs of staff is "tremendous" and that they say I am "the only man whose judgement they trust".'[7]

The Parliamentary debate on the Norway debacle was scheduled for 7–8 May and the opposition had turned it into a vote of confidence in his government. Realising that many MPs did not share the judgement of the Chiefs of Staff, Chamberlain was extremely anxious about the debate and the vote. To deal with the acute pressure-cooker environment in Number 10 he took long walks in St James's Park, where he was able to take time to think while pursuing his favourite hobby, birdwatching. Chamberlain had been searching in vain for the nest of the kestrel he had seen some weeks previously. Remarkably, on the 8 May, midway through the two-day debate, he still found the time to tell one his private secretaries, to send a letter to his birdwatching mentor, Gilbert Collett, asking if he could help him locate the bird.

8 May 1940
10 Downing Street
Whitehall

Dear Sir
Some weeks ago you wrote to the Prime Minister about the kestrel in St. James's Park and mentioned that it was fond of perching on the top of a very high tree, rising from the water's edge opposite the incinerator. Mr Chamberlain has since tried to identify the tree but without success. Could you therefore give him more particulars? What sort of tree is it, a popular or a plane? Is it on the island or the main shore and is it on the North side of the lake or the South? Mr Chamberlain himself has not seen the kestrel again since he wrote to you.

Yours truly
C.M. Campbell
Private Secretary[8]

The kestrel *Falco tinnunculus* is a falcon, best known for its habit of hovering in flight in search of prey. Like all birds of prey, it has excellent eyesight and once its victim is sighted the kestrel makes a short, steep dive towards its target. Their prey consists mainly of voles, shrews and mice associated with rough grassland and as a result kestrels have adapted well to living in urban areas. However, a kestrel nesting in St James's Park would have been a notable sighting given the sheer number of people visiting the grounds, not to mention its location in the heart of London. The kestrel also features in the famous poem 'Into Battle' written by Julian Grenfell who, like Chamberlain's cousin, Norman, was killed in the First World War. The poem was well known to Chamberlain and juxtaposes the horrors of war with the beauty of birds:

> The kestrel hovering by day,
> And the little owls that call by night,
> Bid him be swift and keen as they,
> As keen of ear, as swift of sight.
>
> The blackbird sings to him: Brother, brother,
> If this be the last song you shall sing,
> Sing well, for you may not sing another;
> Brother, sing.[9]
>
> The thundering line of battle stands,
> And in the air Death moans and sings;
> But Day shall clasp him with strong hands,
> And Night shall fold him in soft wings.

As Chamberlain had predicted, in the ensuing debate on 7-8 May in Parliament, MPs remorselessly attacked his war leadership and were savage in their criticism of him. Taking his place in the chamber he was greeted by cries of 'Missed the bus?' His old nemesis, David Lloyd George, was particularly scathing:

> The Prime Minister must remember that he has met this formidable foe of ours in peace and in war. He has always been worsted. He is not in a position to appeal on the ground of friendship. He has appealed for sacrifice. The nation is prepared for every sacrifice so long as it has leadership, so long as the government show clearly what they are aiming at and so long as the nation is confident that those who are leading it are doing their best. I say solemnly that the Prime Minister should give an

example of sacrifice, because there is nothing which can contribute more to victory in this war than that he should sacrifice the seals of office.

But it was Leo Amery, the fiery Conservative MP who Chamberlain had passed over for promotion, who delivered the fatal blow:

> Somehow or other we must get into the government, men who can match our enemies in fighting spirit, in daring, in resolution and in thirst for victory. Some 300 years ago, when this house found that its troops were being beaten by the dash and daring of Prince Rupert's cavalry, Oliver Cromwell spoke to John Hampden. In one of his speeches he recounted what he said. It was this: "I said to him, 'Your troops are most of them old, decayed serving men and tapsters and such kind of fellows ... You must get men of a spirit that are likely to go as far as they will go, or you will be beaten still." It may not be easy to find these men. They can be found only by trial and by ruthlessly discarding all who fail. We are fighting today for our life, for our liberty, for our all; we cannot go on being led as we are. I have quoted certain words of Oliver Cromwell. I will quote certain other words. This is what Cromwell said to the Long Parliament when he thought it was no longer fit to conduct the affairs of the nation: 'You have sat too long here for any good you have been doing. Depart, I say, and let us have done with you. In the name of God, go.'[10]

The government survived the vote of confidence, but with a greatly reduced majority of just eighty-one. Devastatingly for Chamberlain, over a quarter of Conservative MPs voted with the opposition or abstained. As he left the Commons, cries of 'Go' could be heard echoing around the Chamber. Two days later the attack that everyone, apart from Chamberlain, had been predicting for so long took place when Hitler's *Blitzkreig* was unleashed on the Low Countries, closely followed by the first air raids on British soil. The 'Phoney War' and Chamberlain's Premiership were over.

At 9pm on 10 May 1940, Chamberlain officially announced his resignation in a radio broadcast. The speech was punctuated with long pauses and Chamberlain couldn't hide his sadness when referring to this as his last message to the British people from Number 10, a sniff clearly audible on the broadcast. However, at the end, his voice rising noticeably, he finally showed the fighting spirit that the nation had been longing for: 'The hour has come when we are to be put to the test as the innocent people of Holland and Belgium and France are being tested already and you and I must rally behind our new leader and with our united strength and with unshakeable courage fight and work until this wild beast that has sprung out of his lair upon us be finally disarmed and overthrown.' It was almost Churchillian.

The speech was one of Chamberlain's best but, ironically for a man who had always rated his own oratory so highly, the next day he was desolate. Writing to Ida from Downing Street, he said, 'Things move at such a giddy pace that your letter seems already out of date and you will know from the press and the radio what has happened since you wrote.' He continued, 'The debate was a very painful affair to many besides myself, and in particular for its exhibition of personal and party passion. It was supposed to be about Norway but I think that, as you say, it was recognised that the Government had a pretty good case there, and no doubt that impression must have been greatly strengthened by the events which have occurred since on the Continent. How fortunate that we have not got large forces of men and guns and planes locked up on Trondheim when we want them so badly here.'[11] Yet, for most MPs, the retreat from Norway was not a strategic withdrawal but a humiliating defeat. The debate about the military setback in Norway had turned into a final vote of no confidence in Chamberlain's Premiership.

Chapter 21

Guilty Men

> 'When you approach a city to fight against it, you shall offer it terms
> of peace … if it does not make peace with you, but makes war against
> you, then you shall besiege it.' Deuteronomy 20:10-12

Following the House of Commons debate on the military withdrawal from
Norway, Chamberlain knew the time had come to form a new National
Government but the opposition had flatly refused to serve under him. So he
offered his resignation and proposed his favoured successor, Lord Halifax, in his
place. But Halifax had come to the conclusion that he could not command the
support or lead the country from the Lords in a time of war. Instead, following
discussions with Labour, Chamberlain had gone to see the King and put forward
Churchill's name: 'The King was as nice as possible and on behalf of the Queen
as well as himself he expressed what I know were very genuine regrets as well
as his own pleasure at my remaining in the Government.'[1] (Chamberlain had
been offered and accepted from Churchill the position of Lord President of the
Council, and he was also part of Churchill's five-man War Cabinet).

On returning from the palace, he had 'scribbled off my broadcast', which
had been commended by everyone for its sincerity. Churchill had also been
magnanimous towards him, telling him in a letter that 'My fate depends largely
on you'. It was another classic Churchill double-edged comment. However,
Chamberlain, as he had done so often in the past when dealing with Churchill,
preferred to take it at face value. To placate his predecessor, Churchill offered
Chamberlain his old role of Chancellor of the Exchequer. However, knowing this
would be strongly opposed by the Labour Party, Chamberlain felt that the best
option would be to accept the post of Lord President of the Council, a position
that would not bring him into direct conflict with the opposition.

Reflecting on the last few tumultuous days, Chamberlain told Ida that
his feelings had been 'overshadowed by the new aggression,' and until this
dissipated, 'everything else seems small and petty.' But though the weight of
responsibility had now been lifted from his shoulders, he felt little relief. While
Churchill continued to be friendly, those round him were more hostile, '[The]
stories that come to me of the method of Government making which is going

now on are disagreeably reminiscent of Lloyd Georgian ways.' His old nemesis continued with his Machiavellian plots, 'Ll.G.s speech yesterday … in which he sought to justify Hitler on the grounds that we had broken faith with Germany was deliberately made to separate himself from the new Government and stake out a position from which ultimately he might be called to make the peace … I know that he thinks we shall be beaten in this war.'

Following the announcement of Chamberlain's resignation, the public, unlike the politicians, had been kinder to him. 'I am getting an enormous number of letters and so is Annie. Many of them are very painful reading for the distress they reveal and almost without exception they declare their complete and unbroken confidence … But it does depress me much more than if they were all letters of abuse.' It was hard on Annie but, he wrote, 'She is standing up to it like a heroine.' To ease the painful transition, Churchill had agreed to them staying on at Number 10 for a month before going back to Number 11, a move Chamberlain caveated with the phrase 'if the Govt still stands.' What he would really miss, though, was his beloved Chequers, 'I shall have to go there some time to collect my things and say goodbye. It will be a bad wrench to part with that place where I have been so happy.'[2]

One of the letters Chamberlain received was from his birdwatching friend, Gilbert Collett, enclosing a sketch map of the tree where Chamberlain could find the kestrel he had been searching for in St James's Park during the Norway debate. The reply read:

> 13 May 1940
> 10 Downing Street
> Whitehall
>
> Dear Sir
> Mr. Chamberlain asks me to thank you very much for your letter and for the sketch, from which he had no difficulty at all in identifying the tree, a poplar which you described with the dead branch at the top. Mr Chamberlain will look out for the kestrel when he is walking by.
>
> Yours truly
> C.M. Campbell
> Private Secretary[3]

Gilbert wrote again two days later, sensitively expressing his regret at Chamberlain's resignation and asking if he would like to continue receiving bird reports from St James's Park. The next day the hard-working Private Secretary, C.M. Campbell, replied on Chamberlain's behalf:

16 May 1940
10 Downing Street
Whitehall

Dear Sir
Thank you for your note of May 15th, which I have been able to show to the Lord President.
 Mr. Chamberlain would be very glad if you would be so kind as to continue to send him any notes of interest about the Park. Mr. and Mrs. Chamberlain expect to be at this address for several weeks yet, but will be moving back eventually to No.11 Downing Street. No doubt the move will be made public.

Yours truly
C.M. Campbell[4]

Whatever was happening to him personally or politically, Chamberlain was not going to give up on a hobby that had helped him cope with his 'heavy burden of anxiety and responsibility'. The next day, Chamberlain wrote to his sister Hilda, apologising that, due the stress of the last few days, he had forgotten her birthday, 'To send you the customary wishes seems a mockery; I don't know if we should not rather all condole with one another on having lived into another Armageddon.' That day he had taken a longer than usual walk around St James's Park and watched carefree Londoners enjoying the sunshine, still blissfully unaware of what was to come. 'We shall try to bring them a little nearer to a sense of reality, though I daresay events will do more towards that end than anything we can think of.'
 Despite it all, he was glad to no longer have the responsibility, 'All my world has tumbled to bits in a moment. The national peril has so swamped all personal feelings that no bitterness remains. Indeed I used to say to Annie before the war came that if such a thing happened I thought I should have to hand over to someone else, for I knew what agony of mind it would mean for me to give directions that would bring death and mutilation and misery to so many.' Putting on a brave face, he told her it was 'providential that the revolution which overturned me coincided with the entry of the real thing.' Magnanimously, he praised his successor, saying that 'Winston has shown up well so far.'[5]

The old bitterness he felt towards a man he had kept out of the Cabinet for so long was dissipating quickly in the face of the hope that Churchill's appointment had generated around the world. 'He does take the opinions of the staff and doesn't attempt to force different views upon them or to shoulder off his colleagues,' he wrote to Hilda. It was a complete reversal of his view of Churchill from just a few weeks previously, reflecting the fact that their respective positions had also been reversed. Chamberlain was now the outsider in the Cabinet, a position reinforced when Churchill agreed to make the Labour leader, Clement Attlee, Deputy Leader of the House, 'Although W's first idea was that I should do this the Labour Party made trouble about it. So I gave it up without a sigh.' Astutely, Churchill did allow Chamberlain to retain leadership of the party, thus allowing him to concentrate on running the war. 'There has been much resentment among those who are personally devoted to me,' Chamberlain wrote, 'Both at my treatment and at the way the "treachery bench" has been given office. This would certainly have broken out if there had been any change in the Leadership but I hope now that our party will loyally accept the change and follow my example.'

Letters of support continued to pour in. Chamberlain calculated that he and Annie between them had received over 2,000, but unlike on previous occasions they felt 'too numbed' to answer many of them. Depression had also set in, Chamberlain morbidly admitting to Hilda, 'In fact my only desire is to get out of this horrible condition of chronic misery and I frankly envy Austen's peace. But there it is. One just goes on doing what lies in front to the best of one's ability without troubling to think of the future in this world or the next.' He signed off by referring back to the First World War, 'How vile that our children should have to go through what our generation suffered, as we thought, to make such things impossible again.'[6]

By the middle of May 1940, the battle for France was all but over. The British Expeditionary Force had been pushed back to the sea and surrounded in a pocket at Dunkirk. Hitler's Blitzkreig machine seemed all conquering. Writing on 25 May, Chamberlain told Ida, 'I am afraid that there has certainly been incompetence among the generals and the quality of the French troops does not seem as good as that of the Belgians.' This depressed him terribly and he confided, 'There is no pleasure in life for us just now. Week ends cannot be distinguished from week days; one works through each day wondering what new crisis will arise and only during the hours of sleep is the mind at rest.'

Looking ahead to his legacy, he told his sister, 'Whatever the outcome it is clear as daylight that if we had to fight in 1938 the results would have been far worse. It would be rash to prophesy the verdict of history, but if full access is obtained to all records it will be seen that I realised from the beginning our military weakness and did my best to postpone if I could not avert the war.' Again he blamed the dire situation on the Labour and Liberal opposition leaders who, 'denounced me for trying to maintain good relations with Italy and Japan, for refusing to back Republican Spain against Franco and for not "standing up to Hitler" at each successive act of aggression.' He concluded bitterly, 'It is they who ought to be held responsible for this fight, but they won't admit it naturally.'[7]

The day after Chamberlain wrote to his sister, the evacuation of Dunkirk started. From 26 May to 4 June over 338,000 troops were evacuated from the beaches by the Royal Navy and an armada of small ships in what became known as the 'Miracle of Dunkirk'. Reflecting on the withdrawal in his next letter, dated 1 June, he told Hilda, 'This has indeed been a terrible week. I knew early of Sunday that there was no chance of a French offensive on the Somme and that there was nothing else for the B.E.F. but to try and get out.' After attending a prayer service at Westminster Abbey he received the news, in a hastily arranged Cabinet meeting, that the Belgians had surrendered unconditionally. 'There seems to have been hardly any mistake that the French did not make,' he told his sister. 'Their generals were beneath contempt and with some notable exceptions the soldiers would not fight and would not even march. The Belgians were better but not steady in short as usual the brunt of all the hard fighting and the hard work fell upon the British.'[8]

He continued his letter the following day, Sunday 2 June, having read the morning papers and this only fuelled his sense of injustice, particularly the accusation that the 'glorious B.E.F was flung into the inferno "unarmored" owing to the lethargy of the late Government.' To put the record straight, he had asked Viscount Gort (6th Viscount Gort, 1886-1946, Commander of the British Expeditionary Force) in person if this was the case and, ever the diplomat, the Field Marshall had replied that the equipment had stood up 'extraordinarily well'. Believing the slur was groundless, he told his sister, 'The people who have been building up a "hate" campaign against me have not in any way given up .... I hear for instance that a party meet every evening at the Reform Club under the chairmanship of Clement Davies [1884-1962, Liberal MP for Montgomeryshire, chair of the All-Party Parliamentary Action Group], that treacherous Welshman who ratted from the last Government and worked his hardest to whip up opposition to it.'[9] Worse still, Churchill had approached him about bringing back into government another 'treacherous Welshman', David Lloyd George. Chamberlain threatened to retire and Churchill, fearing it would destabilise his new War Cabinet, parked the idea.

On Saturday, 8 June Chamberlain wrote to Ida from 10 Downing Street for the last time. It was a sad and poignant day. 'We don't actually make the move until Monday, but since we could not go to Chequers this week end we decided to utilise it for the exhausting task of getting our things across from the one house to the other and sorting them out in their new abode.' Reflecting on the move, Chamberlain wondered how long they would be there, an anxiety made worse after he learnt that Churchill had called a secret session without inviting him. To head off another Labour attack, he had gone to Churchill and offered to 'resign without reproaches'. Churchill refused to accept his resignation but asked him to reconsider his objection to bringing Lloyd George back. Reluctantly, Chamberlain agreed, on the condition that Lloyd George end their personal feud and the press campaign against him.

On Monday 10 June, as the French government fled to Bordeaux and Paris became an open city, Mussolini finally declared war on Britain and France. Fearing the conflict would soon be over and he would miss out on the spoils, Mussolini told his Army Chief-of-Staff, Marshal Badoglio, 'I only need a few thousand dead so that I can sit at the peace conference as a man who has fought.' The man who Chamberlain had spent most of his Premiership trying to win over had finally stabbed him in the back.[10]

On Saturday 15 June, Operation Ariel, the codename for the Allied evacuation of military staff and civilians from France, began. Writing to Hilda on the same day from 11 Downing Street, he told her, 'This has again been a terrible week and one night, for the first time, I was hardly able to get any sleep having "the horrors" all the time.' In particular he couldn't get the 'horror' of the 'treacherous Welshman' Lloyd George joining the government out of his mind. 'If there is a good chance of winning he will come in and get his share of the glory,' he told Hilda, 'If it goes the other way he will stay out so as to be ready to form another Govt and make peace for the terms of which he would be able to blame the maladministration of his predecessors.'

Chamberlain kept busy writing letters of sympathy to the families of men killed in the battle. 'It is too awful to have to do that twice in a lifetime. Thrice accursed Hitler.' Contemplating Hitler's next move, an invasion of Britain, he told Hilda, 'Our fate depends on our capacity to prevent invasion, as in Napoleon's day, but with many circumstances altered to our disadvantage. The key lies in the air.' Continuing the letter the next day, he confided that the outlook was grim, 'But no grimmer than before in reality for I have long seen this coming.'[11] It was an amazing statement coming from someone who had predicted so often there would not be an attack in the west. He signed off dejectedly, 'We keep well here but there is no pleasure in life and no prospect of any.'

On 18 June, Churchill addressed the House of Commons on the forthcoming Battle of Britain and, with Chamberlain listening, delivered one of his most famous speeches, declaring, 'If the British Commonwealth and Empire lasts for a thousand years men will still say, "This was their finest hour".' In France, the Government had capitulated and the Germans had moved the original 'Wagon de l'Armistice', used to sign the German surrender in 1918, back to exactly the same location in the Compiègne forest. The next day, a victorious Hitler signed the armistice and blew up the carriage, thus sealing the most humiliating defeat in French history.

Reflecting on the defeat, Chamberlain told Ida, 'As a matter of fact they never seem to have fought seriously anywhere where our troops were in contact with them, though we read much of their "heroic resistance" elsewhere ... I suppose we must expect an attempt at invasion pretty soon now and one always feels that it may come in an unexpected form. But I am confident that it will be heavily resisted by men in a very different mood from those the Germans have overrun so easily.' Writing at 11.30pm, he could 'hear the drone of our fighter planes overhead, probably going down the Thames estuary to meet the raiders.' As precaution, he was having his own and Annie's wills remade. He ended by telling his sister about his last trip to his beloved Chequers, which he had found heartbreaking, 'We managed to get down to Chequers last Wednesday and had 1½ hours there to say goodbye to the staff and to Spot and to look round my trees and the gardens. I am content now I have done that, and shall put Chequers out of my mind. We have had some happy days there but they are over anyhow and it is difficult to see how there can be much more happiness for any of us.'[12]

On Saturday 29 June, at 1.15am, just as Chamberlain had finished the last of three Cabinet meetings, the air raid sirens had sounded, so he, Annie and 'the servants' had run for the shelter. They were stuck there until about 2am, 'to my great annoyance', and not long after finally getting to sleep they were awoken again at 4am by the all-clear sirens wailing. Unlike his sleepless father, Chamberlain's son, Frank, was having a good war, despite two bombs having dropped near his field gun, falling just 300yds from his ammunition store. 'Frank makes no other comment on this incident than that it was "funny". Dorothy says he is in roaring spirits; in fact he seems to be enjoying the war thoroughly. One gets a different side of it when one is continually writing letters of sympathy to people who have lost their sons in France.'

To boost morale in the face of invasion, he had been asked to make a radio broadcast, but rather to his consternation, he had been limited to five minutes, 'which somewhat cramps my style'. Writing to Hilda the next day, he said, 'We are in fact alone and we are at any rate free of our obligations to the French who have been nothing but a liability to us. It would have been far better if they were neutral from the beginning.'[13] The one consolation of not being in power was more free time. The day before, he had wandered around Lady Stanley's (Sibyl Stanley known as Portia, 1893-1969) gardens at Sevenoaks, where he read books on the lawn, admired the view and had partaken of her 'sumptuous tea'.

On 5 July, the campaign to remove Chamberlain from office reached its zenith with the publication of the polemic *Guilty Men* by 'Cato'.[14] Cato was, in fact, three journalists: Michael Foot, the future Labour Leader, Frank Owen, a former Liberal MP, and Peter Howard, a Conservative MP. It was written under a pseudonym because their employer, the media tycoon Lord Beaverbrook, banned his journalists from writing for other publications. Beaverbrook was also guilty of being a supporter of both Chamberlain and appeasement but, unsurprisingly, did not feature in the book.

Guilty Men was written in the form of a tragic play which featured a cast of fifteen 'guilty' men who had failed to stand up to Hitler's 'blatant bullying' and rearm sufficiently in the face of increasing Nazi aggression. The cast were all members of the National Government and while most were Conservatives, some were Liberal Nationals and one was Labour. The play charted the history of Britain's appeasement of Hitler to the point that the government found itself staring invasion and defeat in the face. While Cato found many of the guilty men wanting, the scalp they really wanted was that of Chamberlain, who featured as the 'Umbrella Man'. The play concluded in pronounced capital letters:

ONE FINAL AND ABSOLUTE GUARANTEE IS STILL IMPERATIVELY DEMANDED BY A PEOPLE DETERMINED TO RESIST AND CONQUER: NAMELY, THAT THE MEN WHO ARE NOW REPAIRING THE BREACHES IN OUR WALLS SHOULD NOT CARRY ALONG WITH THEM THOSE WHO LET THE WALLS FALL INTO RUIN. THE NATION IS UNITED TO A MAN IN ITS DESIRE TO PROSECUTE THE WAR IN TOTAL FORM: THERE MUST BE A SIMILAR UNITY IN THE NATIONAL CONFIDENCE. LET THE GUILTY MEN RETIRE, THEN, OF THEIR OWN VOLITION, AND SO MAKE AN ESSENTIAL CONTRIBUTION TO THE VICTORY UPON WHICH ALL ARE IMPLACABLY RESOLVED.

Guilty Men soon became the classic denunciation of appeasement, with 200,000 copies sold in a matter of weeks from shops, news-stands and street barrows. In July 1940 alone it went through twelve print runs and effectively destroyed what remained of Chamberlain's battered reputation.

Chapter 22

I regret nothing

'I have fought the good fight, I have finished the race, I have kept the faith.' 2 Timothy 4:7

Two days after publication of *Guilty Men* Chamberlain wrote to Ida, wondering whether it would be his last letter before the invasion, '5 July was the date fixed by many prophets and seers with great precision and confidence. But here I am two days later writing peacefully on a lovely morning with no visible trace of war except the protected windows about me.' He continued, 'There is no doubt that preparations for an invasion are being carried on and all the indications point to its being attempted very shortly.' In spite of this he told his sister that, Churchill, who had been a dinner guest the day before, and Beaverbrook (Lord, Minister of Aircraft Production, 1879-1964) who had lunched with Chamberlain on the same day, both thought that Hitler would not risk it.

On the Home Front he told Ida, 'The Beaver gave me confidential figures and facts about aircraft production which, I must say, filled me with encouragement. I believe that we alone are now exceeding German output in our own production, i.e. without counting anything we get from the U.S.A.'[1] (While it was true that the British were producing planes faster than the Germans, in fact Fighter Command had calculated that the Luftwaffe had over 2,500 operational planes whereas the RAF could only muster 1,963). Three days later, on 10 July, the Battle of Britain began in earnest when the Luftwaffe attacked convoys in the Channel.

Contrasting the bravery of the RAF and the Fleet Air Arm with the cowardly attacks of his opponents, Chamberlain commented reproachfully, 'If I am personally responsible for deficiencies of tanks and A.A. guns I must be equally personally responsible for the efficiency of the Air Force and the Navy.' The French defeat still weighed heavily on his mind and, despite all his efforts, Ireland remained defiantly neutral. 'It may be that in the end we shall have to seize the Irish ports and land by force, but I am very anxious to avoid that if possible. The Irish have a terrible memory for grievances and I don't want to give them another to add to Strongbow and Cromwell and William III and the Black and Tans.'[2]

The 14 July found Chamberlain at 11 Downing Street, tired of waiting for Hitler to invade. 'I am disposed to think that the immediate prospect of invasion on a big scale has dimmed considerably ... And every week that passes makes it more difficult for such an operation to be carried out.' He felt that such an attack, 'After all the songs and propaganda must succeed or Hitler's prestige would suffer an alarming blow.' In the Far East the Japanese had demanded the closure of the Burma Road supply link to China, with whom they were at war, and fearing an attack, the British had agreed. Commenting, Chamberlain said wryly, 'We have not got the forces to fight Japs Germans and Italians at once.' The Americans had been insistent that the British took a 'bold line' with the Japanese but were 'not prepared to use force to help us'. It was a dilemma that Churchill was going to address in a broadcast that evening.

Chamberlain was also lined up to do a broadcast but complained to his sister that before the recording his throat had gone dry and he had only just been able to finish it. He did not know what had caused it, did not feel particularly tired and his friends had all told him he looked well. Yet deep down he knew something was wrong and it depressed him. 'But I have lost my spring and my spirits. All my recreations, flowers, fishing and shooting, country life have been taken from me and there is nothing to look forward to.' His only remaining pleasures were his walks in St James's Park and birdwatching. It was not just his interests that he missed but his beloved Chequers. His sisters, Hilda and Ida, had to put down their dog and he had expressed his sympathy, adding mournfully, 'I miss my Spot too'.[3]

The next day, 15 July, to cheer himself up, Chamberlain took a long walk around Green Park in the afternoon and, while there, watched two swifts screaming around the grounds. The following day he saw four more. Thrilling birds who spend most of their life on the wing, swifts stay in Britain for just three months of the year before migrating to central and southern Africa. Swifts thrived in wartime London. The magnificent Victorian buildings in Whitehall provided good nesting sites, as did prewar homes and bombed-out buildings. Like the tawny owl he heard hooting in the garden at No 10, Chamberlain would also have been familiar with the swift's place in folklore where it is known as 'The Devil Swallow' or 'The Devil's Screecher'. Long associated with the supernatural, the devil connection probably came about from its black plumage, scythe-like shape, and its habit of ascending from the heavens at dusk and screeching around buildings. As a result of seeing them, Chamberlain got his ornithological private secretary to send off a letter to Gilbert Collett:

11 Downing Street
Whitehall. S.W.

Dear Sir,
Mr. Chamberlain, remembering that once before his observation of a
swift over Horse Guards Parade was considered worth noting, thinks
you may care to know that he saw two swifts in Green Park yesterday
(July 15) afternoon and that this morning he saw at least four over the
partly dried lake in St. James's Park.

Yours truly
C.M. Campbell
Private Secretary.[4]

Gilbert Collett duly replied two days later, on 18 July, commending Chamberlain
on his observations of swifts and telling him about one of Britain's rarest and most
beautiful birds, the black redstart *Phoenicurus ochruros*, which had started nesting
in Whitehall. About the size of a robin, its name comes from the male's slate-grey
and black plumage, which contrasts with a striking red rump and tail. The black
redstart had first bred in London at the Wembley Exhibition Centre in 1926 and
during the Second World War the population boomed as a direct consequence of
the Blitz. Ironically, the bomb sites, with their large areas of sparsely vegetated
land between the shells of buildings, mimicked the black redstart's preferred
habitat of the scree slopes in the Alps. If ever there was a bird associated with the
war it was the black redstart, but unfortunately Chamberlain had not yet seen
one. Replying to Collett the next day, the indispensable Miss Campbell wrote:

11 Downing Street
Whitehall. S.W.
19th July, 1940

Dear Sir,
I am much obliged to you for your letter of the 18th which I have
handed to Mr. Chamberlain. He would like me to add that on the 17th
he saw a number of Swifts – perhaps seven or eight – flying over the
lake in the park, but yesterday he could only see one.
    Mr. Chamberlain had heard about the Black Redstarts in London
and was aware that a pair were frequenting the neighbourhood of

Whitehall and had even been heard in Downing Street. He himself has not however been fortunate enough to come across them.

Yours truly
(Miss) C.M. Campbell
Private Secretary[5]

Though neither Chamberlain nor Collett knew it at the time, it would be the last letter that they would ever exchange on birds. Over nearly three years – encompassing the most tumultuous events of Chamberlain's Premiership – an intimate relationship had developed between them. Although they probably never met in person, both men had come to know and respect each other through their shared love of ornithology. For Collett, it must have very flattering to have corresponded directly with the Prime Minister and to count him as a pen friend. For Chamberlain, the bird sightings sent to him by Collett and writing back about his own observations helped him cope during extraordinary times. Escaping from Number 10 and going birdwatching in St James's Park had been Chamberlain's antidote to living with the reoccurring nightmare that was Adolf Hitler.

That nightmare became a reality when, on 19 July, Hitler made a long and rambling speech in the Reichstag at the Kroll Opera House in Berlin. Entitled 'A Final Appeal for Peace and Sanity', it was a 'Declaration of Victory over France and the British Forces in the Western Campaign'.[6] The speech offered Britain 'peace or destruction'. 'In this hour and before this body,' said the Führer triumphantly in the presence of Chamberlain's former confidant, the Italian Foreign Minister, Count Galeazzo Ciano, 'I feel myself obliged to make one more appeal to reason to England.' He then made it clear that a rejection of his 'appeal to reason' would result in a final attack upon Britain with every resource that Germany could muster. To emphasise the point, the Luftwaffe dropped copies of the whole speech over southern England. It was the beginning of Britain's darkest hour.

Friday 19 July, was also the date when Chamberlain put his signature to a document that was to prove one of his greatest wartime legacies. After the fall of France, Churchill had asked chosen members of the government to coordinate resistance in France and in the other occupied countries. On 1 July at the Foreign Office a meeting had been held, chaired by Lord Halifax and attended by, among others, the Labour MP and economist, Dr Hugh Dalton (1887-1962), the Minister for Economic Warfare. Dalton had strongly opposed Chamberlain's policy of appeasement and had been instrumental in moving his party from a position of pacifism to armed resistance. The next day he wrote to

Halifax saying, 'We have got to organise movements in enemy–occupied territory comparable to the Sinn Fein movement in Ireland, to the Chinese Guerrillas now operating against Japan, to the Spanish Irregulars who played a notable part in Wellington's campaign or – one might admit it – to the organisations which the Nazis themselves have developed so remarkably in almost every country in the world. This 'democratic international' must use many different methods, including industrial and military sabotage, labour agitation and strikes, continuous propaganda, terrorist acts against traitors and German leaders, boycotts and riots.'

This recommendation was taken to Churchill, who agreed and asked Chamberlain to put together the rules of engagement for the new body, with Dalton at its head. Chamberlain drew up a draft and circulated it on 13 July, six days later, putting his signature to a secret paper which became the founding charter of the Special Operations Executive. 'A new organisation shall be established forthwith to co-ordinate all action, by way of subversion and sabotage, against the enemy overseas ... it will be important that the general plan for irregular offensive operations should be in step with the general strategic conduct of the war,' Chamberlain wrote.[7] It was the last great act of a statesman who, against all the odds, had made his way to the top of politics, but one for which he would get no credit (The SOE would go on to play a decisive part in winning the war, but as the organisation remained clandestine no one outside the War Cabinet and the senior echelons of the Foreign Office knew of its existence until the war was over).

The next day, Saturday 20 July 1940, Chamberlain was weighed down by an unfamiliar feeling, that of being in office but not in power. On hearing Hitler's speech the previous day, he wrote to Ida, 'It seems that he only repeated the same old distortion of history, the same abuse and threats and an even more astounding exhibition than usual of his power of self deception ... I believe he really thinks that he has always been generous, forgiving and anxious for friendship and that he is able to entirely forget or ignore the conditions on which that friendship was offered, just as, if his offer had been accepted, he would later on have forgotten his peace pledges whenever it suited him. It is just that power of thinking in blinkers which makes him so utterly ruthless and untrustworthy.' Chamberlain had at last got the measure of Hitler, but three years too late.

He continued to doubt that the invasion would now happen, writing, 'The German bully only enjoys war and slaughter and destruction when it falls on people who can't hit back.' Dismissing the book *Guilty Men*, he asked his sister, 'By the way does it occur to you when you read of the "Men of Munich who brought us into this mess" that the exploits of the Navy R.A.F. and B.E.F. must have been made possible by the "Men of Munich"? For no one can suppose that our equipment has all been turned out in the last six weeks. However, it would be foolish to expect from these blind partisans either reason or logic since those things are not allowed to interfere with their emotions.' It was a spirited defence of his Premiership, but in the face of invasion and defeat it rang very hollow. Chamberlain signed off, 'We have had two luncheon parties this week which went off very well but I am in considerable trouble with my inside which hasn't been working properly. Horder [Chamberlain's physician] is attending to me and doesn't take it seriously but it is very tiresome and adds a good deal to the miseries of life.'[8]

A week later, on Saturday 27 July 1940, Chamberlain wrote to Hilda, again from 11 Downing Street:

> I mentioned in my last letter that I was having trouble in my inside. As a matter of fact it has been going on for some time, gradually getting worse and Horder at last thought it best that I should be X rayed. That was done this week and the result is that I am to enter a nursing home next Monday for an operation that afternoon. It is not in itself a serious operation and I should be out again in a fortnight but the consequences will not be altogether pleasant and I shall have to adjust myself to a new condition of things.

In fact the X-ray revealed that Chamberlain was suffering from advanced colon cancer, but not wishing to alarm his sisters, he had down played his condition, writing in his own diary that it was a major operation and he had 'even chances'. He continued stoically, 'I understand that you will be coming up during the week and Annie will be able to tell you then more about it. 1940 has not been one of my happiest years, but it has been much worse for many other people than it has for me.'

Despite being tired and in pain, he flew up to Norwich and then inspected coastal defences at Ipswich. 'Of course I don't view these things with a professional eye but I came away with a very definite opinion that if the Germans tried to land there they would have a very rough time.' This made him doubt more than ever whether Hitler would risk an invasion. 'The long delay in undertaking an invasion while we go on strengthening our defence does make one wonder more than ever whether Hitler has not got some other plan in his head and I can't help thinking that he may be preparing in Norway for an attack on the line Iceland, Faroes, Shetlands, Orkneys and Caithness.' He added, 'You had better write here next week, for though I shall be at Nuffield House [a convalescence nursing home] Annie will bring my letters along.'[9]

On Monday 29 July, Chamberlain entered the nursing home where he underwent a major operation to cut out the cancerous tissue. However, the cancer had spread too far and the operation merely bought him more time. The truth was deliberately concealed from him by his doctors and although Chamberlain knew he was gravely ill, he did not know it was terminal. He left on 12 August after two weeks of 'fair hell' and retired to Highfield Park near Basingstoke, an estate owned by his aunt Lilian. There he spent six weeks convalescing, during which time Churchill, who had been saddened by the news, continued to send him Cabinet papers. He finally returned on 9 September, a shadow of his former self, writing in his diary:

> I still have to adjust myself to the new life of a partially crippled man, which is what I am. Any ideas which may have been in my mind about possibilities of further political activity and even a possibility of another Premiership after the war, have gone … At present, I have come into the very centre of the battle for Britain and the next few weeks may well see the turn of the tide one way or another. If we are still alive and free as I think we have every reason to hope I should like to go on working in my present capacity till the end of the war and then get out; and try and fill up the remainder without further public responsibilities.[10]

The Blitz on London had started on 7 September 1940, with government buildings in Whitehall, Parliament Street and the area around Downing Street targeted by the Luftwaffe in a series of day and night raids. On 11 September 1940, an unexploded anti-aircraft shell fell on Horse Guards Avenue inflicting several casualties. On 12 September, Horse Guards Avenue and the Ministry of Transport were struck by high-explosive bombs. The following day another anti-aircraft shell hit Horse Guards Parade, causing minor damage to Number 10's windows and roof.[11]

On Sunday 15 September, Chamberlain wrote his last letter to his sister, Ida, from 11 Downing Street. The heavy bombing raids had disrupted Cabinet meetings and he had spent long periods in the air raid shelter, still weak but determined to carry on. To make matters worse, Chamberlain was suffering from severe toothache and his dentist hadn't been able to help, so the problem tooth had to be extracted. It was 'another M(inor) M(isery) of which I seem to have rather an accumulation just now,' he wrote. On the subject of the invasion, Chamberlain told Ida, 'All Hitler's preparations for invasion are going on as though he meant to have a go at us. But I always return to the same conclusion, that failure would be so disastrous that he would hardly attempt it unless he was very sure of success and I can't see how he can have that certainty unless he can first subdue the R.A.F. He has not done that yet and I don't see how he is going to do it.'

His stepmother, Mary, had been to visit him. Despite being bombed out twice, she continued to sleep in her bed and Chamberlain told his sister that he admired her courage. 'The greatest danger appears now to come from the fragments of our own A.A. shells. I have picked up several ugly bits embedded in the lawn of our garden and one piece smashed a hole through a window of the Cabinet room, so our meetings are henceforth to be in another place.' Confiding to his sister that he was finding work difficult, he said, 'I am doing a certain amount of work but still manage to get my afternoon rest, though it is apt to broken up by the wailing of the sirens. Annie is I think feeling the strain but she stands up to it heroically.' He went on to tell Ida that the Germans continued to put out 'feelers for peace', but they were merely an attempt to get 'victors' terms without paying for them. 'As long as that is the case they will get no response here. Horder was here this morning after a night spent in going round shelters in the east end. His account of the conditions was rather appalling but he reports that the spirit was quite undefeated. We are going to see this bloody thing through, was what was said to him.'[12]

On Tuesday 10 September 1940, he had been granted an audience with the King and Queen. Visibly shocked at Chamberlain's appearance, George VI was moved that a person he counted as a friend and confidant was so gravely ill. 'I saw the King on Tuesday and he showed me the damage done by a delay action bomb. Since then a more determined attack has been made but happily with no loss of life or serious damage. It is bad tactics on the part of the Germans for it only makes our people more angry and excites the indignation of the Americans. I don't know when this will reach you, but Mary's letter of the 7th to Highfield reached me on the 14th. I wonder what I shall have to write about next week! Your affectionate brother, Neville.'[13]

In considerable pain and in constant need of medication, he left Downing Street for the last time on Thursday, 19 September 1940, resigned to his fate and recording in his diary that he had 'nothing to look forward to but a progressive deterioration during which … I shall be an increasing burden and nuisance to those about me.' Going back to Highfield Park on 22 September, he tended his resignation, which was initially rejected by Churchill so they could 'go on together through the storm', but later reluctantly accepted due to Chamberlain's failing health. The press reaction to his resignation was 'not before time', which hurt him greatly as it was 'without the slightest sign of sympathy for the man or even any comprehension that there may be a human tragedy in the background.' On 29 September, in recognition of his service, Churchill offered Chamberlain the highest honour for chivalry, The Order of the Garter, but Chamberlain refused, saying he wanted, like his father, to die as plain Mr Chamberlain.[14] On 11 October he made a final broadcast, not mentioning his illness but instead defiantly stating 'It is not conceivable that human civilisation should be permanently overcome by such evil men and evil things, and I feel proud that the British Empire, though left to fight alone, still stands across their path unconquered and unconquerable.'

Reflecting on his life he wrote:

> It was the hope of doing something to improve the conditions of life for the poorer people that brought me at past middle life into politics, and it is some satisfaction to me that I was able to carry out some part of my ambition, even though its permanency may be challenged by the destruction of the war. For the rest I regret nothing that I have done and I can see nothing undone that I ought to have done. I am therefore content to accept the fate that has so suddenly overtaken me and only trust that I may not have to bear my disabilities too long.[15]

Chamberlain was too weak to travel so, at his request, a few of his closest friends visited him at Highfield. They included the King and Queen who drove over on 14 October specially to say goodbye to a faithful public servant who, over time, had gone from being a politician to a friend. Another welcome visitor was his friend and confidant, Sir Horace Wilson, who had shared his ill-fated flights to Germany to appease Hitler. On 31 October, Chamberlain resigned from being chair of the Conservative Research Department after ten eventful years. While his mind remained alert, his condition now deteriorated rapidly as the cancer aggressively spread throughout his body. One of the last persons to see him who were not family was Lord Halifax, on 7 November, who noted, 'It was a melancholy visit, but he was very brave and contented. And much touched by the kindness of his friends – and indeed of hundreds more who had written.'[16] Two days later, on 9 November 1940 at 5.30 p.m., Neville Chamberlain died quietly in his sleep with his wife Annie and his two sisters, Hilda and Ida, at his side. He was 71 years old. In life he had declared peace for our time but it had eluded him. In death he had finally found peace for all time.

Epilogue

Chamberlain's death was a release for a man who, in his final six months as Prime Minister, had been vilified and blamed for everything that had gone wrong in the war, and who in his final six weeks of life, had seen his body ravaged by cancer. On the day after his death, 10 November, the celebrated diarist and fanatical supporter of Chamberlain, Henry 'Chips' Channon (1897-1958), marked his passing. He had once memorably described Chamberlain as 'The greatest Englishman alive', now in death he wrote, 'Though I loved him, I am glad: the shafts of malice had hurt him and probably killed him. Now the reaction, already begun, will have added impetus, and his place in history will be more secure. He had nothing to live for; for all his hopes had gone.'[1] More forgivingly Mr. Hore-Belisha, the former Secretary of State for War, also paid tribute saying 'I am glad now to feel that when, after four months of war, a breach in our association came … I was able to meet his request in the circumstances of the time to refrain from controversy and thus to spare him additional anxiety. History will judge his achievements but his contemporaries will be of one accord in praising his high character, his elevated standards of duty, and his industrious devotion to the service of the State.'[2]

On 12 November in Church House, the temporary home of the House of Commons, Churchill paid tribute to him. In a long and moving address to a silent House of Commons he said, 'It fell to Neville Chamberlain in one of the supreme crises of the world to be contradicted by events, to be disappointed in his hopes, and to be deceived and cheated by a wicked man.'[3] It was a magnanimous speech from a man who had been held back in his political career by Chamberlain, but who also admired many of his qualities, not least his devotion to work and loyalty to party. Yet, pointedly, he also said, 'No one is obliged to alter the opinions which he has formed or expressed upon issues which have become a part of history,' adding, 'A few years later, when the perspective of time has lengthened, all stands in a different setting.' Churchill was to be true to his word when, just seven months after Chamberlain's death, the old enmity returned when he described him as 'the narrowest, most ignorant, most ungenerous of men,' who 'knew not the first thing about war, Europe or foreign politics.'[4]

On 13 November, a Memorial Service was held at Birmingham Parish Church addressed by the Lord Mayor of Birmingham, Sir Wilfrid Martineau. On the same day, Chamberlain's body was cremated at Golders Green crematorium in London. There was no ceremony and only two members of his family were present, his wife, Annie, and his daughter, Dorothy. In a break with tradition, the cremation took place before the funeral service because of security considerations, and at the insistence of the Dean of Westminster Abbey, Paul de Labilliere, who required anybody interred there to be cremated because of lack of space.[5] The next day his ashes were brought to Westminster Abbey under the tightest security, for fear that a solitary German bomb could take out leading members of the government. The abbey had already suffered blast damage from a nearby bomb and many of its great stained glass windows were boarded up. Elaborate and top secret evacuation plans had been drawn up by the government and the Dean to ensure the safety of those attending. *Pathé News* filmed those arriving at the abbey and, in a brief commentary entitled 'He strove for peace', said: 'To Westminster Abbey come representatives of all phases of public life to pay homage to the ashes of Neville Chamberlain, the man of peace. The Duke of Gloucester represents His Majesty, Mr. Churchill, who succeeded Mr. Chamberlain as Prime Minister, joins his Cabinet colleagues in mourning the loss of the man who sought peace to the limit of human endurance. So a true Briton passes, a man of peace has found the peace which must come to us all.'[6]

Among those of his family in attendance were his devoted wife Annie and daughter Dorothy, her husband, Stephen Lloyd, his stepmother, Mary, and his two sisters, Ida and Hilda, with whom he had corresponded nearly every week of his adult life. Chamberlain's son, Frank, was on active service in Malta and unable to attend. Among the politicians in attendance were Sir Horace Wilson, Chamberlain's confidant, and Alexander Cadogan, the most senior official at the Foreign Office and a vocal opponent of appeasement. The pall bearers included Churchill, members of the War Cabinet and Chamberlain's cousin, Arthur. Inappropriately, there was even a suggestion that Chamberlain's nemesis, Lloyd George should be one, but this was sensibly dropped. At the service, which began at noon, Churchill was moved to tears, but Cadogan, sitting at the back among the shattered windows of the abbey, later wrote, 'Coldest thing I've ever known,' and 'Rather too long a service'.[7] What Cadogan considered a lengthy service included the stirring verses of 'I vow to thee, my country' and the hymn 'Now the labourer's task is o'ver'. After the Lord's Prayer, Bible verses Matthew 5:8-9 and Matthew 5:6, from an introduction to the Sermon on the Mount, were read out:

Blessed are the pure in heart
For they shall see God

Blessed are the peacemakers
For they shall be called the children of God
Blessed are they that hunger and thirst after righteousness
For they shall be filled

The service had been drawn up by the Dean in close cooperation with Churchill to ensure that Chamberlain's supporters, already aggrieved that he was being scapegoated, were not given further cause for complaint. The Dean was also very aware that Chamberlain was a lapsed Unitarian who had never had an easy relationship with religion. Yet in his youth Chamberlain had been a regular churchgoer and he had never publicly renounced his faith. Perhaps more appropriate to Chamberlain's memory would have been the verse 5:10 from Matthew:

Blessed are those who are persecuted because of righteousness
For theirs is the kingdom of heaven

Among the hundreds of letters of commiseration received by Chamberlain's widow was one from Chamberlain's birdwatching friend, Gilbert Collett. In it he recalled the happy times they had spent sharing bird reports and how it had been a privilege to have known such a knowledgeable and enthusiastic ornithologist. On the black-bordered condolence note, which was sent to back to Collett, Annie added in her own hand, 'I am so glad to have your message, for I knew how interested my husband was in exchanging news of birds with you.'

It was a view echoed in a long and thoughtful obituary which was published in *Nature* magazine on 16 November 1940, which read:

The death of Mr. Neville Chamberlain on November 9, occurring at so short an interval after his retirement from political life, has afforded him little opportunity for the enjoyment of that leisure that he has earned by his strenuous life. The tragedies of the three years 1937-40 need no recapitulation. The death knell of the League of Nations as a political force had already sounded when Mr. Chamberlain accepted office as Prime Minister, and he turned to the policy of 'appeasement' and the formation of a 'peace front'. The policy achieved its greatest success with Mr. Chamberlain's almost superhuman effort at Munich which was "to secure peace in our time" – and it was its greatest failure. Although the career of Mr. Neville Chamberlain was political, a considerable amount of his time was devoted to amateur natural history.

In later years in London he maintained this interest in entomology and recorded the wood-leopard moth in the garden in Downing Street; but then his interests were more devoted to ornithology and he contributed to the annual report on the bird sanctuaries in the Royal Parks, published by H.M Stationery Office … St. James's Park was his special venue, where his early morning walks during his office as wartime premier were reminiscent of the walks of the late Lord Grey of Fallodon during the War of 1914-18. In addition to the pied wagtail and the redwing, Mr Chamberlain recorded the lesser black-backed gull, the carrion crow, the swift, the kestrel, the grey wagtail and the wheatear in St. James's Park. He also recorded a melanic form of pied wagtail in Downing Street, and in the garden common to No.10 and No.11 he maintained a bird table and bird-boxes, inducing the blue tit to nest there and blackbirds and song thrushes to become resident. He also shared Lord Grey's fondness for fly-fishing.[8]

It was an obituary that came close to summing up his true legacy: the politician whose efforts to win peace were thwarted by Hitler, Munich and the path to war and the natural historian whose love of nature helped him to deal with some of the most momentous events of the twentieth century.

On 15 February 1941 Gilbert Collett received a letter out of the blue. It read:

Highfield Park
Heckfield
Basingstoke

Dear Mr Collett
Mrs. Chamberlain asks me tell you how much she appreciated the message which you sent to her last November. She is wondering whether you happen to have kept all the communications and messages which Mr. Chamberlain sent you during the past years either through myself or any other secretaries, noting his observations on birds in St.James's Park.

In this case would you be willing to send them here to me in order that I might take copies of these communications for Mrs. Chamberlain? Mrs. Chamberlain would be very grateful if you would arrange this and it would of course be wise to send the letters by registered post.

Can you by chance remember the name of the big gull which Mr. Chamberlain was always so delighted to see returning each year?

Was it the Greater Black-backed gull and had it a habit of standing on the rock facing into the west wind?

Yours very truly
C.M. Campbell[9]

Collett duly sent the correspondence to Mrs Chamberlain and received a grateful reply a week later on 21 February 1941:

Highfield Park
Heckfield
Basingstoke

Dear Mr Collett
Thank you so much for sending me through Miss Campbell your letters from Mr. Chamberlain and for telling me that the bird I remember his noticing afresh each year was the Greater Black-backed Gull which used to stand on the rock facing into the wind.

With regard to your letters to Mr. Chamberlain I am afraid that unfortunately he would not have kept these any more than he kept copies of his letters to you. His correspondence was so very large that he was only able to keep a small proportion of it and in any case his memory was so good over the things which interested him in natural history that he would he would have no need to refer to the written word.

I remember seeing the newspaper cutting about the scaup. Mr. Chamberlain was very much surprised that there should be a scaup on the lake – and your letter accounts for this.

Yours sincerely
Anne Chamberlain[10]

Gilbert Collett was to die on July 24 1964, at the age of 76, in hospital at Chippenham, Wiltshire. He is best remembered for his contribution to philately, in particular for being the first President of the British West Indies Study Circle, and his collection of Jamaican stamps, considered one of the finest of its kind.[11] However, his contribution to natural history, and ornithology in particular, has been largely forgotten. As well as keeping meticulous records of the birds he discovered in St James's Park from 1932-1940, he also kept a very detailed bird record of his travels, including clippings from many journals and magazines. They include an article dated 13 July 1935 on golden eagles *Aquila chrysaetos* from the *Field* magazine by the famous Scottish naturalist, Seton Gordon (1886-1977). It contains the prophetic line, 'I have christened the eaglets Hitler and Mussolini, for they early begin to learn the art of war.'

Chamberlain's love of nature was the one constant strand running through his personal, professional and political life. A dedicated and committed conservationist who was years ahead of his time, Chamberlain's interests in the natural world were truly eclectic and encompassed botany, lepidopterology, entomology, ornithology, fishing, shooting and forestry. He was one of the early members of the Society for the Promotion of Nature Reserves, and a founding member of the Council for the Preservation of Rural England. Today, in their modern guises as The Wildlife Trusts and the Campaign to Protect Rural England, they count between them over 850,000 members and among their long list of achievements are the creation of Britain's national parks, the green belt, the Town and Country Planning Act 1947 and the creation of over 2,300 nature reserves protecting wildlife. Through his support and encouragement of these fledgling organisations, Chamberlain can rightly claim these outstanding achievements to be an important part of his legacy.

Sadly, the list of birds Chamberlain recorded at Downing Street has been lost with the passage of time. However, throughout his life he kept a range of detailed diaries and notebooks on subjects he loved, from entomology to orchids, fishing to furnishings, game to gardening and sports to wines. In his fishing diary the final entry is dated 22 June 1940, when he caught two trout before being summoned back to the War Cabinet to discuss the Fall of France. 'I really can't consent to die,' he once reportedly said, 'before they arrange some fishing in the next world.'[12] Yet it was to birdwatching that he turned as Prime Minister, time and again, in response to the immense pressure he found himself under as he tried in vain to appease Hitler and prevent a Second World War. His daily walks in St James's Park became more than just exercise or an opportunity to escape the suffocating confines of Number 10, they were his way of coping with an evil tyrant heading inexorably towards war. Munich and appeasement may have defined Neville Chamberlain's Premiership but nature and birds defined his personality.

References

Chapter 1

1. Silk handkerchief, 1938, author's collection
2. *The Daily Telegraph and Morning Post*, Saturday, October 1 1938, p11
3. Cato, *Guilty Men* (1940), p53
4. Neville Chamberlain to Hilda, 1923 British Industries Fair, *Papers of Neville Chamberlain*, NC18/1/1-1168, University of Birmingham
5. George Meredith, *Poems and Lyrics of the Joy of Earth/Lark Ascending* (1883), https://en.wikisource.org
6. W, Mandy *Seeking information on Captain C. N. Pelly - my grandfather*, (2011), https://www.pprune.org
7. Press photo, 1940, author's collection
8. Heston Aerodrome, https://en.wikipedia.org
9. *Chips: The Diaries of Sir Henry Channon* 29 September 1938, p166 Earl Winterton (who Chamberlain had fallen out with over rearmament of the airforce)
10. Faber, D., *Munich:Appeasement and World War II* (2008)
11. Gibbs, Sir Philip, *This Nettle Danger*, (1939), Hutchinson
12. Goldstein, E., Lukes, I., eds, *The Munich Crisis, 1938: Prelude to World War II* (1999), p289
13. Cato, *Guilty Men* (1940), p52
14. Winston Churchill, in a letter to Lloyd George 13 August 1938, https://richardlangworth.com
15. Haigh, Morris and Peters, *The Guardian book of Munich* (1988), p240
16. Mullin, G., 'Peace for our time' plane ticket for Neville Chamberlain's flight to 1938 Munich conference with Hitler to try to prevent Second World War sells for £17,000, *Daily Mail*, 21 July 2014
17. *BBC Archive*, Chamberlain returns from Munich with Anglo-German Agreement, 30 September 1938, http://www.bbc.co.uk/archive
18. Rodgson, S., *The Man Who Made The Peace* (1938), p108
19. Oster conspiracy, https://en.wikipedia.org

20. Neville Chamberlain, 30 September 1938, '*Peace for our time*', https://en.wikipedia.org
21. *The London Illustrated News*, 8 October 1938
22. Neville Chamberlain to Hilda, 2 October 1938, *Papers of Neville Chamberlain*, NC18/1/1-1168, University of Birmingham
23. Haigh, Morris and Peters, *The Guardian book of Munich* (1988), p231
24. Ibid
25. *Daily Herald*, 1 October 1938
26. Self, R., *Neville Chamberlain - A Biography* (2006), p235
27. *Weekly Illustrated*, 8 October 1938
28. *The Daily Telegraph and Morning Post*, October 1 1938, p10
29. *Nature* magazine, vol. 142, No. 3597, October 8, 1938
30. *Leicester Mercury*, 30 September 1938
31. *The Daily Telegraph and Morning Post*, 1 October 1938, p6

Chapter 2

1. Municipal Dreams, *Municipal Housing in Liverpool before 1914: the 'first council houses in Europe'*, (2013), https://municipaldreams.wordpress.com
2. Dargue, W., A History of Birmingham Places & Place names . . . from A to Y, *Victorian Britain 1837-1901*, https://billdargue.jimdo.com
3. Feiling, K., *The Life of Neville Chamberlain* (1946), p37
4. Ward, R., *The Chamberlains* (2015), p108
5. Church of the Messiah, Birmingham, https://en.wikipedia.org
6. Plant, Helen, *'ye are all one in Christ Jesus': aspects of unitarianism and feminism in Birmingham, c. 1869–90*, (2007), http://www.tandfonline.com
7. *Cavalcade The British News Magazine*, February 19 1938, p22
8. Ruston, Alan, *Neville Chamberlain, Dictionary of Unitarian & Universalist Biography*, (2006), http://uudb.org
9. Dilks, D., *Neville Chamberlain, Vol One 1869-1929* (2010)
10. Wilmot, F., *The History of Harborne Hall* (1991)
11. Ibid
12. Feiling, K., *The Life of Neville Chamberlain* (1946), p7
13. The Chamberlain Highbury Trust, *History of Highbury and the Grounds* https://chamberlainhighburytrust.co.uk
14. *Where is it?*, Entomology books belonging to Neville Chamberlain, Birmingham Museum Archive
15. Seger, Donna *Mary Endicott: Puritan Princess*, (2017), https://streetsofsalem.com

16. Feiling, K., *The Life of Neville Chamberlain* (1946), p16
17. *The Entomologists Monthly Magazine*, Vol xxvi, 1890
18. *Pyrisitia Chamberlaini* Chamberlain's Yellow, Butler, (1878), https://www.butterfliesofcuba.com
19. Feiling, K., *The Life of Neville Chamberlain* (1946) p30
20. Anthony, Paul, *A Nightingale Sang in Highbury Park: Chamberlain's Birds*, (2016), http://highburyparkfriends.org.uk

Chapter 3

1. Feiling, K., *The Life of Neville Chamberlain* (1946), p34
2. Joseph Chamberlain, https://en.wikipedia.org
3. Feiling, K., *The Life of Neville Chamberlain* (1946), p41
4. Hardman, R., 'King of the Pranksters – The Uproarious Story of the Prime Minister's Brother-in-law', *Daily Mail*, 23 November 2008
5. Hodgson, S., *The Man who made the Peace* (1938), p23
6. Kenrick, K.L., *Birmingham Natural History and Philosophical Society Centenary Celebrations: the records of the society and the story they tell.* Birmingham Natural History and Philosophical Society (1958)
7. Hodgson, S., *The Man who made the Peace* (1938), p12
8. Northumberland Wildlife Trust, *A 'rather grand' idea 100 years ago*, 2012, http://www.nwt.org.uk
9. Chamberlain, I &H., *Common Objects of the Riviera* (George Rutledge and Sons, 1913)
10. Royal Society for the Protection of Birds, *Our history - A history of the RSPB, from its humble beginnings, to the thriving far-reaching organisation it is today*, https://www.rspb.org.uk
11. Marsh, P., *The Chamberlain Litany* (2010), p117

Chapter 4

1. Neville Chamberlain to Hilda, 2 August 1915, *Papers of Neville Chamberlain*, NC18/1/1-1168, University of Birmingham
2. Neville Chamberlain to Hilda, 14 March 1915, *Papers of Neville Chamberlain*, NC18/1/1-1168, University of Birmingham
3. Neville Chamberlain to Hilda, 4 September 1915, *Papers of Neville Chamberlain*, NC18/1/1-1168, University of Birmingham
4. Neville Chamberlain to Hilda, 17 October 1915, *Papers of Neville Chamberlain*, NC18/1/1-1168, University of Birmingham

5. Neville Chamberlain to Ida, 19 February 1916, *Papers of Neville Chamberlain*, NC18/1/1-1168, University of Birmingham
6. Neville Chamberlain to Beatrice, 26 March 1916, *Papers of Neville Chamberlain*, NC1/13/3/39-40, University of Birmingham
7. Neville Chamberlain to Hilda, 15 April 1916, *Papers of Neville Chamberlain*, NC18/1/1-1168, University of Birmingham
8. Neville Chamberlain to Hilda, 14 May 1916, *Papers of Neville Chamberlain*, NC18/1/1-1168, University of Birmingham
9. Neville Chamberlain to Hilda, 2 September 1916, *Papers of Neville Chamberlain*, NC18/1/1-1168, University of Birmingham
10. Neville Chamberlain to Hilda, 16 July 1916, *Papers of Neville Chamberlain*, NC18/1/1-1168, University of Birmingham
11. Neville Chamberlain to Hilda, 18 October 1916, *Papers of Neville Chamberlain*, NC18/1/1-1168, University of Birmingham
12. Neville Chamberlain to Hilda, 8 July 1916, *Papers of Neville Chamberlain*, NC18/1/1-1168, University of Birmingham
13. Neville Chamberlain to Hilda, 16 July 1916, *Papers of Neville Chamberlain*, NC18/1/1-1168, University of Birmingham
14. Birmingham City Council, *Lady Mayoress's Depot Committee Report*, 26 April 1917
15. Neville Chamberlain to Hilda, 3 December 1916, *Papers of Neville Chamberlain*, NC18/1/1-1168, University of Birmingham
16. Neville Chamberlain to Hilda, 3 December 1916, *Papers of Neville Chamberlain*, NC18/1/1-1168, University of Birmingham
17. Neville Chamberlain to Hilda, 12 August 1917, *Papers of Neville Chamberlain*, NC18/1/1-1168, University of Birmingham
18. Feiling, K., *Life of Neville Chamberlain* (1946), p65
19. Chamberlain, N. *Norman Chamberlain, A Memoir* (John Murray, 1923)

Chapter 5

1. Crawford, Elizabeth, *Suffrage Stories: 'From Frederick Street to Winson Green': The Birmingham Women's Suffrage Campaign*, 2008, https://womanandhersphere.com
2. Harrison, B., *Separate Spheres: The Opposition to Women's Suffrage in Britain* (1978), p121
3. Feiling, K., *Life of Neville Chamberlain* (1946), p84
4. Neville Chamberlain to Hilda, 20 March 1922, *Papers of Neville Chamberlain*, NC18/1/1-1168, University of Birmingham

5. *Birmingham Conservative and Unionist Association*, Management Committee Minutes, 29 December 1922
6. Moseley, O., *My Life* (1968) pp184–185
7. Neville Chamberlain to Hilda, 1 November 1924, *Papers of Neville Chamberlain*, NC18/1/1-1168, University of Birmingham
8. Neville Chamberlain to Hilda, 15 November 1924, *Papers of Neville Chamberlain*, NC18/1/1-1168, University of Birmingham
9. Broxton, Anthony, *Let's Build The Houses Quick! How Labour tackled previous housing crises*, 20 August 2017 https://tidesofhistory.wordpress.com
10. Neville Chamberlain to Hilda, 23 May 1925, *Papers of Neville Chamberlain*, NC18/1/1-1168, University of Birmingham
11. Rating and Valuation Act 1925, http://www.legislation.gov.uk
12. Hodgson, S., *The Man who made the Peace* (1938), p35
13. Neville Chamberlain to Hilda, 1 November 1925, *Papers of Neville Chamberlain*, NC18/1/1-1168, University of Birmingham
14. Sharp, Clifford, 'Shall we hang Mr. Churchill or not?' *New Statesman* 1926, https://www.newstatesman.com
15. *Manchester Guardian* 'War on ugly buildings', 3 September 1926
16. Campaign to Protect Rural England, *Horrors, atrocities and monstrosities, Neville Chamberlain* 7 September 1926, http://www.cpre.org.uk

Chapter 6

1. Self, R., *Neville Chamberlain* (2006), p133
2. Neville Chamberlain to Hilda, 2 June 1929, *Papers of Neville Chamberlain*, NC18/1/1-1168, University of Birmingham
3. Ibid
4. Lord Lexden, *'Neville Chamberlain – the unappreciated merits'*, Conservative Home, 13 April 2018, https://www.conservativehome.com
5. Feiling, K., *The Life of Neville Chamberlain* (1946), p180
6. Neville Chamberlain to Hilda, 24 October 1931, *Papers of Neville Chamberlain*, NC18/1/1-1168, University of Birmingham
7. Neville Chamberlain to Hilda, 7 November 1931, *Papers of Neville Chamberlain*, NC18/1/1-1168, University of Birmingham
8. Austen to Neville Chamberlain, 5 November 1931, *Papers of Neville Chamberlain*, NC1/27/1-131, University of Birmingham
9. Hansard Import Duties, 4 February 1932, https://api.parliament.uk

10. Titcomb, James, How the Bank of England abandoned the gold standard, *The Daily Telegraph*, 7 January 2015
11. Rogers, R., Order!Order! A Parliamentary Miscellany *The Times* letters, 24 January 1933, (2009), p73
12. Neville Chamberlain to Hilda, 29 January 1933, *Papers of Neville Chamberlain*, NC18/1/1-1168, University of Birmingham
13. Webb, Sam, Adolf gives Germany the thumbs-up: Chilling footage shows Hitler take office as Nazis swept into power 80 years ago, *Daily Mail*, 30 January 2013
14. Self, R., *Neville Chamberlain* (2006), p203

Chapter 7

1. Neville Chamberlain to Ida, 29 April 1933, *Papers of Neville Chamberlain*, NC18/1/1-1168, University of Birmingham
2. Neville Chamberlain to lda, 28 October 1933, *Papers of Neville Chamberlain*, NC18/1/1-1168, University of Birmingham
3. Neville Chamberlain to lda, 11November 1933, *Papers of Neville Chamberlain*, NC18/1/1-1168, University of Birmingham
4. Neville Chamberlain to lda, 12 May 1934, *Papers of Neville Chamberlain*, NC18/1/1-1168, University of Birmingham
5. Neville Chamberlain to Hilda, 2 January 1934, *Papers of Neville Chamberlain*, NC18/1/1-1168, University of Birmingham
6. Neville Chamberlain to Hilda 7 January 1934, *Papers of Neville Chamberlain*, NC18/1/1-1168, University of Birmingham
7. Lord Lexden, *Neville Chamberlain – the unappreciated merits*, Conservative Home, 13 April 2018 https://www.conservativehome.com
8. Neville Chamberlain to Hilda, 25 February 1934, *Papers of Neville Chamberlain*, NC18/1/1-1168, University of Birmingham
9. Neville Chamberlain to lda, 17 March 1934, *Papers of Neville Chamberlain*, NC18/1/1-1168, University of Birmingham
10. Neville Chamberlain to Hilda, 9 June 1934, *Papers of Neville Chamberlain*, NC18/1/1-1168, University of Birmingham
11. Neville Chamberlain to Hilda, 28 July 1934, *Papers of Neville Chamberlain*, NC18/1/1-1168, University of Birmingham
12. Ibid
13. Neville Chamberlain to Hilda, 4 August 1934, 1938 *Papers of Neville Chamberlain*, NC18/1/1-1168, University of Birmingham

14. Neville Chamberlain to lda, 24 November 1934, *Papers of Neville Chamberlain*, NC18/1/1-1168, University of Birmingham
15. Neville Chamberlain to Hilda, 18 March 1935, *Papers of Neville Chamberlain*, NC18/1/1-1168, University of Birmingham
16. Neville Chamberlain to Hilda, 23 March 1935, *Papers of Neville Chamberlain*, NC18/1/1-1168, University of Birmingham
17. Neville Chamberlain to Hilda, 21 April 1935, *Papers of Neville Chamberlain*, NC18/1/1-1168, University of Birmingham
18. Neville Chamberlain to Hilda, 18 January 1936, *Papers of Neville Chamberlain*, NC18/1/1-1168, University of Birmingham
19. Ibid
20. Neville Chamberlain to Hilda, 1 February 1936, *Papers of Neville Chamberlain*, NC18/1/1-1168, University of Birmingham
21. Neville Chamberlain to Hilda, 9 February 1936, *Papers of Neville Chamberlain*, NC18/1/1-1168, University of Birmingham
22. British Birds *Notes reed-buntings flocking in Spring*, Vol. XV,1922, https://britishbirds.co.uk

Chapter 8

1. Neville Chamberlain to Hilda, 19 April 1936, *Papers of Neville Chamberlain*, NC18/1/1-1168, University of Birmingham
2. Neville Chamberlain to lda, 24 May 1936, *Papers of Neville Chamberlain*, NC18/1/1-1168, University of Birmingham
3. Petrie, C., *The Chamberlain Tradition* (1938), p270
4. Neville Chamberlain to Hilda, 23 September 1936, *Papers of Neville Chamberlain*, NC18/1/1-1168, University of Birmingham
5. Neville Chamberlain to lda, 31 October 1936, *Papers of Neville Chamberlain*, NC18/1/1-1168, University of Birmingham
6. Neville Chamberlain to Hilda, 14 November 1938, *Papers of Neville Chamberlain*, NC18/1/1-1168, University of Birmingham
7. Ibid
8. Neville Chamberlain to Hilda, 28 November 1936, *Papers of Neville Chamberlain*, NC18/1/1-1168, University of Birmingham
9. Neville Chamberlain to lda, 1 December 1936, *Papers of Neville Chamberlain*, NC18/1/1-1168, University of Birmingham
10. Junkers Ju-88, https://en.wikipedia.org
11. Neville Chamberlain to lda, 16 January 1937, *Papers of Neville Chamberlain*, NC18/1/1-1168, University of Birmingham

12. Neville Chamberlain to lda, 6 February 1937, *Papers of Neville Chamberlain*, NC18/1/1-1168, University of Birmingham
13. Neville Chamberlain to lda, 21 March 1937, *Papers of Neville Chamberlain*, NC18/1/1-1168, University of Birmingham
14. Neville Chamberlain to lda, 10 April 1937, *Papers of Neville Chamberlain*, NC18/1/1-1168, University of Birmingham
15. Neville Chamberlain to Hilda, 25 April 1937, *Papers of Neville Chamberlain*, NC18/1/1-1168, University of Birmingham
16. Neville Chamberlain to Hilda, 15 May 1937, *Papers of Neville Chamberlain*, NC18/1/1-1168, University of Birmingham
17. Neville Chamberlain to lda, 22 May 1937, *Papers of Neville Chamberlain*, NC18/1/1-1168, University of Birmingham

Chapter 9

1. Neville Chamberlain to Hilda, 30 May 1937, *Papers of Neville Chamberlain*, NC18/1/1-1168, University of Birmingham
2. Ibid
3. Neville Chamberlain to lda, 6 June 1937, *Papers of Neville Chamberlain*, NC18/1/1-1168, University of Birmingham
4. Chequers, https://en.wikipedia.org
5. Neville Chamberlain to Hilda, 25 June 1937, *Papers of Neville Chamberlain*, NC18/1/1-1168, University of Birmingham
6. *The Countryman*, Vol XVI No 1, 'Natural History at Downing Street', 1937 Oct-Nov-Dec, pp45-47
7. *New Scientist*, Acid comments on a cause célèbre, 8 November 1984, p37
8. Neville Chamberlain to Hilda, 26 June 1937, *Papers of Neville Chamberlain*, NC18/1/1-1168, University of Birmingham
9. Neville Chamberlain to lda, 4 July 1937, *Papers of Neville Chamberlain*, NC18/1/1-1168, University of Birmingham
10. Neville Chamberlain to Hilda, 18 July 1937, *Papers of Neville Chamberlain*, NC18/1/1-1168, University of Birmingham
11. Neville Chamberlain to lda, 24 July 1937, *Papers of Neville Chamberlain*, NC18/1/1-1168, University of Birmingham
12. Ibid
13. Neville Chamberlain to Hilda, 1 August 1937, *Papers of Neville Chamberlain*, NC18/1/1-1168, University of Birmingham
14. Neville Chamberlain to lda, 8 August 1937, *Papers of Neville Chamberlain*, NC18/1/1-1168, University of Birmingham

15. Ibid
16. Neville Chamberlain to Hilda, 29 August 1937, *Papers of Neville Chamberlain*, NC18/1/1-1168, University of Birmingham
17. Neville Chamberlain to Hilda, 12 September 1937, *Papers of Neville Chamberlain*, NC18/1/1-1168, University of Birmingham
18. Ibid
19. Neville Chamberlain to Gilbert Collett, 29 September 1937, Sarah Kelly Private Collection
20 Campaign to Protect Rural England, *10th anniversary of the CPRE*, https://www.cpre.org.uk
21. Neville Chamberlain to Hilda, 9 October 1937, *Papers of Neville Chamberlain*, NC18/1/1-1168, University of Birmingham
22. Neville Chamberlain to Ida, 16 October 1937, *Papers of Neville Chamberlain*, NC18/1/1-1168, University of Birmingham
23. Edward Wood,1st Earl of Halifax https://en.wikipedia.org/wiki/
24. Neville Chamberlain to Ida, 6 November 1937, *Papers of Neville Chamberlain*, NC18/1/1-1168, University of Birmingham
25. Neville Chamberlain to Gilbert Collett, 19 November 1937, Sarah Kelly Private Collection
26. Royal Society for the Protection of Birds, Common Redpoll, https://www.rspb.org.uk
27. Neville Chamberlain to Hilda, 21 November 1937, *Papers of Neville Chamberlain*, NC18/1/1-1168, University of Birmingham
28. Neville Chamberlain to Ida, 26 November 1937, *Papers of Neville Chamberlain*, NC18/1/1-1168, University of Birmingham
29. Neville Chamberlain to Ida, 12 December 1937, *Papers of Neville Chamberlain*, NC18/1/1-1168, University of Birmingham

Chapter 10

1. Neville Chamberlain to Ida, 23 January 1938, *Papers of Neville Chamberlain*, NC18/1/1-1168, University of Birmingham
2. Neville Chamberlain's letter to the Hitler Youth, http://www.freerepublic.com
3. Gardham Duncan, MI5 suspected Nazi Youth of organising cycling tours as cover for spying, *The Daily Telegraph* 7 March 2010
4. Neville Chamberlain to Hilda, 13 February 1938, *Papers of Neville Chamberlain*, NC18/1/1-1168, University of Birmingham

5. National Archives, Letter from Anthony Eden to Neville Chamberlain, 1938 (CAB/23/92 f252), http://www.nationalarchives.gov.uk

6. Edward Wood, 1st Earl of Halifax, https://en.wikipedia.org/wiki

7. Bennett, G. *What's the context? The resignation of Anthony Eden, 20 February 1938*, History of government blog 20 February 2018, https://history.blog.gov.uk

8. Neville Chamberlain to Hilda, 27 February 1938, *Papers of Neville Chamberlain*, NC18/1/1-1168, University of Birmingham

9. Gary Willis, *'An Arena of Glorious Work': The Protection of the Rural Landscape Against the Demands of Britain's Second World War Effort.* Rural History (2018) 29, 2, 259–280.

10. Ibid

11. Ibid

12. Campaign to Protect Rural England, *CPRE Monthly Report*, February, 1938

13. Abercrombie, P., unpublished account, No 20, Part VI, 18 months of activities 1938 to August 1939, (SCA D439/11/4/8/19-220), p16

14. Ibid

15. Neville Chamberlain to Hilda, 13 March 1938, *Papers of Neville Chamberlain*, NC18/1/1-1168, University of Birmingham

16. Ibid

17. Neville Chamberlain to lda, 20 March 1938, *Papers of Neville Chamberlain*, NC18/1/1-1168, University of Birmingham

18. Hansard, 24 March 1938, 'Foreign Affairs and Rearmament'

19. Neville Chamberlain to Hilda, 27 March 1938, *Papers of Neville Chamberlain*, NC18/1/1-1168, University of Birmingham

20. Neville Chamberlain to lda, 3 April 1938, *Papers of Neville Chamberlain*, NC18/1/1-1168, University of Birmingham

21. Neville Chamberlain to lda, 16 April 1938, *Papers of Neville Chamberlain*, NC18/1/1-1168, University of Birmingham

22. Neville Chamberlain to Hilda, 24 April 1938, *Papers of Neville Chamberlain*, NC18/1/1-1168, University of Birmingham

23. Neville Chamberlain to lda, 1 May 1938, *Papers of Neville Chamberlain*, NC18/1/1-1168, University of Birmingham

24. Neville Chamberlain to Hilda, 22 May 1938, *Papers of Neville Chamberlain*, NC18/1/1-1168, University of Birmingham

25. Neville Chamberlain to lda, 28 May 1938, *Papers of Neville Chamberlain*, NC18/1/1-1168, University of Birmingham

Chapter 11

1. Neville Chamberlain to lda, 18 June 1938, *Papers of Neville Chamberlain*, NC18/1/1-1168, University of Birmingham
2. Neville Chamberlain to Hilda, 25 June 1938, *Papers of Neville Chamberlain*, NC18/1/1-1168, University of Birmingham
3. Ibid
4. Neville Chamberlain to Hilda, 4 July 1938, *Papers of Neville Chamberlain*, NC18/1/1-1168, University of Birmingham
5. Neville Chamberlain to Gilbert Collett, 13 July 1939, Sarah Kelly Private Collection
6. Neville Chamberlain to lda, 16 July 1938, *Papers of Neville Chamberlain*, NC18/1/1-1168, University of Birmingham
7. Pageant of Birmingham, Birmingham Centenary Celebrations 1938, Illustrated Souvenir Booklet
8. Neville Chamberlain to Hilda, 27 August 1938, *Papers of Neville Chamberlain*, NC18/1/1-1168, University of Birmingham
9. Neville Chamberlain to Hilda, 3 September 1938, *Papers of Neville Chamberlain*, NC18/1/1-1168, University of Birmingham
10. Neville Chamberlain to Hilda, 11 September 1938, *Papers of Neville Chamberlain*, NC18/1/1-1168, University of Birmingham
11. Ibid

Chapter 12

1. Neville Chamberlain to Ida, 19 September 1938, *Papers of Neville Chamberlain*, NC18/1/1-1168, University of Birmingham
2. *News Review*, 22 September 1938
3. Neville Chamberlain to lda, 19 September 1938, *Papers of Neville Chamberlain*, NC18/1/1-1168, University of Birmingham
4. Schmidt, Dr P., *Hitler's Interpreter* (1951), p90
5. Ibid
6. *News Review*, 22 September 1938
7. Chamberlain letter to Ida, 19 September 1938, *Papers of Neville Chamberlain*, NC18/1/1-1168, University of Birmingham
8. Ibid
9. Ibid
10. Schmidt, Dr P., *Hitler's Interpreter* (1951), p91
11. Neville Chamberlain to Ida, 19 September 1938, *Papers of Neville Chamberlain*, NC18/1/1-1168, University of Birmingham

12. Minute of the conversation between Neville Chamberlain and Adolf Hitler at Berchtesgaden, FO 371/21738, 1938
13. Schmidt, Dr P., *Hitler's Interpreter* (1951), p92
14. Ibid
15. Schmidt, Dr P., *Hitler's Interpreter* (1951), p93
16. Ibid
17. Ibid
18. Neville Chamberlain to Ida, 19 September 1938, *Papers of Neville Chamberlain*, NC18/1/1-1168, University of Birmingham
19. Schmidt, Dr P., *Hitler's Interpreter* (1951), p94
20. Neville Chamberlain to Ida, 19 September 1938, *Papers of Neville Chamberlain*, NC18/1/1-1168, University of Birmingham
21. Ibid

Chapter 13

1. Ibid
2. Schmidt, Dr P., *Hitler's Interpreter* (1951), p96
3. Ibid
4. Ibid
5. Documents on German Foreign Policy 3/II, No. 1048, British delegation (Godesburg) to Halifax, 23 September 1938, p482
6. Shirer, W., *This is Berlin – Reporting from Nazi Germany 1938-40*, p24
7. Feiling, K., *The Life of Neville Chamberlain*, p39
8. Schmidt, Dr P., *Hitler's Interpreter* (1951), p99
9. Documents on German Foreign Policy 3/II No. 1058 Halifax to British delegation (Godesburg), 23 September 1938, p490
10. Schmidt, Dr P., *Hitler's Interpreter* (1951), p99
11. Schmidt, Dr P., *Hitler's Interpreter* (1951), p102
12. *Irish Times*, Editorial, 24 September 1938
13. Neville Chamberlain to Hilda, 2 October 1939, *Papers of Neville Chamberlain*, NC18/1/1-1168, University of Birmingham
14. Hansard, 28 September 1938, Prime Minister's Statement
15. Ibid
16. Neville Chamberlain to Hilda, 2 October 1938, *Papers of Neville Chamberlain*, NC18/1/1-1168, University of Birmingham
17. Ibid
18. Ibid
19. Ibid
20. Hansard, 3 October 1938, Prime Minister's Statement

Chapter 14

1. Hodgson, S., *The Man who made the Peace* (1938), p112
2. Carla Pass, 'The Lasting Legacy of Munich: British Public Perceptions of Neville Chamberlain During the Phoney War', Master of Arts, Dalhousie University, Halifax, Nova Scotia, August 2014, p138
3. Ibid
4. Hansard, House of Commons debate, 6 October 1938, Cols. 545-546
5. *Papers of Neville Chamberlain*, NC13/7, University of Birmingham
6. *Papers of Neville Chamberlain*, NC13/7/939, University of Birmingham
7. *Papers of Neville Chamberlain*, NC13/7/943, University of Birmingham
8. *Papers of Neville Chamberlain*, NC13/7/946, University of Birmingham
9. *Papers of Neville Chamberlain*, NC13/7/209, University of Birmingham
10. *Papers of Neville Chamberlain*, NC13/7/210, University of Birmingham
11. *Papers of Neville Chamberlain*, NC13/7/211, University of Birmingham
12. *Papers of Neville Chamberlain*, NC13/7/154, University of Birmingham

Chapter 15

1. *Picture Post*, 1 October 1938, Vol 1, No 1, Hulton's National Weekly
2. *Picture Post*, 8 October 1938, Vol 1, No 2, Hulton's National Weekly
3. Neville Chamberlain to Ida, 9 October 1938, *Papers of Neville Chamberlain*, NC18/1/1-1168, University of Birmingham
4. Ibid
5. Neville Chamberlain to Hilda, 15 October 1938, *Papers of Neville Chamberlain*, NC18/1/1-1168, University of Birmingham
6. Neville Chamberlain to Ida, 24 October 1938, *Papers of Neville Chamberlain*, NC18/1/1-1168, University of Birmingham
7. Oxford by-election, 1938, https://en.wikipedia.org
8. *Picture Post*, 5 November 1938, Vol 1, No 6, Hulton's National Weekly
9. Neville Chamberlain to Gilbert Collett, 22 October 1938, Sarah Kelly Private Collection
10. Hansard, International Situation, 1 November 1938
11. Neville Chamberlain to Hilda, 6 November 1938, *Papers of Neville Chamberlain*, NC18/1/1-1168, University of Birmingham
12. Neville Chamberlain to Ida, 13 November 1938, *Papers of Neville Chamberlain*, NC18/1/1-1168, University of Birmingham
13. Neville Chamberlain to Hilda, 27 November 1938, *Papers of Neville Chamberlain*, NC18/1/1-1168, University of Birmingham

14. Neville Chamberlain to Ida, 4 November 1938, *Papers of Neville Chamberlain*, NC18/1/1-1168, University of Birmingham
15. Ibid
16. Neville Chamberlain to Gilbert Collett, 9 December 1938, Sarah Kelly Private Collection
17. *The Times*, 'From the Sea', 9 December 1938
18. Neville Chamberlain to Ida, 17 December 1938, *Papers of Neville Chamberlain*, NC18/1/1-1168, University of Birmingham
19. Ibid
20. Ibid
21. *The Guardian*, 'Christmas cards from politicians past and present', 17 December 2010

Chapter 16

1. Neville Chamberlain to Ida, 8 January 1939, *Papers of Neville Chamberlain*, NC18/1/1-1168, University of Birmingham
2. Neville Chamberlain to Hilda, 15 January 1939, *Papers of Neville Chamberlain*, NC18/1/1-1168, University of Birmingham
3. Neville Chamberlain to Hilda, 5 February 1939, *Papers of Neville Chamberlain*, NC18/1/1-1168, University of Birmingham
4. Neville Chamberlain to Hilda, 19 February 1939, *Papers of Neville Chamberlain*, NC18/1/1-1168, University of Birmingham
5. Neville Chamberlain to Ida, 26 February 1939, *Papers of Neville Chamberlain*, NC18/1/1-1168, University of Birmingham
6. Neville Chamberlain to Hilda, 5 March 1939, *Papers of Neville Chamberlain*, NC18/1/1-1168, University of Birmingham
7. Neville Chamberlain to Ida, 12 March 1939, *Papers of Neville Chamberlain*, NC18/1/1-1168, University of Birmingham
8. Neville Chamberlain to Hilda, 19 March 1939, *Papers of Neville Chamberlain*, NC18/1/1-1168, University of Birmingham
9. Neville Chamberlain to Ida, 26 March 1939, *Papers of Neville Chamberlain*, NC18/1/1-1168, University of Birmingham
10. Neville Chamberlain to Hilda, 1-2 April 1939, *Papers of Neville Chamberlain*, NC18/1/1-1168, University of Birmingham
11. Neville Chamberlain to Ida, 9 April 1939, *Papers of Neville Chamberlain*, NC18/1/1-1168, University of Birmingham
12. Ibid

13. Neville Chamberlain to lda, 13 April 1939, *Papers of Neville Chamberlain*, NC18/1/1-1168, University of Birmingham
14. Ibid
15. Roosevelt, F., Press Conference, 15 April 1939, http://www.presidency.ucsb.edu
16. Neville Chamberlain to lda, 23 April 1939, *Papers of Neville Chamberlain*, NC18/1/1-1168, University of Birmingham
17. Neville Chamberlain to lda, 29 April 1939, *Papers of Neville Chamberlain*, NC18/1/1-1168, University of Birmingham

Chapter 17

1. Neville Chamberlain to Hilda, 29 April 1939, *Papers of Neville Chamberlain*, NC18/1/1-1168, University of Birmingham
2. Ibid
3. Neville Chamberlain to lda, 7 May 1939, *Papers of Neville Chamberlain*, NC18/1/1-1168, University of Birmingham
4. Neville Chamberlain to Hilda, 14 May 1939, *Papers of Neville Chamberlain*, NC18/1/1-1168, University of Birmingham
5. Neville Chamberlain to lda, 21 May 1939, *Papers of Neville Chamberlain*, NC18/1/1-1168, University of Birmingham
6. Neville Chamberlain to Hilda, 28 May 1939, *Papers of Neville Chamberlain*, NC18/1/1-1168, University of Birmingham
7. Ibid
8. Anonymous 1939: [Kenrick, G. H.] *Entomologist's Record & Journal of Variation*, 51, p116
9. Neville Chamberlain to Hilda, 17 June 1939, *Papers of Neville Chamberlain*, NC18/1/1-1168, University of Birmingham
10. Neville Chamberlain to lda, 25 June 1939, *Papers of Neville Chamberlain*, NC18/1/1-1168, University of Birmingham
11. Neville Chamberlain to Hilda, 2 July 1939, *Papers of Neville Chamberlain*, NC18/1/1-1168, University of Birmingham
12. Neville Chamberlain to lda, 8 July 1939, *Papers of Neville Chamberlain*, NC18/1/1-1168, University of Birmingham
13. Neville Chamberlain to Hilda, 15 July 1939, *Papers of Neville Chamberlain*, NC18/1/1-1168, University of Birmingham
14. Ibid
15. Neville Chamberlain to lda, 23 July 1939, *Papers of Neville Chamberlain*, NC18/1/1-1168, University of Birmingham

16. Biografie Max Sichel, (1896 - 1942), https://www3.sachsen.schule
17. Neville Chamberlain to Hilda, 30 July 1939, *Papers of Neville Chamberlain*, NC18/1/1-1168, University of Birmingham
18. Ibid
19. Ibid
20. Neville Chamberlain to lda, 5 August 1939, *Papers of Neville Chamberlain*, NC18/1/1-1168, University of Birmingham
21. Neville Chamberlain to Hilda, 13 August 1939, *Papers of Neville Chamberlain*, NC18/1/1-1168, University of Birmingham
22. Neville Chamberlain to lda, 19 August 1939, *Papers of Neville Chamberlain*, NC18/1/1-1168, University of Birmingham
23. Ibid

Chapter 18

1. Flying Visit of Truth to Berlin in the form of an RAF leaflet, 7 January 2017, Barron Maps Blog, http://www.barronmaps.com
2. *Daily Telegraph*, text of note to the German people, 9 September 1939, https://www.telegraph.co.uk
3. Neville Chamberlain to lda, 10 September 1939, *Papers of Neville Chamberlain*, NC18/1/1-1168, University of Birmingham
4. Ibid
5. Ibid
6. Neville Chamberlain to Hilda, 17 September 1939, Papers of Neville Chamberlain, NC18/1/1-1168, University of Birmingham
7. Ibid
8. Ibid
9. Neville Chamberlain to lda, 23 September 1939, *Papers of Neville Chamberlain*, NC18/1/1-1168, University of Birmingham
10. Neville Chamberlain to Hilda, 1 October 1939, *Papers of Neville Chamberlain*, NC18/1/1-1168, University of Birmingham
11. Neville Chamberlain to lda, 8 October 1939, *Papers of Neville Chamberlain*, NC18/1/1-1168, University of Birmingham
12. U-boat warfare, HC Deb 17 October 1939, vol 352, cc686-90, https://api.parliament.uk/historic-hansard
13. Neville Chamberlain to Hilda, 15 October 1939, *Papers of Neville Chamberlain*, NC18/1/1-1168, University of Birmingham
14. Ibid

15. Neville Chamberlain to Ida, 22 October 1939, *Papers of Neville Chamberlain*, NC18/1/1-1168, University of Birmingham
16. Ibid
17. Annie Chamberlain to Hilda, 24 October 1939, *Papers of Neville Chamberlain*, NC18/1/1-1168, University of Birmingham
18. Neville Chamberlain to Ida, 5 November 1939, *Papers of Neville Chamberlain*, NC18/1/1-1168, University of Birmingham
19. Neville Chamberlain to Hilda, 19 November 1939, *Papers of Neville Chamberlain*, NC18/1/1-1168, University of Birmingham
20. Neville Chamberlain to Ida, 3 December 1939, *Papers of Neville Chamberlain*, NC18/1/1-1168, University of Birmingham
21. Ibid
22. Neville Chamberlain to Hilda, 10 December 1939, *Papers of Neville Chamberlain*, NC18/1/1-1168, University of Birmingham
23. Neville Chamberlain to Ida, 20 December 1939, *Papers of Neville Chamberlain*, NC18/1/1-1168, University of Birmingham
24. Mrs Chamberlain's Broadcast to the Women of France, 31 December 1939, *Papers of Neville Chamberlain*, NC11/11, University of Birmingham

Chapter 19

1. Dorril, S., *Blackshirt: Sir Oswald Mosley and British Fascism* (2007), p475.
2. Neville Chamberlain to Ida, 7 January 1940, *Papers of Neville Chamberlain*, NC18/1/1-1168, University of Birmingham
3. Ibid
4. Neville Chamberlain to Hilda, 13 January 1940, *Papers of Neville Chamberlain*, NC18/1/1-1168, University of Birmingham
5. Ibid
6. Neville Chamberlain to Ida, 20 January 1940, *Papers of Neville Chamberlain*, NC18/1/1-1168, University of Birmingham
7. Ibid
8. Neville Chamberlain to Gilbert Collett, 21 January 1940, Sarah Kelly Private Collection
9. This is supposition, but there is strong supporting evidence in his letters to Collett and his sisters that he would have done this despite the security risks.
10. Neville Chamberlain to Hilda, 27 January 1940, *Papers of Neville Chamberlain*, NC18/1/1-1168, University of Birmingham

11. Neville Chamberlain to Gilbert Collett, 1 February 1940, Sarah Kelly Private Collection
12. Shakespeare, W., *Julius Caesar*, Act 1: Scene 3
13. Neville Chamberlain to Ida, 3 February 1940, *Papers of Neville Chamberlain*, NC18/1/1-1168, University of Birmingham
14. Neville Chamberlain to Hilda, 9 February 1940, *Papers of Neville Chamberlain*, NC18/1/1-1168, University of Birmingham
15. Neville Chamberlain to Ida, 17 February 1940, *Papers of Neville Chamberlain*, NC18/1/1-1168, University of Birmingham
16. *Malaya Tribune*, 26 February 1940, p15 http://eresources.nlb.gov.sg
17. Neville Chamberlain to Hilda, 25 February 1940, *Papers of Neville Chamberlain*, NC18/1/1-1168, University of Birmingham
18. Ibid
19. Neville Chamberlain to Ida, 2 March 1940, *Papers of Neville Chamberlain*, NC18/1/1-1168, University of Birmingham
20. Neville Chamberlain to Hilda, 10 March 1940, *Papers of Neville Chamberlain*, NC18/1/1-1168, University of Birmingham
21. Anon., London Zoo during World War Two Blog, *Zoological Society of London*, 1 September 2013, www.zsl.org
22. Neville Chamberlain to Ida, 16 March 1940, *Papers of Neville Chamberlain*, NC18/1/1-1168, University of Birmingham
23. Neville Chamberlain to Ida, 30 March 1940, *Papers of Neville Chamberlain*, NC18/1/1-1168, University of Birmingham
24. Kennedy, P.G., 'Habits of the Tree-Creeper', *British Birds Vol XXX*, 1 June 1936
25. Theobold, P., 'The Divisive Rook', *Shooting UK*, 3 June 2014
26. Neville Chamberlain to Ida, 30 March 1940, *Papers of Neville Chamberlain*, NC18/1/1-1168, University of Birmingham
27. Ibid
28. Neville Chamberlain to Ida, 6 April 1940, *Papers of Neville Chamberlain*, NC18/1/1-1168, University of Birmingham

Chapter 20

1. Neville Chamberlain to Ida, 13 April 1940, *Papers of Neville Chamberlain*, NC18/1/1-1168, University of Birmingham
2. Ibid
3. Neville Chamberlain to Gilbert Collett, 13 April 1940, Sarah Kelly Private Collection

4. Neville Chamberlain to Hilda, 20 April 1940, *Papers of Neville Chamberlain*, NC18/1/1-1168, University of Birmingham
5. Ibid
6. Neville Chamberlain to lda, 27 April 1940, *Papers of Neville Chamberlain*, NC18/1/1-1168, University of Birmingham
7. Neville Chamberlain to Hilda, 4 May 1940, *Papers of Neville Chamberlain*, NC18/1/1-1168, University of Birmingham
8. Neville Chamberlain to Gilbert Collett, 8 May 1940, Sarah Kelly Private Collection
9. Grenfell, J., *Into Battle* (1915) in Meynell, Viola *Julian Grenfell* (1917)
10. Hansard, 7-8 May 1940, Conduct of the War
11. Neville Chamberlain to lda, 11 May 1940, *Papers of Neville Chamberlain*, NC18/1/1-1168, University of Birmingham

Chapter 21

1. Neville Chamberlain to lda, 11 May 1940, *Papers of Neville Chamberlain*, NC18/1/1-1168, University of Birmingham
2. Ibid
3. Neville Chamberlain to Gilbert Collett, 13 May 1940, Sarah Kelly Private Collection
4. Neville Chamberlain to Gilbert Collett, 16 May 1940, Sarah Kelly Private Collection
5. Neville Chamberlain to Hilda, 17 May 1940, *Papers of Neville Chamberlain*, NC18/1/1-1168, University of Birmingham
6. Ibid
7. Neville Chamberlain to lda, 25 May 1940, *Papers of Neville Chamberlain*, NC18/1/1-1168, University of Birmingham
8. Neville Chamberlain to lda, 1 June 1940, NC Collection 1/18/1-1168 *Papers of Neville Chamberlain*, NC18/1/1-1168, University of Birmingham
9. Ibid
10. Badoglio, P., *L'Italia nella seconda guerra mondiale* (Mondadori, Milan, 1946), p37
11. Neville Chamberlain to Hilda, 15 June 1940, *Papers of Neville Chamberlain*, NC18/1/1-1168, University of Birmingham
12. Neville Chamberlain to lda, 21 June 1940, *Papers of Neville Chamberlain*, NC18/1/1-1168, University of Birmingham

13. Neville Chamberlain to Ida, 29 June 1940, *Papers of Neville Chamberlain*, NC18/1/1-1168, University of Birmingham
14. Cato, *Guilty Men* (Victor Gollancz, 1940)

Chapter 22

1. Neville Chamberlain to Ida, 7 July 1940, *Papers of Neville Chamberlain*, NC18/1/1-1168, University of Birmingham
2. Ibid
3. Neville Chamberlain to Hilda, 14 July 1940, *Papers of Neville Chamberlain*, NC18/1/1-1168, University of Birmingham
4. Neville Chamberlain to Gilbert Collett, 16 July 1940, Sarah Kelly Private Collection
5. Neville Chamberlain to Gilbert Collett, 19 July 1940, Private Collection
6. Propaganda leaflet, 'A Last Appeal to Reason by Adolf Hitler', Speech before the Reichstag, 19 July 1940
7. Foot, M.R.D., *SOE in France: An Account of the Work of the British Special Operations in France 1940-1944* (2004), p9-10
8. Neville Chamberlain to Ida, 20 July 1940, *Papers of Neville Chamberlain*, NC18/1/1-1168, University of Birmingham
9. Neville Chamberlain to Hilda, 27 July 1940, *Papers of Neville Chamberlain*, NC18/1/1-1168, University of Birmingham
10. Self, R., *Neville Chamberlain: A Biography* (2005) p443
11. Thomas, Rohan, 10 Downing Street, 2011, http://www.westendatwar.org.uk
12. Neville Chamberlain to Ida, 15 September 1940, *Papers of Neville Chamberlain*, NC18/1/1-1168, University of Birmingham
13. Ibid
14. Self, R., *Neville Chamberlain: A Biography* (2005), p445
15. Self, R., *Neville Chamberlain: A Biography* (2005), p446
16. Self, R., *Neville Chamberlain: A Biography* (2005), p447

Epilogue

1. *Chips: The Diaries of Sir Henry Channon*, 10 November 1940
2. *The Yorkshire Post* Death of Mr. Chamberlain Service to the State: Tributes to a Great Patriot. Monday 11 November 1940, p1
3. Churchill War Time Speeches, *Upon the death of Neville Chamberlain*, House of Commons, 12 November 1940, The Churchill Society, London

4. Self, R., *Neville Chamberlain: A Biography* (2005), p450

5. Cowling, C., *The PM who was cremated before his funeral*, 2 December 2014

6. *British Pathe*, 'Chamberlain – He Strove For Peace', 18 November 1940, www.britishpathe.com

7. Baker, N., *Human Smoke: The Beginnings of World War II, the End of Civilization* (2008), p249

8. *Nature*, Vol 146, News and Views, 16 November 1940

9. Anne Chamberlain to Gilbert Collett, 15 February 1941, Sarah Kelly Private Collection

10. Anne Chamberlain to Gilbert Collett, 21 February 1941, Sarah Kelly Private Collection

11. Gilbert William Collett, British West Indies Study Circle, Bulletin September 1964, https://bwisc.org/biography-gilbert-collett

12. Self, R., *Neville Chamberlain: A Biography* (2005), p29

Further Reading

Bryant, Arthur, *In Search of Peace* (Hutchinson, 1938)

Chamberlain, I. & H., *Common Objects of the Riviera* (Routledge, 1913)

Cato, *Guilty Men* (Victor Gollancz, 1940)

Faber, D., *Munich The 1938 Appeasement Crisis* (Simon & Schuster, 2008)

Feiling, Keith, *The life of Neville Chamberlain* (Macmillan, 1946)

Haigh, R. H., Morris D. S., Peters, A.R., *The Guardian Book of Munich* (Wildwood House, 1988)

Henderson, Sir Nevile, *Failure of a Mission* (Hodder and Stoughton Ltd, 1940)

Marsh, Peter T., *The Chamberlain Family* (Haus Publishing, 2010)

Max Everset-Phillips, *Neville Chamberlain and the Art of Appeasement* (i2f Publishing, 2013)

Schmidt, Dr Paul, *Hitler's Interpreter* (Heinemann, 1951)

Self, Robert, *Neville Chamberlain A Biography* (Ashgate, 2006)

Self, Robert, *The Neville Chamberlain Diary Letters*, 4 Vols (Ashgate, 2000-2005)

Ward, Roger, *The Chamberlains* (Fonthill, 2015)

Index

(Greenwood 'disastrous speech')
105, 110, (Coopers resignation) 136,
(Chamberlain urged bring Labour
members into gov) 154, (Oxford
by-election) 155, (Attlee attacks
Munich agreement) 157, (Attlee
describes Chamberlain as a Fascist)
165, (tables debate Czechoslovakia)
166, (calls Chamberlain's resignation)
168, (done with sharing confidences)
169, 173, (brings vote censure)
177, 178, ('speak for England')
181, 188, (attacks over Hore-
Belisha resignation) 193, 196, 197,
(Chamberlains resignation) 213,
(Churchill makes Attlee Deputy
Leader) 216, (blamed for war)
217, 218, 220, (Dalton heads
up SOE) 224

Lally, Gwen (pageant master) 111

Large copper butterfly 27 (*Lycaena
dispar*)

Lark Ascending, The (poem) 3

Laski, Professor 107

Latvia 170

Law, Andrew Bonar (MP, PM) 42, 43,
44, 46

League of Nations (votes for sanctions
against Italy) 66, 86, (Italy withdraws
from) 93, (value questioned) 103,
(Hitler denigrates) 120, (Gilbert
Murray letter) 165, 173, 232

Lee, Lord and Lady of Fareham 81

Lenormand, Henri-René 12

Leopard moth (*Zeuzera pyrina*) viii,
81-82, 233

Lepidoptera (study of butterflies
and moths) (George Kenrick) 17-18,
23, 235

Liberal party 4, 14-15, 26, (Corbett
stands 1918 election) 41, 42, (Labour
governs with support of) 44, 52,
53, (1931 National Gov) 54, 57,
63, 66, (Chamberlain's Cabinet)
79, 104, (Lord Runciman mission
Czechoslovakia) 112, 118, 155, 165,
170, (blames for war) 217, 220

Lilliput (magazine) 153

Lindley, Sir Francis Oswald 173

Lindsay, Sandie 155

Lister, Mrs (niece Lord Halifax)
151, 152

Little blue heron (*Egretta caerulea*) 22

Lloyd, Geoffrey MP 11

Lloyd George, David (MP, PM) x, 4,
(offers Chamberlain Dir of Dept
National Service) 38-39, 42, (resigns)
43, (time taken reach front bench) 44,
52, (champions public works) 61, 63,
(Chamberlain has terrific duel with)
98-99, (visits Hitler) 118, 163, (belief
Russia is key to salvation) 168, 173,
(attacks Chamberlain Norway debate)
210, (Churchill brings back into gov)
217-218, 231

Lloyd, Lord 4

Lloyd, Stephen (son-in-law) 65, 231

Local Government Bill (1929) 51

Locarno Pact 46, 97

Lockheed, British Airways
(Model 10 and 14) (flights to
Germany) 2-3, (Dimbleby describes
as 'the machine') 5, (first flight
Germany) 115-116, (Christmas card)
162, 190

Londonderry, Lord 105, 116

London Illustrated News (special
Munich issue) 9-10